The

Effects

of

Mass

Communication

The Effects of Mass Communication
is the third volume in the series on
FOUNDATIONS OF COMMUNICATIONS RESEARCH

EDITED BY
Paul F. Lazarsfeld and Bernard Berelson

The two previous volumes in the series are
Content Analysis in Communication Research
BY BERNARD BERELSON
Personal Influence
BY ELIHU KATZ AND PAUL F. LAZARSFELD

JOSEPH T. KLAPPER

The Free Press, New York

The

Effects

of

Mass

Communication

To
Rosalind Kean Wallace

Fifth Printing January 1965

Copyright © 1960 by The Free Press, a Corporation

Printed in the United States of America

Library of Congress Catalog No.: 60-14402

Designed by Sidney Solomon

Preface

NATURE OF THE BOOK

*T*HIS BOOK attempts to collate and integrate the findings of published research, and some provocative conjecture, regarding certain social and psychological effects of mass communication.

More specifically, the book is concerned with two major areas of such effect. Part I deals with mass communication as an agent of persuasion and attempts to cite its known capabilities and limitations in that regard. Part II deals with the effects of specific kinds of media content which have been alleged to produce socially and psychologically important consequences. An introductory chapter, which is largely subjective, discusses the current state of knowledge of the effects of mass communication in general and proposes a primitive theoretical scheme which is further discussed at various other explicitly labeled places in the book and in the conclusion. Except for the introduction and conclusion, the entire work is primarily a collection of the findings of others.

The book at times draws heavily upon an earlier work by the same author (Klapper, 1949). The present volume, however, is by no means a mere up-dating of the earlier one. It differs from the earlier work in its inclusion and discussion of the proposed theoretical scheme, in its far greater concern with extra-communication conditions which influence the effect of communications, and in the areas of effect which are discussed. Of the five topics discussed in the earlier volume, three have been retained and two of these are treated in much greater detail, and two have been omitted. Three topics not treated in the earlier volume are here accorded a chapter each.[1]

LITERATURE SURVEYED

The source material for this book consisted mainly of the vast array of learned and semi-learned journals and of relevant books. Traditional techniques of library research were employed in culling this literature. Journals of abstracts, bibliographies, and works known to the author were used as starting points; the works cited contained bibliographies and references which led to additional material; and this snowballing was continued until the returns became so slight that it was clearly unprofitable to continue.

This process led to the identification and investigation of over 1000 studies, essays, and reports. More than 270 of these, which contributed directly to the present volume, are cited in the bibliography. The others were found to be either wholly irrelevant to the topics of the book, to be so methodologically culpable as to be useless, or, in some cases, to provide only one more confirmation of some highly specific finding or point of view that had been widely confirmed or better expressed in other cited works.

The primary object of the literature search was to locate all *published reports* of *disciplined social research* dealing with *effects of mass communication* in certain specific areas. However, several unpublished works have found their way into the text and the bibliography. These include occasional doctoral dissertations which have attained some recognition outside the departments in which they were written, and several reports issued in unpublished form by academic, commercial, and government agencies. No attempt has been made, however, exhaustively to explore such sources of unpublished material; the almost limitless volume, the frequently privileged status, and, above all, the sheer difficulty of tracking down and obtaining these little-known works rendered any attempt at exhaustive examination beyond the budgetary and physical capabilities of the present study. The value to the research fraternity of a central clearing house or information center for such materials has often been noted; unless and until the concept is somehow implemented, knowledge of the materials, and thus their potential usefulness, will remain severely limited.

It must also be noted that a considerable number of the cited works are not reports of research at all, but rather present the considered conjecture of reputable and acute thinkers. In addition, articles from popular sources (e.g., *Parents Magazine*) are occasionally cited as evidence of popular concern about particular effects of the media.

Finally, and perhaps most importantly, a considerable number of the cited research studies do not deal with mass communications per se, but with laboratory approximations thereof or with some form of interpersonal communication; they have been included as source material because their findings appear to be at least hypothetically applicable to mass communication as well.

The author has assiduously attempted to indicate, in referring to any document, whether it is empirical or nonempirical, and the specific sort of communication to which it refers.

A NOTE ON EXCLUSIONS

The specific topics treated in this book and the relative emphasis accorded them are easily ascertainable from the extended Table of Contents. Brief introductory notes at the beginning of

Part I and Part II also provide quick overviews of those sections.

A few words are in order, however, as to what this book does *not* cover. Several topics have been excluded for one or more of a variety of reasons, prime among which, perhaps, was the need of limiting the areas of concern. To explore and collate the literature relative to all possible social or psychological effects of mass communication would require a decade, an interdisciplinary team, and an astronomical budget. The present study has enjoyed none of these boundless goods, and the author has thus been forced to limit its scope to a few areas which have been much discussed, which could be explored in a reasonable time and reported within reasonable space, and which form a convenient whole. Of the many areas thus excluded, three seem to merit particular mention.

1. The book does not deal with the use of mass media in formal pedagogy, whether presented in classrooms or on closed or open broadcast systems. Consideration of the problems peculiar to that field and of the already vast literature would clearly require a separate study, of duration, length, and complexity at least equal to the one here reported.

2. Relatively little mention is made of either the effects of mass communication in international psychological warfare, or the effects of domestic mass communication in countries other than the United States.[2] The problems which would be evoked by so broadly expanding the width of concern are compounded by the fact that foreign communication systems are organized and controlled in various dissimilar ways, and by the fact that the audiences exist in milieus culturally different from that of the United States. Proper consideration of the effects of mass communication under such conditions would involve taking account of such an array of variables as to render the task unfeasible within the limitations of the present study.

3. No attempt is made to deal with the effects of the media as instruments of consumer advertising. Not only is much of that vast research privileged, but the lion's share presents findings which can be regarded as valid only in reference to the specific situation

researched and which are in general too precisely "applied" to be particularly useful for this more basically oriented volume. By the same token, the findings of the research which are cited in this volume cannot be assumed to be generalizable to the effects of consumer advertising. The goals of such advertising and the psychological significance to the audience member of the decisions involved are often quite unlike the goals and decisions involved in the kind of persuasive communications here discussed.

REFERENCE AND FOOTNOTE SYSTEM

Being primarily a collation of the findings of published research, the book naturally and necessarily makes continual reference to other studies. To provide maximum reading ease, such studies are identified within the text itself by author or authors and year of publication, e.g. "Maccoby (1954)." Notes are added only when additional information (such as the locus of a quotation) is provided, or to indicate that the present author has been impelled to comment further. A series of short quotes from the same pages of the same work is flagged by a single footnote at the end of the series. All notes appear at the end of the book starting on page 258. Full bibliographical listings of the works cited are relegated to the Bibliography itself, where the works are arranged alphabetically by author. Multiple entries for the same author or groups of authors are arranged in *chronological order by publication dates, not alphabetically by titles*.

ACKNOWLEDGEMENTS

The preparation of this volume was made possible by a grant from the Columbia Broadcasting System, Inc., and on behalf of both myself and the Bureau of Applied Social Research, Columbia University, sponsor of the study, I am glad to acknowledge that support.

In the course of this project's conception, its struggles into life, its growth, and its completion, many people have provided many kinds of aid. To attempt to categorize such aid is futile, for many people helped in multiple ways. For reasons best known to them and to me, therefore, I am happy to record my great indebtedness and my extreme gratitude:

—to Paul F. Lazarsfeld, Herbert Hyman, Sigmund Diamond, David Sills, Sidney S. Spivack, and Clara Shapiro, all of Columbia University or its Bureau of Applied Social Research; to Charles Y. Glock, formerly of that Bureau and now of the University of California; and to York Lucci, also formerly of the Bureau and now of Stanford Research Institute.

—to Joseph M. Bertotti and Lawrence L. Ferguson of the General Electric Company;

—to Hope Lunin Klapper of New York University;

—to the late Rosalind Kean Wallace of Market Planning Corporation, and to Helen J. Kaufmann, formerly of that organization;

—and to Denise Bistryn Kandel, M. Jean Herman, Sheila Spaulding, Uriel G. Hurwitz, Marjorie Leary, Patrick Smith, Jimmie Yvonne Duncan, and Ann Medrick, all of whom contributed their several and various skills.

Finally, I am extremely grateful for the opportunity afforded me to complete this work while developing a communications research program at the General Electric Company.

Despite the aid and advice provided by these individuals and institutions, I must of course accept complete responsibility for the research procedures used in preparing this volume, and for the presentation and interpretation of the cited research findings.

JOSEPH T. KLAPPER

New York City, April 15, 1960

Contents

Introduction[1]*

*T*WENTY YEARS AGO, writers who undertook to discuss mass communication typically felt obliged to define that then unfamiliar term. In the intervening years, conjecture and research upon the topic, particularly in reference to the *effects* of mass communication, have burgeoned. The literature has reached that stage of profusion and disarray, characteristic of all proliferating disciplines, at which researchers and research administrators speak wistfully of establishing centers where the accumulating data might be sifted and stored. The field has grown to the point at which its practitioners are periodically asked by other researchers to attempt to assess the cascade, to determine whither we are tumbling, to attempt to assess, in short "what we know about the effects of mass communication."

What we know of course varies, depending on whether we are discussing one type of effect or another. In regard to some

* All notes appear at the end of the book.

points, the evidence is remarkably consistent. In regard to others, the data contain apparent anomalies or apparent outright contradictions. These characteristics of the data are by now well known, and they have given rise to a widespread pessimism about the possibility of ever bringing any order to the field.

The author acknowledges and will here briefly document the pessimism, but he neither condones nor shares it. He will rather propose that we have arrived at the brink of hope. More specifically, he will here propose that we have reached the point at which certain empirical generalizations may be tentatively formulated. A few such generalizations will be presented, and it will be further proposed that they are capable of ordering a good deal of the data, of resolving certain apparent anomalies, and of indicating avenues for new and logically relevant research.

The Bases of Pessimism

The pessimism, at present, is widespread, and it exists both among the interested lay public and within the research fraternity.

Some degree of pessimism, or even cynicism, is surely to be expected from the lay public, whose questions we have failed to answer. Teachers, preachers, parents, and legislators have asked us a thousand times over these past fifteen years whether violence in the media produces delinquency, whether the escapist nature of much of the fare does not blind people to reality, and just what the media can do to the political persuasions of their audiences. To these questions we have not only failed to provide definitive answers, but we have done something worse: we have provided evidence in partial support of every hue of every view. We have claimed, on the one hand, and on empirical grounds, that escapist material provides its audience with blinders and with an unrealistic view of life,[2] and, on the other hand, that it helps them meet life's real problems.[3] We have hedged on the crime and violence question, typically saying, "Well, probably there is no causative relationship, but there just might be a triggering effect."[4] In reference to persuasion, we have maintained that the media are after all not so terribly powerful,[5] and yet we have reported their impressive successes in promoting such varied phenomena as religious intolerance,[6] the sale of war bonds,[7] belief in the American Way,[8] and disenchantment with Boy Scout activities.[9] It is surely no wonder that a bewildered public should regard with cynicism a research tradition which supplies, instead of definitive answers, a plethora of relevant but inconclusive and at times seemingly contradictory findings.

Considerable pessimism, of a different order, is also to be expected within the research fraternity itself. Such anomalous findings as have been cited above seemed to us at first to betoken merely the need of more penetrating and rigorous research. We shaped insights into hypotheses and eagerly set up research designs in quest of the additional variables which we were sure would bring order out of chaos and enable us to describe the process of effect with sufficient precision to diagnose and predict. But the variables emerged in such a cataract that we almost drowned. The relatively placid waters of "who says what to whom"[10] were early seen to be muddied by audience predispositions, "self-selection," and selective perception. More recent studies, both in the laboratory and the social world, documented the influence of a host of other variables including various aspects of contextual organization;[11] the audiences' image of the sources;[12] the simple passage of time;[13] the group orientation of the audience member and the degree to which he values group membership;[14] the activity of opinion leaders;[15] the social aspects of the situation during and after exposure to the media,[16] and the degree to which the audience member is forced to play a role;[17] the personality pattern of the audience member,[18] his social class, and the level of his frustrations;[19] the nature of the media in a free enterprise system;[20] and the availability of "social mechanism[s] for implementing action drives."[21] The list, if not endless, is at least overwhelming, and it continues to grow. Almost every aspect of the life of the audience member and the culture in which the communication occurs seems susceptible of relation to the process of communication effect. As early as 1948, Berelson, cogitating on what was then known, came to the accurate if perhaps moody conclusion that "some kinds of *communication* on some kinds of *issues,* brought to the attention of some kinds of *people* under some kinds of *conditions,* have some kinds of *effects.*"[22] It is surely no wonder that today, after another decade at the inexhaustible fount of variables, some researchers should feel that the formulation of any systematic description of what effects are how effected, and the predictive application of such principles, are goals which become the more distant as they are the more vigorously pursued.

But, as has been said, the present author takes no such pessimistic view. He rather proposes that we already know a good deal more about communication than we thought we did, and that we are on the verge of being able to proceed toward more abundant and more fruitful knowledge.

The Bases of Hope

This optimism is based on two phenomena. The first of these is a new orientation toward the study of communication effects which has recently become conspicuous in the literature. And the second phenomenon is the emergence, from this new approach, of a few tentative generalizations.

In describing the new approach, and in presenting the generalizations, the author submits rather than asserts. He hopes to be extremely suggestive, but he cannot yet be conclusive. And if these pages bespeak optimism, they also bespeak the tentativeness of exploratory rather than exhaustive thought. Explicit note will in fact be taken, both in this chapter and elsewhere in the volume, of wide areas to which the generalizations do not seem to apply, and warnings will be sounded against the pitfalls of regarding them as all-inclusive or axiomatic.

THE "PHENOMENISTIC" APPROACH

The new orientation, which has of course been hitherto and variously formulated, can perhaps be described, in a confessedly oversimplified way, as a shift away from the concept of "hypodermic effect" toward an approach which might be called "situational" or "functional."[23] Because of the specific, and for our purposes sometimes irrelevant, connotations attached to these two terms, we will here use a word coined by the present author in an earlier publication and refer to the approach as "phenomenistic."[24] Whatever it be called, it is in essence a shift *away* from the tendency to regard mass communication as a necessary and sufficient cause of audience effects, toward a view of the media as influences, working amid other influences, in a total situation. The old quest of specific effects stemming from the communication has given way to the observation of existing conditions or changes, followed by an inquiry into the factors, *including* mass communication, which produced those conditions and changes, and the roles which these factors played relative to each other. In short, attempts to assess a stimulus which was presumed to work alone have given way to an assessment of the role of that stimulus in a total observed phenomenon.

Examples of the new approach are becoming fairly numerous. The so-called Elmira[25] and Decatur[26] studies, for example, set out to determine the critical factors in various types of observed decisions, rather than to focus exclusively on whether media did or did not have effects. The Rileys and Maccoby focus on the varying functions which media serve for different sorts of children, rather than inquiring whether media do or do not affect them.[27] Some of the more laboratory-oriented researchers, in particular the Hovland school, have been conducting ingeniously designed controlled experiments in which the communication stimulus is a constant, and various extra-communication factors are the variables.[28]

This new approach, which views mass media as one among a series of factors working in patterned ways their wonders to perform, seems to the author already to have been extremely useful, and to have made possible a series of generalizations which will very shortly be advanced.

Before the generalizations are advanced, however, a few words of preliminary warning about the phenomenistic approach seem highly in order. For that approach, despite its usefulness, may, if relied upon too exclusively, tend to obscure the very issues it is intended to elucidate.

It is possible that the phenomenistic approach may so divert our attention to the factors with which mass communication is in interplay, or to the fact that interplay exists, that we forget our original goal of determining the effects of mass communication itself. For example, we shall see, in Part One of this book, that the effects of mass communication are likely to differ, depending upon whether the communication is or is not in accord with the norms of groups to which the audience members belong. In a later chapter, we shall see that the effects of fantasy and of media depictions of crime and violence are likely to have different effects among children who are primarily oriented toward different types of groups. This is valuable information which contributes greatly to our knowledge of the processes and types of mass communication effect. But if research is to provide socially meaningful answers to questions about the effects of mass communication, it must inquire into the relative prevalence of these different conditions under which mass communication has different effects. Unfortunately, communication research has not often addressed itself to such questions, and this book will necessarily reflect that limitation. It may, however, be noted that if the phenomenistic approach thus tends to delay the provision of definitive answers, it does so in the interests of the eventual answers being the more meaningful.

It must also be remembered that though mass communication seems usually to be a *contributory* cause of effects, it is often a major or necessary cause and in some instances a sufficient cause. The fact that its effect is often mediated, or that it often works among other influences, must not blind us to the fact that mass communication possesses qualities which distinguish it from other influences, and that by virtue of these qualities, it is likely to have characteristic effects. Neither the phenomenistic approach nor the proposed generalizations deny these possibilities; they are, in fact, explicitly stated in the third and fourth generalizations below. But there seems some danger that attention may at times become too exclusively focused on the other factors to which the phenomenistic approach points, and the dangers of such neglect must be kept in mind.

Precautions can, of course, be taken against such dangers as have here been outlined, and given such precautions, the phenomenistic approach seems to the present author to offer good hope that the disarray of communications research findings may to some degree be ordered. He feels, as has already been noted, that the approach has in fact made possible a series of generalizations which will now be advanced. They are submitted very gingerly. They seem to the author at once extremely generic and quite immature; they seem on the one hand to involve little that has not been said, and on the other hand to be frightfully daring. They do seem, however, to be capable of relating a good deal of data about the processes, factors, and directions of communication effects, and of doing this in such a way that findings which hitherto appeared to be at best anomalous, if not actually contradictory, begin to look like orderly variations on a few basic themes.

EMERGING GENERALIZATIONS

The generalizations will first be presented in their bare bones and without intervening comment. Various later sections of the book will be devoted to indicating their apparent capabilities and limitations. Without further ado, then, it is tentatively proposed that:

1. Mass communication *ordinarily* does not serve as a necessary and sufficient cause of audience effects,[29] but rather functions among and through a nexus of mediating factors and influences.

2. These mediating factors are such that they typically render mass communication a contributory agent, but not the sole cause, in a process of reinforcing the existing conditions. (Regardless of the condition in question—be it the vote intentions of audience members, their tendency toward or away from delinquent behavior, or their general orientation toward life and its problems—and regardless of whether the effect in question be social or individual, the media are more likely to reinforce than to change.)

3. On such occasions as mass communication does function in the service of change, one of two conditions is likely to exist. Either:

a. the mediating factors will be found to be inoperative and the effect of the media will be found to be direct; *or*

b. the mediating factors, which normally favor reinforcement, will be found to be themselves impelling toward change.

4. There are certain residual situations in which mass communication seems to produce direct effects, or directly and of itself to serve certain psycho-physical functions.

5. The efficacy of mass communication, either as a contributory agent or as an agent of direct effect, is affected by various aspects of the media and communications themselves or of the communication situation (including, for example, aspects of textual organization, the nature of the source and medium, the existing climate of public opinion, and the like).

Neither the generalizations nor their implications will be further discussed in this chapter. They are attempts to account for and order existing research findings, and they will accordingly be discussed, at several points, after various bodies of findings have been themselves presented. The reporting of the findings remains the major purpose of the book; the theoretical orientation of the author is a wholly secondary matter.

The author would like to make clear, however, that he is in no way committed to these particular generalizations, let alone to the exact form in which they here appear. He hopes, in fact, that further thought and research will modify and perhaps annihilate the schema. He is far less concerned with insuring the viability of these generalizations than he is with indicating that the time for generalization is at hand.

THE EFFECTS
OF PERSUASIVE
COMMUNICATION

Introductory Note

Concern about the possible influence of mass communication upon the opinions and attitudes of men has been prevalent for several decades and has existed, in a less intense way, as long as there have been mass or quasi-mass communications. The figure of the pen as mightier than the sword has been modernized by social observers who have claimed that the mass media are more powerful than the atom bomb. Other social observers have scoffed. As the more fearful have pointed to the impressive successes of various propaganda campaigns, the more phlegmatic have pointed to the impressive failures of other campaigns. Neither group has been hard put to it to find evidence to support its position.

Communications research has reflected this preoccupation with the persuasive power of mass communication. Case studies, laboratory experiments with small groups, and surveys involving thousands of respondents have all been undertaken to determine whether given communications have had effects, what effects, if any, they have had, and what conditions have apparently handicapped or facilitated the persuasion.

The accumulated literature is vast in scope and varied in regard to topics, scientific validity, and findings. It attests occasions on which persuasive communication, transmitted by any given medium, has succeeded; occasions on which it has had no impact; and occasions on which it has produced "boomerang" effects, precisely opposite to those intended. Some of the causes of these phenomena have been at least tentatively identified.

The four chapters of Part One of this volume discuss the findings of this research. The data are organized, and the chapters titled, according to a simple typology of possible "directions of effect."[1]

Chapter II deals with the relative frequency of the several types of attitude effect and then focuses upon the most common, viz., reinforcement. Certain factors which have been identified as contributing to the likelihood of reinforcement are cited and discussed. The chapter also deals with two phenomena which seem closely related to reinforcement, viz., minor attitude change and the resistance to change of "ego-involved" attitudes.

Chapter III discusses the efficacy of mass communication in creating opinions and attitudes on new issues.

Chapter IV considers the phenomenon of conversion.

Chapter V cites and discusses various characteristics of communications, media, and communication situations which have been found to be related to the efficiency of persuasion, regardless of whether the effect is reinforcement or conversion.

Throughout Part One we will be almost exclusively concerned with what Katz and Lazarsfeld (1955) have aptly called "campaign" effects,[2] i.e., such short term opinon and attitude effects as are typically the goals of campaigns—political, civic, or institutional. There are virtually no objective studies of the role played by mass communication in long term attitude change.

We will also be concerned almost exclusively with changes in *attitude,* rather than in overt behavior. Whether or not an attitude is manifested in overt behavior obviously depends upon numerous extra-communication factors, including, for example, the degree to which action is physically or socially feasible.

Reinforcement,

Minor Change,

and Related Phenomena

The Relative Incidence of Reinforcement, Minor Change, and Conversion

A NUMBER OF STUDIES, some performed in the laboratory and some in the social world, indicate that persuasive mass communication functions far more frequently as an agent of reinforcement than as an agent of change. Within a given audience exposed to particular communications, reinforcement, or at least constancy of opinion, is typically found to be the dominant effect; minor change, as in intensity of opinion, is found to be the next most common; and conversion is typically found to be the most rare. It would appear to be no exaggeration to say that the efficacy of mass communication in influencing existing opinions and attitudes is inversely correlated with the degree of change.[1]

This is in no way to say that major changes and conversions do not occur, nor that under particular conditions they may not be widespread. It is rather to say that by comparison they are rare, and that persuasive mass communication normally tends to serve far more heavily in the interests of reinforcement and of minor change.

These tendencies have been elaborately documented in two studies of the effect of pre-election campaigns.

In the first and now classic study, Lazarsfeld, Berelson, and Gaudet (1948) employed a panel technique to trace the effects of the 1940 presidential campaign upon residents of Erie County, Ohio. Among approximately 600 respondents whose vote intentions were ascertained in May (before the national conventions) and in October, exposure to months of campaign propaganda was found to have reinforced the original, pre-campaign intentions of 53 per cent. An additional 26 per cent switched from adherence to a particular party to "undecided," or from "undecided" to a particular party. Only 5 per cent were definitely found to have been converted, i.e., to have crossed party lines.[2]

In a second study, of greater complexity and wider topical scope, Berelson, Lazarsfeld, and McPhee (1954) investigated the decision-making processes of voters in Elmira, N.Y. during the presidential campaign of 1948. Respondents were classified along a five-point scale ranging from "strong Republican," through "moderate Republican" and "neutral," to "strong Democrat." Their position on the scale in June was compared, by panel procedures, with their position in August, and their position in August was later compared with their position in October.

Reinforcement, modification, and conversion were found to have occurred with the same relative incidence as they had in the earlier study. Between June and August, 66 per cent of a panel of 760 respondents maintained their original party adherence, 17 per cent wavered between a given party and "neutral," or vice versa, and only 8 per cent were actually converted. During the second half of the campaign, the incidence of reinforcement was about the same (68 per cent), and that of conversion even lower (3 per cent).[3] Those who were more highly exposed to the campaign, furthermore, were found to be more selective in their exposure and to be less likely to undergo conversion than were those who were less highly exposed.[4] Berelson, Lazarsfeld, and McPhee conclude, in what seems something of an understatement, that media "exposure crystallizes and reinforces more than it converts."[5] An appendix to the study indicates that these findings are confirmed in one or another degree by three other independent studies of elections.

It has been suggested that these election studies may undervalue the *total* effect of mass communications. Lang and Lang (1959), for example, have suggested that the mass media may exercise a more indirect and perhaps more extensive effect on vote intentions during the period *between* political campaigns, and these authors have called for research designed to explore this hypothesis. Their provocative argument is, however, as yet neither substantiated nor refuted by empirical findings, and it is accordingly discussed, along with other as yet speculative matters, in the conclusion to this volume.[6]

The tendency of mass communication to reinforce rather than convert has, in any case, been documented by various other studies, and in reference to communications on political and non-political topics. The Bureau of Applied Social Research, for example, interviewed 560 adult residents of Springfield, Missouri, before and after a week-long media and public relations campaign designed to improve their attitude toward the oil industry. Seventy eight per cent of the panel retained their original "pro" or "anti" classification, 13 per cent switched from "anti" to "pro," and 9 per cent switched in the opposite direction.[7] In a recent study of rather limited scope, Schramm and Carter (1959) found that an election campaign telecast had changed the vote intention of only *one* out of 65 interviewed viewers. Other studies which indicate that mass communication is more likely to reinforce than it is to convert are cited in the succeeding sections of this chapter, which focus on the process of reinforcement rather than upon the mere fact of its occurrence.

Considerably greater incidence of minor change, as opposed to conversion, has been noted in various laboratory studies. As early as 1938, Sims reported that among a group of persons opposed to the TVA whom he exposed to counterpropaganda, intensity of opposition was reduced far more often than conversion was effected. Similar findings were reported by Asher and Sargent (1941) in relation to the effect of "cartoon caricatures." More recently, Janis and King (1954), investigating the effects of role-playing upon opinion change, observed that all forms of all communications used in the experiments produced minor changes considerably more frequently than they produced major changes.[8]

Thus, persuasive mass communication has been observed, on different occasions, to create attitudes, to reinforce or modify existing attitudes, and to change attitudes. Research has pretty well established that such mass communication is more likely to reinforce existing opinions than to change them, and more likely to produce modifications than conversions. Happily, communications research has gone beyond the fact and thrown considerable light upon the *process*.

Mediating Factors in the Service of Reinforcement

INTRODUCTION

Two decades of research, some focused directly upon the problem and some peripherally pertinent, indicate that the tendency of persuasive mass communication to reinforce existing opinion is anything but hypodermic. The communication itself appears to be no sufficient cause of the effect, but rather to function amid other factors and conditions which, though external to the communication, seem to mediate its influence in such a way as to render it an agent of reinforcement rather than change.[9]

We shall here cite five mediating factors and conditions, including both those whose operation is most widely documented in the literature and some others which, though not as copiously documented, seem to the present author to be particularly important and implicative. Specifically, we shall note how reinforcement is or may be abetted by (1) predispositions and the related processes of selective exposure, selective perception, and selective retention; (2) the groups, and the norms of groups, to which the audience members belong; (3) interpersonal dissemination of the content of communications; (4) the exercise of opinion leadership; and (5) the nature of mass media in a free enterprise society.

None of this will alter or amend the basic proposition that reinforcement is a more likely effect of persuasive communication than is conversion. The discussion to follow will rather help to explain why this is so. It will accordingly add little to what has already been said regarding the actual effects of mass communication, but will deal instead with how the effect occurs.

PREDISPOSITIONS AND RELATED PROCESSES: SELECTIVE EXPOSURE, SELECTIVE PERCEPTION, AND SELECTIVE RETENTION

The existing opinions and interests of people, or, more generally, their predispositions, have been shown profoundly to influence their behavior vis-à-vis mass communications and the effects which such communications are likely to have upon them. By and large, people tend to expose themselves to those mass communications which are in accord with their existing attitudes and interests. Consciously or unconsciously, they avoid communications of opposite hue. In the event of their being nevertheless exposed to unsympathetic material, they often seem not to perceive it, or to recast and interpret it to fit their existing views, or to forget it more readily than they forget sympathetic material. The processes involved in these self-protective exercises have become known as selective exposure (or, more classically, "self-selection"[10]), selective perception, and selective retention.

Selective exposure.—The tendency of people to expose themselves to mass communications in accord with their existing opinions and interests and to avoid unsympathetic material, has been widely demonstrated. Among the voters of Erie County in 1940, for example, Lazarsfeld, Berelson, and Gaudet (1948) found that

> . . . actual exposure to [partisan propaganda] does *not* parallel availability. Availability *plus* predispositions determines exposure—and predispositions lead people to select communications which are congenial, which support their previous position. More Republicans than Democrats listened to Willkie and more Democrats than Republicans listened to Roosevelt. The universe of campaign communications—political speeches, newspaper stories, newscasts, editorials, columns, magazine articles—was open to virtually everyone. But exposure was consistently partisan. . . .

> By and large about two-thirds of the constant partisans—the people who were either Republican or Democratic from May right through to Election Day—managed to see and hear more of their own side's propaganda than the opposition's. About one-fifth of them happened to expose more frequently to the other side, and the rest were neutral in their exposure. But—and this is important—the more strongly partisan the person, the more likely he is to insulate himself from contrary points of view. The constants with great interest and with most concern in the election of their own candidate were *more* partisan in exposure than the constants with less interest and less concern. Such partisan exposure can only serve to reinforce the partisan's previous attitudes. In short, the most partisan people protect themselves from the disturbing experience presented by opposition arguments by paying little attention to them. Instead, they turn to that propaganda which reaffirms the validity and wisdom of their original decision—which is then reinforced.

> One of the assumptions of a two-party democratic system is that considerable inter-communication goes on between the supporters of the opposing sides. This evidence indicates that such inter-communication may go on in public—in the media of communication—without reaching very far into the ranks of the strongly partisan, on either side. In recent years, there has been a good deal of talk by men of good will about the desirability and necessity of guaranteeing the free exchange of ideas in the market-place of public opinion. Such talk has centered upon the problem of keeping free the channels of expression and communication. Now we find that the consumers of ideas, if they have made a decision on the issue, themselves erect high tariff walls against alien notions.[11]

Similar findings have been reported by other investigators, in reference to various topics. Cartwright (1949), for example, reports upon a test made by the Treasury Department of a documentary film designed to heighten citizen identification with such home front activities as bond purchasing and donating blood; a well touted free public showing in Bridgeport, Connecticut, was attended by only 5 per cent of the adult population, and the audience later was found to consist in the main of already more active citizens. A media campaign designed to increase information about the UN and improve attitudes toward it was found by Star and Hughes (1950) to have been most widely attended by persons whose interest in and opinion of the organization were high to begin with. Cannell and MacDonald (1956) discovered that articles on health, including those dealing with the possible relationship between smoking and cancer, were consistently read by 60 per cent of the non-smoking males among a probability sample of Ann Arbor adults, but by only 32 per cent of the male smokers, to whom the material presented more of a threat; among women, for whom the threat was considerably less, the respective percentages were 69 and 59. Recently Schramm and Carter (1959) found that Republicans were about twice as likely as were Democrats to have watched a Republican sponsored campaign telecast. An old and now classic story of selective exposure indicates that

> . . . even so-called educational programs are not free from this tendency. Some time ago there was a program on the air which showed in different installments how all the nationalities in this country have contributed to American culture. The purpose was to teach tolerance of other nationalities. The indications were, however, that the audience for each program consisted mainly of the national group which was currently being praised. There was little chance for the program to teach tolerance, because the self-selection of each audience produced a body of listeners who heard only about the contributions of a country which each already approved.[12]

Selective perception.—Objective demonstrations of selective perception antedate communications research. Laboratory experiments have established that perception of moving lights, relative size of coins, relative length of lines, and the like, is in part or whole determined by what persons want to perceive, have habitually perceived, or expect some form of social or physical reward for perceiving.[13] Various devices have been successfully used to elicit apparently wholly sincere reports of perception quite out of accord with fact.

Similar processes, in regard to communications stemming both from mass media and from other sources, have been long noted and often detailed.

Allport and Postman (1945), in a now classic study of the metamorphoses of rumors, presented virtual case histories of oral messages being changed in the process of social diffusion to fit existing spheres of knowledge and attitudes. In one phase of the study, for example, a picture of an altercation in a train, in which a white man is holding a razor and arguing with a Negro, was shown to subjects who were required to describe it to other subjects, who were in turn required to describe it to others, and so on. In the course of these successive narrations, the razor typically shifted to the hand of the Negro. Allport and Postman note, among other conclusions, that material which does not fit the predispositions of a perceiver is likely to be

> recast to fit not only his span of comprehension and . . . retention, but, likewise, his own personal needs and interests. What was outer becomes inner; what was objective becomes subjective.[14]

Mass communication has been found vulnerable to similarly selective perception. Hyman and Sheatsley (1947) found that people who thought the Soviet Union entirely to blame for poor Soviet-U.S. relations were less apt to think the papers they read were over-critical of the Soviet Union than were those who placed the blame on the United States or on both countries. The authors note that this tendency existed despite the presumed selective reading of the different groups. The pro-Soviet group, for example, presumably tended to read pro-Soviet papers, but they were nevertheless *more* likely than the others to consider that their papers treated the Soviet Union *unfavorably.* Cooper and Jahoda (1947) and Kendall and Wolf (1946 and 1949) all report on a study in which cartoons ridiculing racial and religious prejudice were misperceived by prejudiced persons as glorifications of pure American lineage, devices employed by Jews to stir up religious strife, and the like; misunderstanding was two-and-a-half times as common among the prejudiced as among the unprejudiced, and three times as common among those prejudiced persons who were least aware of the social implications of prejudice. Somewhat similar findings are reported by Wilner (1951), whose subjects interpreted the expressions and motives of characters in a pro-tolerance film (*Home of the Brave*) in ways which were largely predictable on the basis of their scores on a racial tolerance test. More recently, Cannell and MacDonald (1956) asked 228 adult residents of Ann Arbor, Michigan whether newspaper and magazine reports had convinced them that smoking was a cause of cancer. The relationship was accepted (i.e., "perceived") by 54 per cent of the non-smokers, but by only 28 per cent of the smokers, for whom it presumably constituted a considerable threat. Other examples of selective perception are attested in the literature, although its occurrence is not the central finding of very many studies.[15]

Selective retention.—Some of the studies cited above in connection with selective perception may obviously involve selective retention as well. The line of demarcation between the two processes is, in fact, often difficult and in some instances impossible to draw. When, for example, a person who has been exposed to a communication a few minutes before presents a distorted or incomplete report of its contents, it is difficult to determine whether the content was selectively perceived in the first place, whether it was correctly perceived but not retained, or whether the two processes complemented one another. The difficulty of making such distinctions is obviously far greater if the period between exposure and report is a matter of days or weeks.

A number of studies, however, have focused more on selective retention than on perception or interpretation.

Levine and Murphy (1943) presented both a pro-Communist

prose passage and an anti-Communist prose passage to five pro-Communist college students and five anti-Communist college students. A few minutes after each presentation the subjects were asked to reproduce the passage as accurately as possible and the whole procedure was repeated "at weekly intervals for four weeks. Then, at weekly intervals for five weeks, memory of the selection was tested without submitting the paragraph to the subject."[16] The pro-Soviet group consistently recalled more of the pro-Soviet material than did the anti-Communist group, and the gap between them increased over time, although the difference never reached the .01 level of significance. During the five weeks of "forgetting," the anti-Communist group forgot the pro-Soviet material faster than the pro-Communist group, and the gap again increased over time, reaching the .01 significance level after three weeks.

Similar tendencies occurred in relation to the anti-Soviet passage, but to a more marked degree.[17] The anti-Soviet group learned more than the pro-Soviet group, and the pro-Soviet group forgot faster than did the anti-Soviet group, with all differences throughout the nine weeks significant at the .01 level. In brief, the material was more readily learned by the sympathetic group, and more readily forgotten by the unsympathetic group.

Selective retention of pictorial material in accord with attitudes on race was reported by Seeleman (1941). A finding which reflects selective retention or selective exposure or both was noted by Hyman and Sheatsley (1947). These authors asked a sample of adults whether they had heard about certain documents (e.g., a communique in which England, France, and the United States had denounced the Franco government). Regardless of their replies, all respondents were then told the gist of the documents and asked how they felt about the topic in question. Persons who had recalled the document to begin with were consistently found to be more likely to approve of the position taken by the document.

The phenomenon of selective retention is now widely regarded as axiomatic and has received little research attention in recent years. Zimmerman and Bauer (1956), however, have incidentally redocumented the occurrence of selective retention in a study focused on other matters, and their findings have since been replicated in an unpublished study by Schramm (1958).

Conclusions.—Selective exposure, selective perception, and selective retention do not, of course, occur among all people in all communication situations. The twenty-odd studies cited above typically indicate that one or more of these processes occurred among a stipulated percentage of the group, but that it did not occur among the rest of the group. Approximately one third of the "constant partisans" observed by Lazarsfeld, Berelson, and Gaudet (1948), for example, did not practice selective exposure, and about one fifth were in fact exposed more to communications opposing their party position.[18] Immunity to the selective processes can be documented in almost any of the studies cited.

Little is known, furthermore, about the functioning of the selective processes over very long periods of exposure to unsympathetic communications. Some of the studies cited here involved a single exposure to a single communication, some involved several exposures or several communications, and some involved exposure to several months of propaganda. None, however, involved exposure to years of propaganda. What might happen to the selective processes over such a period is as yet largely a matter of speculation.

Even in relation to limited exposure, furthermore, the selective processes appear to function at times imperfectly or not at all, and on some occasions to serve, atypically, to impel opinion change. Various such situations are discussed in Chapters III and IV which deal, respectively, with the role of mass communication in creating opinions about new issues and in producing conversions.

But, as we have shown, the selective processes do occur extremely frequently, and where they do, they function as a protective net in the service of existing predispositions. In this sense, the processes seem to the present author to be illustrative of the generalizations earlier advanced,[19] which state that mass communications ordinarily work through mediators, rather than producing direct effects, and that the mediators themselves tend to render mass communication an agent, but not the sole cause, of reinforcement rather than conversion.

GROUPS AND GROUP NORMS

Communication research has recently, and somewhat belatedly, been "rediscovering" the group.[20] The profound influence which even casual, let alone primary-type groups, exercise upon the perceptions, opinions, and attitudes of their members has been long a focus of research by social psychology in general and by small group researchers in particular. The conspicuous pertinency of such studies for mass communication research and theory has been asserted by various writers, among them Flowerman (1949), Ford (1953 and 1954), Riley and Riley (1951 and 1959) and Maccoby (1954), and has recently been systematically expounded by Katz and Lazarsfeld (1955).

Drawing upon a host of studies, few of which are in themselves concerned with the effects of communication, Katz and Lazarsfeld propose, with considerable supporting evidence, that many "ostensibly individual opinions and attitudes . . . [are] primarily social [in] character,"[21] i.e., they are the norms of groups to which the individual belongs or wishes to belong. The authors systematically detail conditions under which groups may serve as reinforcing agents and may influence mass communications to do likewise, and conditions under which group influence may be inactive or may even favor opinion change.[22] In reference to groups serving in the interests of reinforcement, various studies are adduced to show that people tend to belong to groups whose opinions are congenial with their own; that the opinions themselves seem to be intensified, or at least made more manifest, by intra-group discussion; and that the benefits, both psychological and social, of continued membership in good standing are likely to act as a deterrent against opinion change.

Several studies indicate that the tendencies cited by Katz and Lazarsfeld do in fact mediate the effects of persuasive communications.

Predispositions on the part of respondents toward opinions characteristic of their family groups, for example, and even a readiness to adhere to a given point of view for no other reason than that it was family-anchored, have been noted in various studies, including Lazarsfeld, Berelson, and Gaudet's (1948) investigation of the 1940 election campaign. For persons such as the young man who reported his intention to "vote Democratic because *my grandfather will skin me if I don't*"—or for his opposite number who explained that "I will vote Republican because *my family are all Republicans so therefore I would have to vote that way*,"[23]—exposure to months of campaign propaganda was found particularly likely to be reinforcing, and particularly unlikely to effect conversion. So strong was the tendency toward family homogeneity that "only 4 per cent of the 413 panel members who voted claimed that someone in their families had voted differently."[24] Similar if less marked homogeneity was found among co-workers and among co-members of formal organizations.

Current theory regarding the resistance of group-anchored attitudes to change and their susceptibility to reinforcement is not yet sufficiently refined, however, to permit wholly accurate prediction. A series of experiments by Kelley and Volkart, for example, strongly suggest that the degree of resistance to change is closely related to the degree to which group members value their membership and to the current saliency of the norms themselves. Certain anomalous findings, however, indicate that our knowledge of these factors, or our techniques of measurement, or both, are as yet highly imperfect. In one of the experiments (Kelley and Volkart, 1952), for example, twelve Boy Scout troops were subjected to a talk which attacked certain pre-validated

Scout norms regarding the relative worth of woodcraft and camp- ing as opposed to more urban activities. The Scouts had been previously classified according to the degree to which they valued their membership, and had been divided into two groups, one of which was assured that its members' reactions to the talk would be kept "private" and the other of which was led to believe that its members' reactions would be made "public." Scouts in the "private" group reacted as might be expected; the more they valued their membership, the less did they change their opin- ions,[25] and among those who most highly valued their member- ship, the communication in fact boomeranged, intensifying the very opinions it was designed to oppose. But among the "public" group, for whom the effect might have been expected to be more marked, no statistically significant differences in resistance be- tween the high and low valuing members were observed, and resistance to the communication was generally less than it had been among the "private" group. Similar on-again-off-again find- ings are reported by Kelley (1958), who exposed various student groups to communications opposing Catholic norms, after first exposing some of the groups to communications designed to raise the saliency of those particular norms. Among the high-school subjects, the "high saliency" Catholics showed significantly greater resistance to change than did the "low-saliency" Catholics or the non-Catholics. Among the college group, however, the expected difference between the high and low-saliency Catholics did not appear, and those Catholics who attended services most regularly showed *less* resistance to the unsympathetic communi- cation than did the less ardent churchgoers.

Kelley and Volkart are unable wholly to account for these findings. They suggest that certain spurious artifacts of the ex- perimental situation, or certain unforeseen complexities in the reactions of subjects, may have affected the results. This is, of course, to say that the experimental variables may have been somewhat impure, or that other variables, as yet unidentified, may have been at work, which is, in turn, a call for further theoretical analysis and further research. At present, it can only be said that it seems logical to postulate a relationship between valuation of group membership and resistance to change, and between saliency of an issue and resistance to change, but that neither relationship has been conclusively demonstrated.

Quite aside from providing anchorage for existing opinions, group membership may facilitate reinforcement and impede conversion by intensifying selective exposure. Intra-group discussion, formal or informal, probably increases the likelihood of given members' being aware of sympathetic media offerings, and actual group exposure to such communications may occur either casually, by virtue of shared interests, or by organizational fiat. The sacrament of teen-age clique and fan club attendance on particular radio, record, and film stars, for example, has been long observed by wearied parents and recently validated by social research,[26] and similar quasi-spontaneous or pre-planned exposure to persuasive communications obviously occurs among groups of all ages. Various highly successful persuasive campaigns, including the rightist attempts of Father Coughlin, the essentially apolitical urgings of Billy Graham, and the continual indoctrination program of Communist states, have urged or demanded that the faithful listen to reinforcing media offerings in groups.

Even if group exposure does not occur, the mere existence of the group facilitates possible reinforcement effects of sympathetic communications by providing a ready-made network for inter-personal dissemination of their contents.[27] The attendant intra-group discussion appears furthermore likely to render the norms more salient, and so to recall drifters back to orthodoxy. In an ingeniously designed experiment by McKeachie (1954), for example, communications (lectures) on controversial topics, and the discussion which the communications engendered, made some group members aware that they had misperceived the pertinent group norms. The great majority of such individuals showed opinion changes in the direction of the norm, which was also the direction intended by the communication. In normal social situations, such increased saliency of the norm may well lead to further dispersion of the communication, producing a kind of self-impelling cycle in the service of reinforcement.

Groups may additionally serve to intensify the reinforcement potential of sympathetic mass communications by providing arenas for the exercise of inter-personal influence (as distinct from mere dissemination of communication content) and opinion leadership. Because of the complexity of these phenomena and because they are not wholly restricted to groups, they are discussed in separate sections of this and later chapters.[28]

Groups and group norms thus serve in various ways to mediate the effects of mass communication in favor of reinforcement. As will be shown in Chapter IV, they also serve on occasions to mediate the effects of communication in favor of conversion. Insofar as they mediate in favor of reinforcement, however, they appear to the author to be, like the selective processes, illustrative of the first two generalizations advanced in the introduction.[29]

INTER-PERSONAL DISSEMINATION OF MASS COMMUNICATION

The common social habit of telling friends about mass communications which they may themselves have missed appears likely to supplement the reinforcing capabilities of the original communications.

Pertinent studies in small group research indicate that communications are likely to be transmitted along social lines defined by friendship, by shared interest, and particularly by shared opinions.[30] Inter-personal dissemination of the contents of a communication thus creates a kind of secondary selective exposure; the audience originally reached by the communication is increased, but the supplement is likely to consist in the main of persons already sympathetic to the views espoused.

Evidence of these tendencies as yet resides in the main in small group research, and the communications involved typically consist of brief bits of highly specific information. But there is some evidence that mass media content, particularly persuasive content, is spread farther abroad through similarly selective channels. In totalitarian countries, for example, the contents of proscribed radio programs, such as those of the Voice of America and Radio Free Europe, are known to be efficiently spread by word of mouth through both casual and semi-formal partisan networks. In reference to democracies there is reason to suspect, but there is no clear-cut evidence, that inter-personal dissemination of mass communication content flows primarily, though not exclusively, along partisan channels. Thus, Berelson, Lazarsfeld, and McPhee (1954) found that during the 1948 election campaign persons most highly exposed to campaign propaganda tended to be most partisan, and that "mass media exposure [also] affects [other] mediating variables like . . . interest, and discussion."[31] They found also that political discussion was pursued in the main by persons with similar views.[32] Neither their study nor any other study of significant scope has clearly shown that persons exposed to partisan communications tend to discuss *those communications or their contents* with persons of similar views.[33]

Inter-personal dissemination may also intensify the reinforcing capabilities of the original communication by the simple fact of its human agency. As will be shown in detail below,[34] such personal influence seems to be generally more persuasive than is mass communication.

Insofar as inter-personal dissemination of persuasive communications abets reinforcement effects, it appears to the present author to be another of the factors cited in the first two of the generalizations earlier advanced,[35]—i.e., the generalizations which proposed that mass communication ordinarily works through mediators, and that these mediators tend to render the effect of the communications reinforcing.

OPINION LEADERSHIP

The reinforcement potential of persuasive mass communication may well be intensified on some occasions by the activity of "opinion leaders," whose role in the process of decision-making has been the focus of considerable recent research. Almost all such research has focused on the role of the opinion leader in processes of opinion or behavior *change*, but there are indications that he functions also in the service of reinforcement.

Both the research and its theoretical implications have been brilliantly summarized by Katz (1957) and will be here resummarized only to the degree necessary for the present argument.

The concept of opinion leadership, or "the two-step flow of communications,"[36] was first clearly formulated by Lazarsfeld, Berelson, and Gaudet (1948). In the course of their analysis of the 1940 election, these investigators discovered that "personal contacts appear to have been . . . more effective than the mass media in influencing voting decisions."[37] The "opinion leaders" who exercised such influence were found to be widely dispersed through all social classes, and to be much like the persons they influence. "Compared with the rest of the population, [however,] opinion leaders were found to be considerably more exposed to the radio, to the newspapers and to magazines, that is, to the formal media of communication."[38] Lazarsfeld, Berelson, and Gaudet (1948) accordingly suggested the possibility that "ideas often flow *from* radio and print *to* the opinion leaders and *from* them to the less active sections of the population."[39]

Subsequent studies, more specifically tailored to explore the phenomenon of opinion leadership, have elaborated upon the original findings and refined the original hypothesis. Research has been focused on the processes by which people come to decisions regarding public issues, change their food purchasing habits and habits of dress, and select the movies they attend. Special studies have inquired into how farmers come to adopt new farming practices and how physicians come to adopt new drugs.[40] In all of these matters, and presumably in others, many people appear to be more crucially influenced by specific other individuals than by pertinent mass communications. These specific others, or "opinion leaders," or "influentials" may serve a following of one, of three or four, or of somewhat more, but they typically do so in reference to only one topic; the fashion leader, for example, is not likely to be a marketing leader, nor is the physician who influences others to adopt a new drug more likely than his colleagues to influence their views on public issues. "Opinion leaders and the people whom they influence are very much alike and typically belong to the same primary groups of family, friends and co-workers."[41] The leader, however, is typically found to be more exposed than are his followers to media appropriate to his sphere of influence and to other sources of pertinent information to which the followers are not exposed. The public affairs leader, for example, is typically more exposed to newspapers and news magazines; the movie leader is more exposed to movie magazines;[42] the physician opinion leader attends more out-of-town meetings than do his followers.

Mass communication may enter this decision-making process at several points, but regardless of its port of entry, it is likely to become susceptible to the mediation of the opinion leader. It may, for example, provide the follower with information, define a point of view, or otherwise provide raw material which is later molded by the opinion leader. Or, after the follower has been influenced by the opinion leader, mass communication may provide material which the follower selectively attends or perceives to buttress his newly adopted opinion. For the opinion leader himself, wide exposure to mass communication[43] provides information and points of view which he may or may not pass on to his less widely exposed followers.[44] The leader's occasions for mediation are multiple.

Existing studies of opinion leadership and personal influence, and particularly those studies which are explicitly related to the effects of mass communication, have focused, as we have noted, primarily on the influence of these factors in attitude and behavior *change,* as, for example, in changes of opinion, purchasing habits, and drug therapy. Practically no attention has been paid to the possible influence of opinion leaders in *discouraging change.* But there is reason to postulate that such leadership does function also in the interests of constancy and reinforcement, and that it may in fact do so quite frequently.

The first and in a sense still the most explicit finding on the subject emphasizes the role of opinion leadership in the process of change. Lazarsfeld, Berelson, and Gaudet (1948) found, in their study of voting decisions, that persons who changed their vote intentions and those who made up their minds late in the campaign mentioned personal influence as a factor in their decisions more often than did those who did not make such changes.[45] It is to be noted, however, that those who did not change their minds also mentioned personal influence, though less often. And, perhaps more importantly, it is to be noted "that those who changed their vote intentions were largely people who early [i.e., earlier] in the campaign, had reported that they intended to vote differently from their family or friends."[46] To whatever degree opinion leadership influenced those particular changes, it functioned to "pull . . . deviates back into line."[47]

This latter consideration, along with certain other findings about opinion leadership, personal influence, and primary groups, provides some grounds for postulating that opinion leadership must serve frequently to reinforce both group norms and individual opinion. The pertinent data provide only inferential evidence for such a position, but the inferences seem highly implicative.

To begin with, the opinion leader has been found, in many studies, to be a kind of super-representative of his group. Comparison of influentials in most of the areas thus far studied reveals that the leader is characteristically more competent, within his specialty, than are his fellows, and that he characteristically has access to wider sources of pertinent information. But he is also typically found to be "like everyone else, only slightly more so"[48] in reference to group norms. The Berelson, Lazarsfeld, and McPhee (1954) voting study, for example, found that opinion leaders were more apt than others to support their party's position. They found that the leaders

> represent or symbolize the given group's norms in the particular sphere—the *given* group's norms, say, labor's and not business', and in the *particular* sphere, say, voting, not running the community's welfare movement or baseball team. Those men can better lead who are traveling the same road as their followers but are a little ahead.[49]

Katz (1957), summing up the findings of studies to that date, concludes that "influence is related . . . [among other things] to the *personification of certain values*"[50] of the group to which leader and follower belong. The leader's guidance seems to be sought or accepted in specific areas partly—or perhaps largely— because it provides his followers with the sort of satisfactions they seek in those areas. The marketing leader, for example, is relied upon because the brands she suggests fulfill the particular needs of her followers. In regard to her field of expertness she appears, like other leaders, to be consciously or unconsciously so intimately familiar with group norms that she can guide other group members toward their attainment.

In reference to group norms, then, opinion leaders seem likely to be conformist. They appear to be, in this respect, very like *group* leaders (as opposed to persons who are merely *opinion* leaders), who have been similarly observed to embody group norms, and thus to be "in a certain sense, the most conformist members of their groups—upholding whatever norms and values are central to the groups."[51] Thus, regardless of the role they play in processes of *individual* opinion change, the influence of opinion leaders in reference to group norms is, theoretically at least, quite likely to be expended often in favor of reinforcement. As a gatekeeper or transmitter of mass communication content, for example, the opinion leader might readily transmit or approve material in accord with group norms, and might fail to transmit, or inveigh against, material opposing such norms.

Now group members, as we have noted at some length earlier in this chapter, tend often to adopt and to remain faithful to opinions and norms of the group. And if we assume that such constancy is not always mere failure to think about the issue, but rather that the members at least on some occasions discuss the matter, then we may postulate that the influence of opinion leaders may often be reinforcing for the individual as well as for the group.

A series of findings reported by Berelson, Lazarsfeld, and McPhee (1954) suggest that constancy *is* often accompanied by discussion, both within and outside the group, and that such discussion is quite apt to be reinforcing. More specifically, the three investigators found that "most political discussion goes on among people of like characteristics—like in friendship, in age . . . in occupation . . . and in political preference itself" and that such "discussions are made up much more of mutual agreement than of disagreement."[52] Analysis of

> . . . the respondents' own recollections, at the end of the campaign, *of what* was talked about in their most recent political discussions [reveals that] in about a third of the cases the discussion centers about topics that do not directly involve political preferences— such as predictions about victory in the election, exchange of information, or neutral observation about the conduct of the campaign. In the remainder of the cases mutual agreement between the discussants outnumbers disagreement ten to one: about 63 per cent amount to reinforcing exchanges about common positions on the candidates or the issues, and only 6 per cent involve some degree of argument between the discussants.[53]

To whatever degree these discussions are influential, they involve the exercise of opinion leadership, and in such instances, opinion leadership would seem to be reinforcing not only for the group, but for a considerable number of individuals as well. Katz (1957), in summing up pertinent research to that date, notes that the

. . . effectiveness of interpersonal influence, as it is revealed in the studies under review, is reflected in the homogeneity of opinions and actions in primary groups. The medium of primary group communication is, by definition, person-to-person. Both of the voting studies indicate the high degree of homogeneity of political opinion among members of the same families, and among co-workers and friends. The effectiveness of such primary groups in pulling potential deviates back into line is demonstrated by the fact that those who changed their vote intentions were largely people who, early in the campaign, had reported that they intended to vote differently from their family or friends.[54]

We may add that personal influence and opinion leadership seem also to function to prevent group members from becoming deviates in the first place.

These several explicit findings and the inferences which may be drawn add up to no firm conclusion. It appears fairly certain that opinion leadership does function in the service of reinforcement as well as in the service of change. But the relative frequency with which it functions in these two ways has not yet been properly investigated. The one explicit datum on relative frequency derives from the pioneer study in the series. The emphasis of subsequent research has been on processes of observed change; in reference to several areas studied, as, for example, those covered by Katz and Lazarsfeld (1955), non-changers are barely discussed. Research on the role of opinion leadership in phenomena of constancy would appear to be a necessary step in increasing and refining our knowledge of personal influence and of "the two-step flow of communication." Particular attention to the interplay of mass communication and opinion leadership in such processes is essential to determining whether and to what degree opinion leadership does in fact increase the reinforcement potential of mass communication.

To whatever degree personal influence does so abet reinforcement, it appears to be another of the mediating factors the existence and influence of which are postulated in the first two of the five generalizations advanced in the introduction to this volume.

THE NATURE OF MASS MEDIA IN A FREE ENTERPRISE SOCIETY

Commercial mass communication in a free enterprise society has been widely claimed to be of necessity a force toward the reinforcement of dominant cultural values, and to be economically constrained from espousing any view which is questioned by any significant portion of its potential audience. The argument was much more popular in the late 40's and early 50's than it is today. It is worth reviewing, however, not only because it was so prevalent, but because it made a good deal of sense, and because the process it envisaged may very well still be occurring.

The argument as typically presented by, for example, Siepman (1948), Lazarsfeld and Merton (1948), Klapper (1948 and 1949), Seldes (1950), and various others, pointed out that commercially competitive mass media in a free enterprise society depended for their life-blood on attracting and holding a vast and highly varied audience. To preclude alienating any significant portion of that audience—and among audiences of several million even a small minority is commercially significant—the media were forced to avoid espousing any point of view which any minority might find distasteful. Since the audience and its views were so varied, the media were perforce either constrained from reflecting any attitudes at all, which was patently impossible, or restricted to echoing those views and values to which there was virtually no objection. Put another way, the media were restricted to echoing what was universally accepted, or to resanctifying the sanctified.[55]

Proponents of this argument generally recognized that it did not apply to newscasts and news commentary, nor to the occasional documentary or information program. They pointed out, however, that media production and media attendance were overwhelmingly devoted to "entertainment" features, and that these, with very rare exceptions, avoided the controversial and re-echoed established values. Elkin (1950 and 1954) claimed, for example, that culturally approved attitudes regarding sex behavior, dress, and the like, were effectively transmitted even by Western films, most of which do not deal with the current scene.

There appears to have been some truth in these claims, at least in regard to the nature of the communication material itself and insofar as the argument was restricted to entertainment fare. Content analyses of daytime serials, TV dramas, short stories in popular magazines, and other entertainment features, consistently revealed that the dramas were typically played out in worlds wherein the best people were native Americans, wherein conflicts stemmed essentially from individual inadequacies and very rarely from social forces, and wherein any deviation from culturally unquestionable behavior led to catastrophe.[56] Films derived from books were found typically to omit or temper any social criticism which might have been in the original, and to tighten the bonds of poetic justice.[57]

Such communication stimuli seem likely to have been reinforcing, both socially and individually. Their potential for conversion was at the very least minimized, or perhaps nullified, by their avoidance of the controversial. Some of the then more vehement proponents of the argument, including Klapper (1948 and 1949), pointed out that the sanctification of existing values enjoyed a "monopoly propaganda position"[58]—i.e., no one opposed it—and that monopoly propaganda was widely believed to be extremely effective.

Whether it actually was so effective, however, was never conclusively demonstrated. At least one study of soap opera audiences suggested that such culturally sanctified moral tenets and myths as the soap operas celebrated did tend to be reinforced among such audience members as already subscribed to such views,[59] but no similar data were adduced in regard to social issues.

Reinforcement of specific social attitudes was also thought to be a likely result of the manner in which mass media on occasion treated topics which they more generally avoided. Several ostensible attacks on race prejudice, for example, were couched in such gentle and ambiguous terms as to be particularly susceptible to wide selective perception and so to be perceived as in accord with virtually any view. A much-exhibited car card, for example, which pictured several white men, a Chinese, and a Negro, captioned "It takes all races to make our city run" surely evoked no resistance among proponents of racial equality; for those who considered themselves unprejudiced but merely believed that non-Caucasians should be assigned to menial labor, the message might have been similarly reinforcing. Other media attacks on race prejudice so exaggerated the phenomenon as to render it inapplicable to any but the wildest extremists. The film *Cross-fire*, for example, portrayed anti-Semitism as a homicidal drive. Such anti-Semites as witnessed the film may well have felt that their own discriminatory practices were not "real" prejudice, and their attitudes, being thus divested of guilt, may well have been reinforced. That some such effect may actually have occurred is suggested by the findings of Raths and Trager (1948) who exposed 114 senior high school students to the film and to before-and-after questionnaires. Prior to seeing the film, 20 per cent and 34 per cent considered anti-Jewish and anti-Negro prejudice, respectively, to be prevalent among young people; after seeing *Cross-fire* only 15 per cent and 21 per cent thought such attitudes prevalent among their contemporaries. The film, in short, seemed to have rendered these persons less sensitive to the existence of racial and religious prejudices.

The foregoing pages have been couched in the past tense, because the picture today is by no means clear. Although no really current content analyses exist to provide precise data,[60] the overall media picture *appears* to have changed considerably. Several current TV and radio programs deliberately seek out and provide voice for exponents of controversial and socially deviant points of view. Current TV dramas do occasionally deal with social issues and not infrequently violate hitherto sanctified taboos; motherhood, for example, is no longer inviolate, and extra-marital relations do not lead unerringly to death, jail, or even social ostracism. Commercial films, both foreign and domestic, have condoned interracial marriage and dealt directly and realistically with racial problems, drug addiction, delinquency, and other matters hitherto more typically avoided. Above all, perhaps, the several media have at least occasionally given to controversy the kind of promition and production—and in the case of radio and TV, the kind of prime time—hitherto almost exclusively reserved for non-controversial entertainment. The Murrows, the Brinkleys, the Wallaces, the UN, and the reporters' interview today rub shoulders with family comedy, variety shows, quizzes, and Westerns.

But this is not necessarily to say that the media may not still be essentially reinforcing.

In the first place, the vast majority of media offerings still obviously fall in the light entertainment category, and probably still avoid the controversial. Although some TV dramas have in recent years treated topics which were previously taboo, these excursions *seem,* in the absence of systematic content analyses, to remain exceptions to the general tendency. The family comedy, for example, to the extent that it espouses any attitudes at all, probably still speaks in favor of sanctified views. A recent report by Winick (1959), which deals primarily with pressures toward censorship in TV and their effect on TV content, cites various recent shows which dealt with controversial topics and a considerably greater number of incidents in which controversial material was deleted, softened, or even changed to conform to traditional TV values. Winick makes no claim to be exhaustive and presents no quantitative data, but concludes that

> There are many examples of courageous innovations in television, but they are far outnumbered by the great mass of programs that refuse to grapple with the themes and issues appropriate to the world today.[61]

> A study of network and station program practices suggests that television is a fairly accurate mirror of the more conservative values of our society.[62]

Thus, although no precise statistics are available, the bulk of media content appears likely to be still speaking in favor of sanctified views. And selective exposure may well shield many devotees of such programs from the more provocative offerings, so that the total effect of media entertainment upon them is predominantly reinforcing.

Secondly, although the controversial programs apparently betoken the growing popularity and audience acceptance of a genre, precisely why that genre is popular and precisely what functions it serves are questions as yet unanswered by research. It is wholly possible that for much of the audience it is not provocative at all, and serves only as a kind of battle scene to be watched from afar by persons more interested in the action than in the topic. It may also serve, in some cases, to provide shocks for those who like to be shocked. In short, for much of the audience, the controversial program may well serve to reinforce some taste or behavior pattern rather than to provoke a weighing of ideas. And even among those who perceive its topical controversy, a considerable number will be likely selectively to perceive the discussion so that it reinforces their existing views.[63]

Finally, the liberalization of dramatic content probably still follows rather than leads the bounds of public acceptance. The recent TV rash of possessive mothers, who are clearly not boys' best friends and not to be honored, may well manifest the seepage of Freudian concepts down to levels of popular culture. The paucity of outraged listeners in any case reveals that the concept is no longer particularly shocking, and that the media are still in accord with popular morality.

It is indeed difficult to see how the situation could be otherwise. The economic character of commercial media in a free enterprise society[64] is such that they appear destined forever to play to, and thus reinforce, socially prevalent attitudes far more often than they are likely to create or convert attitudes. And thus the economic character of the media appears to be one of the several factors which contribute to the likelihood that mass communica-

tion will serve as an agent of reinforcement rather than of conversion. The locus of this influence within the temporal dynamic
of communication effect differs from that of such previously discussed mediators as audience predispositions and the selective
processes, which exert their influence during or after the audience
member's exposure to the communication. The nature of the
media in a free enterprise system affects the communication itself,
and so operates prior to the mediators hitherto discussed. The
direction of its influence appears, however, to be similar to that of
the later operating mediators.

Related Effect Phenomena

Two commonly observed aspects of the effects of persuasive
mass communication are at least tentatively explicable in terms of
the play of the mediating forces which have been described above.
One of these is the incidence of minor attitude change. The other
is the resistance to change of "ego-involved" attitudes.

THE INCIDENCE OF MINOR ATTITUDE CHANGE

The relatively high incidence of minor attitude change among
persons exposed to persuasive mass communication has already
been noted.[65] By way of brief review, two exhaustive studies of
election campaigns found that the percentage of respondents who
wavered between adherence to a particular party and neutrality,
without ever crossing party lines, was much higher than the percentage actually converted and much lower than the percentage remaining wholly constant in their opinions. Similar
results were obtained in a study of the effect of an institutional
advertising campaign and in a considerable number of laboratory
studies.

It is perhaps not remarkable that people should be more inclined to change slightly than they are to change a great deal, and

attempts to explain this fact may seem unnecessary. It may be remarked, however, that such changes are apparently not as deterred by predispositions, group norms, and other extra-media factors as is conversion. The incidence of minor change might be looked upon as manifesting imperfections in the processes which ordinarily hinder change. The fluctuations of opinion, short of conversion, simply may not constitute a psychological threat sufficiently critical to bring all the defensive forces into full play.

The processes of minor attitude change may in this sense resemble the processes involved in another phenomenon which is more fully discussed below in relation to conversion.[66] Several studies have found that communications designed to change opinion have succeeded in communicating the facts which were expected to create the new opinion without, however, changing the opinion itself. Here again the facts per se apparently were not sufficiently threatening to elicit the full screening capabilities of selective exposure, selective perception, and selective retention. But perception, or interpretation, apparently stopped short of allowing the facts to serve the persuasive function of which they were thought capable.

Minor changes of opinion, short of conversion, may similarly fall within the leeway accorded by group norms. They may also represent a degree of drift which the group member experiences without being aware that he is straying from the norm. The McKeachie (1954) study, cited earlier in the chapter,[67] suggests that when such drifters are reminded of the norm, they tend to snap back to the orthodox group point of view.

Minor change, short of conversion, may also be due, in the case of some persons, to the operations of *conflicting* predispositions, conflicting group norms, and the like. Persons under such cross-pressures have been found to be less resistant to conversion than are other persons, and the role played by cross-pressures is accordingly treated in some detail in the course of the later discussion of conversion.[68] As there noted, however, such persons have also been found to be relatively likely to undergo what we have here called minor opinion changes.

THE RESISTANCE TO CHANGE OF "EGO-INVOLVED" ATTITUDES

"It might be stated as Crosby's Law," wrote John Crosby, TV critic of the *New York Herald Tribune,*

> . . . that the more important the subject is, the less influence the guy with the mike has. In matters of the most profound importance to the individual—say, religion—I doubt that the Murrows, or Godfreys, the Winchells or anyone else could sway a single soul a single inch.[69]

Communication researchers have come to similar though by no means so absolute conclusions. A number of studies, cited elsewhere in this volume,[70] have found that in regard to such matters as racial and religious tolerance, for example, persuasive mass communication is particularly unlikely to produce conversions and particularly likely to reinforce existing attitudes. Because attitudes on such topics are, for many people, crucial to their self-images and central to clusters of related attitudes, they have occasionally been called "ego-involved attitudes," and it has become something of a dictum that ego-involved attitudes are peculiarly resistant to conversion by mass communication—or, for that matter, by other agencies.

But attitudes on any topic whatever may be highly ego-involved for one individual and considerably less so, if at all, for others. Belief in white supremacy, or in racial equality, may be central to the self-image of a segregationist or an active integrationist, and his views may involve extensive social and professional commitments. But views on progressive education, or on the intelligence of dogs, may be equally basic and equally committing to a school principal or an animal trainer. To call an attitude "ego-involved," in short, seems to the present author equivalent to saying that the attitude is, for one reason or another, particularly salient and particularly committing to those who hold it.

Tannenbaum (1956) discusses and documents the same general phenomenon without reference to ego-involvement. The findings of a rather complex study involving twenty-seven different combinations and levels of three variables led him to conclude "that . . . susceptibility to change is inversely proportional to the intensity of initial attitude"[71] i.e., that the more intensely an attitude is held, the less likely it is to be changed by persuasive communication. One cannot, of course, simply assume that the term "intensity" is synonymous with "saliency" or "commitment," the words commonly used to describe "ego-involved" attitudes. But it would seem a logical expectation that the three factors would be closely related, and, in any case, the data clearly indicate that attitudes which are intensely held *or* which are particularly salient and extensively committing are particularly resistant to change.[72]

In terms of our present orientation, this is to say that under such conditions, the mediating forces for reinforcement are likely to be particularly active. Salient and committing attitudes would seem particularly likely, for example, to derive from or to determine primary group membership; and in regard to such attitudes, the groups and their opinion leaders would seem likely to be particularly intolerant of deviation. Individuals coming in contact with sympathetic communications on subjects so dear or basic to their hearts would seem more likely to relay the information to others of like views, and more likely to be shocked by and to inveigh against unsympathetic communications on similar issues. Selective exposure, selective perception, and selective retention would seem likely, and appear from the data, to exercise particularly assiduous protection against communications threatening attitudes so crucial to the individual.

We have previously remarked that the findings of research regarding the persuasive capabilities of the media in relation to political, social, and economic issues cannot be generalized to the persuasive capabilities of the media in relation to consumer advertising. The apparently greater power of the media in the consumer advertising sphere may well be due, at least in part, to the fact that persuasion in such cases is usually focused upon matters which are not likely to be particularly ego-involved for many members of the mass audience.

Theoretical Considerations

The several phenomena cited in the preceding section—predispositions and the derived processes of selective exposure, selective perception, and selective retention; groups and group norms; inter-personal dissemination of the contents of communication; the exercise of personal influence and opinion leadership; and the nature of the media in a free-enterprise society—possess, despite their obvious diversity, certain characteristics in common:

(1) They are all external to the communication itself, but clearly mediate the effects of the communication. (The flow of influence is not, of course, unidirectional; the communication often serves to activate or intensify the extra-communication processes, which in turn mediate the effects of the communication.)

(2) They are all likely to exist and become active in normal communication situations. This is in no way to say that they are always active, nor that the extent of their activity cannot be manipulated, but only to say that, all other conditions being equal, they are likely to become active.

(3) They are all likely to increase the native potential of mass communication for reinforcing existing views, and, in general, to reduce the likelihood that such communication will effect conversions.

It is on the basis of these considerations that the present author has advanced the first two of the five generalizations proposed in the introductory chapter. The first of these generalizations, it will be recalled, proposed that "mass communication *ordinarily* does not serve as a necessary and sufficient cause of audience effects, but rather functions among and through a nexus of mediating factors and influences." It is now proposed that all of the factors and influences cited above are integral functioning elements of that nexus.

The second generalization proposed that such mediating factors "typically render mass communication a contributory agent, but not the sole cause, in a process of" reinforcement. All of the mediators cited have been shown to exert such an influence upon the communication.

All five of the generalizations are advanced in a tentative and exploratory way. The author is, in fact, no so much concerned with defending these particular formulations, which must inevitably be emended, as rather with indicating that the time for generalization is at hand and that even exploratory generalizations may be helpful. In that spirit, it is proposed that even these first two generalizations, tentative though they may be, are organizationally and theoretically suggestive. More specifically:

(1) They suggest a relationship between the relative incidence of certain gross effects (reinforcement, minor change, and conversion), or of what we have called the *direction* of effects, and the process of effect.

(2) They are organizationally suggestive in that they call attention to the common characteristics of certain diverse factors and phenomena in the process of effect (audience predispositions, group norms, interpersonal influence, and the like). Such factors are thus seen to belong to a class of factors, as yet only hazily defined, but clearly distinct from such other factors as the textual characteristics of the communication itself or the nature of its source.

(3) They are further organizationally suggestive in that they suggest that certain other phenomena (such as the incidence of minor attitude change and the resistance to change of ego-involved attitudes) are, as it were, specialized manifestations of the basic process. In theoretical jargon, the generalizations "predict"

or "account for" such phenomena, at least conjecturally, and thus help to organize our current knowledge of the effects of mass communication.

(4) They are theoretically and practically helpful in that they promote certain predictive formulations or hypotheses, and so indicate logical avenues for further cumulative research. For example:

(a) Our knowledge of even the best documented of the alleged mediators is far from adequate. Certain of our predictive hypotheses are accordingly as yet essentially untested; the proposition that opinion leadership often *hinders* conversion is a case in point. Other hypotheses are neither clearly confirmed nor invalidated by existing data: the relationship between the salience of opinions and their resistance to change is an example. Further research, based on more refined theory, will test such hypotheses and more accurately define the numerous variables.

(b) If such factors as predispositions, group norms, and the like do indeed define a class of factors, all external to the communication and all mediators in the service of reinforcement, we may be sure that all members of the class have not yet been identified, and that the search for those as yet unknown will progressively illuminate the process of communication effect.

(c) If such mediating factors are in truth largely responsible for the reinforcing tendencies of persuasive mass communication, it may be tentatively predicted that they will either be inoperative or will operate very differently in those situations in which mass communication *does* produce major attitude changes. This prediction will be explored in Chapter IV of this volume.

Summary

1. Communications research strongly indicates that persuasive mass communication is in general more likely to reinforce

the existing opinions of its audience than it is to change such opinions. Minor attitude change appears to be a more likely effect than conversion and a less likely effect than reinforcement. This is not to say, however, that conversion does not occur nor that under certain conditions it may not be widespread.

2. The fact that persuasive mass communication serves more often as an agent of reinforcement than of conversion seems to be due, at least in part, to the way in which its influence is mediated by certain extra-communication factors and conditions. Among these are:

a. *Predispositions and the derived processes of selective exposure, selective perception, and selective retention.* People tend to expose themselves selectively to communications in accord with their existing views and to avoid exposure to unsympathetic communications. If exposed to unsympathetic material, they not infrequently distort (i.e., selectively perceive) its meaning so as to bring it into accord with their existing views. People also tend selectively to retain sympathetic material better than unsympathetic material. Although these phenomena are extremely common, they are rarely if ever experienced by all persons in any communication situation.

b. *The group, and the norms of groups, to which the audience member belongs.* Predispositions which reflect norms of groups to which the audience member belongs seem especially resistant to change. It has been proposed that resistance is particularly high if the norms are currently salient, and among people who particularly value their group membership, but research findings on these two points are inconclusive. Groups themselves may facilitate reinforcement in various other ways. They often increase selective exposure. They also provide arenas for inter-personal dissemination of the content of sympathetic communications, for the exercise of opinion leadership, and for discussion which may render the norms more salient or conspicuous.

c. *Inter-personal dissemination of communication content.* Such dissemination seems more likely to occur among people who share pertinent opinions on the topic in question. It thus seems likely to increase the native potential of the communication for reinforcement without similarly increasing its potential for conversion.

d. *Opinion leadership.* People have been shown to be more crucially influenced in many matters by "opinion leaders" than they are by mass communications. Such opinion leaders are typically "super-normative" members of the same group as their followers, but are more exposed to mass communications and thus serve as transmission agents or interpreters. Although most studies of opinion leadership have to date focused on the leaders' role in producing change, there is good reason to postulate that they frequently exercise their influence in favor of constancy and reinforcement.

e. *The nature of commercial mass media in a free enterprise society.* It has been held that in order to avoid offending any significant portion of their necessarily vast and varied audience, the media were perforce reduced to espousing only such attitudes as were already virtually universal. Content analyses of entertainment fare prevalent in the 1940's and early 1950's bore out these allegations. A resulting sanctification of the status quo—a social and individual reinforcing effect—was widely alleged but never scientifically demonstrated. Some current media material *seems* less orthodox and more daring. No research has identified the effects of such material, and, in any case, it apparently remains the exception rather than the rule. Mass media probably still function predominantly, if less consistently, as socially reinforcing agents, and the economic character of the media and of this society may well render such a situation inevitable.

3. Two phenomena related to the effects of persuasive communication seem at least tentatively explicable in terms of the play of the mediating forces cited above:

a. *Minor changes in attitude frequently follow exposure to persuasive communication.* Such changes may manifest the imperfections of the selective processes and the leeway accorded by group norms. Some cases of minor change seem to result from the operation of *conflicting* predispositions or group norms or from other cross-pressures.

b. *"Ego-involved" attitudes are particularly resistant to change.* Since such attitudes are, by definition, particularly crucial to the audience member, both as an individual and a social being, the reinforcing mediators may be stimulated to unusually vigorous activity.

4. *Theoretical Considerations.* The data adduced in this chapter suggest and support the first two of the five generalizations advanced in the introduction. These, in turn, serve certain stipulated organizational and theoretical functions. In brief, they help to clarify relationships between the data, "predict" or "account for" certain phenomena, and suggest logically related lines of further research.

The Creation of
Opinion on New Issues

The Effectiveness of Mass Communication

" *W* HOEVER SAYS the first word to the world is always right," said Joseph Goebbels,[1] a mass communication practitioner of odious capability. He appears to have been expressing, at the time, his faith in two somewhat different concepts: (1) that mass communication is highly effective in creating attitudes on newly arisen or newly evoked issues, and (2) that the point of view first expressed will prevail over later persuasive communications to the contrary. We shall be concerned, at this point, with only the first of these issues.[2]

Goebbels' faith in the efficacy of mass communication in *creating* attitudes has been shared by a goodly number of researchers. Rose (1948), for example, suggested that films and other vehicles preaching racial tolerance might be particularly effective among children who had not yet thought about the matter. Herz (1949) reflects a fairly popular view in his assertion that propaganda is essentially an offensive rather than a defensive weapon—i.e., it can create opinion far more easily than it can convert. Hovland (1954), after noting that press support of presidential candidates seems to bear no relationship to their success at the polls,[3] hypothesizes that the papers may, however, have considerable influence on public opinion regarding "minor issues and local candidates," about which the readers are less likely to know much or have such highly structured attitudes.

The weight of research evidence clearly tends to support these beliefs, although the data are neither so clear-cut nor abundant as seems generally to be believed. Many of the data commonly presented are, in fact, of questionable pertinency.

Reference is ordinarily made in this connection, for example, to studies which find that persuasive communication is particularly successful among persons who, prior to exposure, either professed to have no opinion on the issue at hand, or who scored in the "neutral" zone on pertinent attitude tests.[4] But at least two questions may be raised about the admission of such data at face value.

On the one hand, it may be argued that unless the classification procedure is exquisitely refined—and often it is not—the "no opinion" or "neutral" label cannot be automatically regarded as valid. Predispositions unrevealed by the questionnaire may be strongly at work. The importance of this argument is underlined by the findings of Berelson, Lazarsfeld, and McPhee (1954). They classified voters, prior to the 1948 campaign, not merely on the basis of overt vote intention, but also on the basis of such factors as sex, religion, and residence, all of which had previously been found to be related to party preference.[5] The "neutrals" in this more refined classification were affected by the campaign considerably *less* often than the moderates.[6] Other less refined studies may well be crediting mass communication with creating opinions on wholly new issues in instances where it is in reality activating (i.e., reinforcing) unconscious predispositions.

On the other hand, both these findings and the earlier findings they contradict may be held to be irrelevant to the present argument because neutrality may be in many instances a reasoned position rather than a lack of opinion. Such considered neutrals, it may be held, should not be expected to be any more susceptible to "conversion" than are those who adhere to a nonneutral opinion. The efficacy of mass communication in creating opinion, it may be argued, can be gauged only in reference to issues on which, at the time of exposure, people are *known to have no opinion at all.*

The author is aware of no data which conform wholly and unquestionably to such specifications. Some data do exist, however, regarding the effect of communications on people who are *unlikely* to have had previous opinions on the matter in question. Annis and Meier (1934), for example, found editorials extremely effective in leading American college students to both favorable and unfavorable opinions of the Prime Minister of Australia. As early as 1948, Berelson, reviewing what was then known of the effects of communication on public opinion, was able to find enough data to conclude that "communication content is more effective in influencing public opinion on new or unstructured issues, i.e., those not particularly correlated with existing attitude clusters."[7] Janis and Feshbach (1953) were able readily to influence people's opinions about the proper method of tooth-brushing by a single communication, and Mandell and Hovland (1952) were more or less equally able to influence college students' opinions on the desirability of devaluating U.S. currency.[8]

Additional pertinent data are provided by certain studies of instances in which mass media contributed to conversion. Some of these conversions seem to be not so much an outright change of opinion as rather the result of the growth of a new opinion which eventually proved incompatible with the old, but which originally stemmed from media definition and treatment of issues about which the "convertees" were previously unaware. The pertinent data are more fully discussed in Chapter IV.[9]

The findings of a study by Lang and Lang (1955) seem to the

author to be closely related to the point at hand, although the study does not involve an absolutely new issue and deals with an interpretation rather than an attitude. The two investigators analyzed the way three television networks covered a night's proceedings during the 1952 Democratic National Convention and found that though the networks reported the same events, they differed in the way they interpreted or "structured" the proceedings. "Monitoring groups" assigned by the Langs to watch particular channels, "tended to take over as their own the interpretations *stressed* on their channel."[10] Although the monitors "rated themselves politically sophisticated"[11] and undoubtedly had some feelings about political conventions, they had not, of course, previously seen the particular events depicted. Their adoption of the interpretation offered by the network thus seems to the present author to be related to the ability of the media to create opinions regarding "new issues." It would seem reasonable to postulate, for example, that media audiences would as easily adopt offered interpretations and points of view about other events or issues with which they were equally unfamiliar.[12] This possibility is explored in a recent conjectural paper by Lang and Lang (1959).

An issue new to the audience was also involved in a study by Janis and Herz (1953) which was, however, primarily focused upon the ability of a communication to "inoculate" its audience against later contrary influences. The experimenters advised subjects of a system, which was not really particularly effective, for working a pinball machine. The great majority of subjects accepted the advice and attempted to employ the system when required to play the machine. Half the group, furthermore, had been specifically forewarned that some failure was inevitable, due to the need of practice and the erratic nature of the machine. The warned group persisted in using the system far longer than the other group. Other studies dealing with inoculation bear on issues on which the subjects were more likely to have previous opinions, and are treated elsewhere in this volume.[13] The fact that inoculation can take place, however, is particularly significant when coupled with the ability of communications to create opinions or attitudes. Such attitudes, it appears, may be quite lasting.

Some additional findings, again of only peripheral relevance to the point under discussion, are provided by Himmelweit, Oppenheim, and Vince (1958) in the course of their elaborate study of British children and British television.[14] They found that in reference to certain topics, television affected the ideas of children who had no other source of information about the matter in hand, but did not affect the views of children who did have previous knowledge of the subject. Thus, TV apparently influenced middle class children's concepts of how wealthy people lived, but it did not affect their ideas about how members of their own class lived.[15] These data are not wholly to the present point, however, since the topics were in no way controversial and the term "persuasion," in the sense that we have been using it here, seems hardly applicable.

A Conjectural Rationale and a Speculation

The basis of media capability in creating opinions relative to new issues seems rather obvious, although it has not been, and perhaps cannot be, explicitly demonstrated. It seems clear, however, that to the degree that the issue is truly new, or unrelated to "existing attitude clusters," it is likely to evade the handicaps which normally beset attempts at conversion.

An individual audience member, for example, is not likely to be predisposed against a recommended point of view on an issue which is new to him. Selective exposure, selective perception, and selective retention are thus unlikely to come into impeding play, although they would seem less likely to *abet* the impact of the message than they would be were the message reinforcing. Neither the individual audience member nor his primary group colleagues is likely *immediately* to perceive a truly new issue as consistent or inconsistent with group norms, and immediate assistance or resistance from such quarters is thus apt to be nil. Opinion leaders are similarly unlikely to be ready to lead. In short, to the degree that the issue is truly new, the extra-communication mediating forces are likely to be inoperative.

Since such mediating forces tend to hinder conversion, it might be predicted that persuasion on new issues is likely, on the whole, to be more widely effective than attempts at conversion. The research cited above suggests that this may well be the case, although the relative frequency of the two effects has not, to the author's knowledge, been specifically investigated. It might also be predicted that since the mediators tend to abet reinforcement, persuasion on new issues is likely to be *less* effective than persuasion which is essentially reinforcing. This last possibility also seems never to have been investigated.

Much the same sort of rationale can be offered in explanation of the ability of mass communication to communicate *facts* without producing the conversions to which such facts were expected to lead the audience. The facts in question may be "new" to the audience and so be free of encumbering predispositions, whereas the opinions are well protected by selective perception, group norms, and the like. The phenomenon is, however, perhaps more closely related to attitude conversion than to attitude creation, and is accordingly discussed at greater length below.[16]

The ability of the media to communicate facts is, in any case, hardly surprising, since the media are known to be highly efficient in imparting factual knowledge and certain types of skills. A vast literature attests the effectiveness of the media in formal classroom pedagogy, closed circuit broadcasts, and other less formal situations. To review that literature and the problems it suggests would require a separate volume.[17] We would here note, however, that when the topic of such instruction is unrelated to "existing attitude clusters," it may be assumed to be, like new issues, unhindered by the extra-communication mediating forces. Given adequate student motivation, learning may be expected to be high. Hovland, Lumsdaine, and Sheffield (1949), for example, found various visual and oral media extremely effective in teaching soldiers how to read maps and how to use the phonetic alphabet. It is at least unlikely that many of the soldiers, prior to exposure, possessed any strong predispositions on these subjects.

The apparent efficacy of the media in creating opinions on new issues suggests that their potential during a time of revolution or social unrest may well be enormous. Opportunities exist, at such a time, not only for the reinforcement of revolutionary views, but also for the introduction or definition of issues to which many audience members have given little or no attention. No research known to the author bears upon the accomplishments of mass communication in such a situation within the American scene and, for reasons previously noted,[18] we have deliberately refrained from extending our survey to cover the effects of mass communication abroad or in the service of international propaganda. Some further speculation on the subject, however, will be found in the Conclusion.[19]

Theoretical Considerations

The rationale advanced above is in accord with the third of the generalizations proposed in the introductory chapter, and is, in fact, one of the bases for that generalization.

The first two generalizations proposed that mass communication ordinarily does not work directly upon its audience, but functions amid a nexus of other factors which abet reinforcement and hinder change. The third generalization proposed that when "mass communication does function in the service of change, one of two conditions is likely to exist: either (1) the mediating forces will be found to be inoperative, and the effect of the media will be found to be direct, *or* (2) the mediating factors will be found, atypically, . . . to be themselves impelling toward change."[20] The ability of mass communication to create opinions on new issues seems to the author to manifest the first of these conditions, i.e., to be an example of "change" occurring while the mediators are quiescent.

It is proposed that the third generalization, like the two that went before it, has already proved theoretically and organizationally helpful. It has accounted for the apparent fact that mass communication can create opinions more easily than it can convert. By the same token, it has nurtured the untested prediction that such opinion creation is a less likely effect than reinforcement. It has also suggested that certain other phenomena, such as mass communication's ability to convey facts without changing opinions, are related manifestations of the same basic process, and susceptible of similar explanation.

Summary

1. Mass communication is widely believed to be quite efficient in creating opinions among people who were not previously inclined one way or another on the issue in question.

2. Some of the data ordinarily advanced to support or to question this belief are probably not wholly pertinent. Some studies, for example, probably include among "neutrals" those who are unconsciously predisposed in one direction or another. Others do not distinguish between lack of opinion and reasoned neutrality. Relatively few studies focus directly upon the effects of mass communication on issues wholly new to the audience.

3. Considerable data are, however, relevant to the point in hand, if not primarily focused upon it. Studies performed both in the laboratory and in the social world indicate that communications are extremely effective in creating opinions on matters about which the audience is *unlikely* to have pre-existing opinions.

Communications on such topics have been found capable of "inoculating" audience members, i.e., of rendering them more resistant to later communications or experiences suggesting a contrary view. Mass communication has also been found effective in "structuring" events for audience members.

4. The basis of mass communication's capability in these regards has not been demonstrated, but seems easily, if tentatively, explicable. To the degree that the issue is really "new," the communication is unlikely to run afoul of unsympathetic predispositions, unsympathetic group norms, or unsympathetic opinion leaders. In short, mediating forces which normally hinder conversion seem likely to be inoperative. By the same token, the mediating forces seem unlikely to assist the persuasive effect, as they frequently do when communications are reinforcing.

5. A similar explanation may apply to mass communication's ability to communicate facts without changing relevant opinions, and to its ability in certain types of instruction.

6. *Theoretical considerations.* The data adduced in this chapter are shown to be illustrative of the third of the five generalizations advanced in the introductory chapter of this volume.

Conversion

The Occurrence of Conversion

ALTHOUGH CONVERSION is a far less frequent effect of mass communication than is reinforcement or minor change, it nevertheless does occur. Among the voters of Erie County whom Lazarsfeld, Berelson, and Gaudet (1948) studied in 1940, for example, 5 per cent were clearly converted.[1] In Elmira, eight years later, 8 per cent of the studied voters switched party adherence between June and August, and 3 per cent switched between August and October.[2]

Conversion has, on some occasions, been quite widespread. Almost three quarters (71 per cent) of a test audience for the British film *Naples Is A Battlefield*, for example, changed their pre-exposure opinion that the U.S. should not send food to Italy, and, at least in regard to this particular issue, not a single case of boomerang occurred.[3] Wilson (1948) found that documentary radio broadcasts on such subjects as juvenile delinquency and health facilities available to Negroes converted no one in reference to some issues, and up to 83 per cent of those originally opposed in reference to other issues. A study by Katz and Lazarsfeld (1955), which will be discussed in detail below, identified 619 changes in opinions regarding public affairs among 800 women interviewed repeatedly over a period of several months, and found that the mass media had frequently played an important role in inducing the changes.[4]

The incidence of conversion, furthermore, may well be cloaked by two reporting techniques, both of which are unfortunately prevalent in the literature of communication research. Many studies which rely on before-and-after tests report only the prevalence of attitude change "in the direction intended by the communication." Great portions of the audience are sometimes reported to be so influenced, but the generic description of the change does not distinguish between those whose attitudes were originally in accord with the communication and whose views were reinforced, and those who were actually converted from an originally contrary position.[5] Equally unhelpful, and at times misleading for our purposes, are reports of "net change" unaccompanied by reports of the integral changes which led to the net effect. It is relatively little use, for example, to learn only that the proportion of a group which agreed with a communication increased from 30 per cent before exposure to 36 per cent after exposure, providing a "net change of 6 per cent."[6] Fuller reports suggest the degree of change at which such reporting may fail even to hint: a study of the effects of a campaign to improve attitudes toward the oil industry, for example, reported a net shift of 4 per cent in the direction intended, and *went on to explain* that in actuality 22 per cent of the respondents had actually changed their opinion, 13 per cent in the direction intended and 9 per cent in the opposite direction.[7] Equally wide or wider conversion has no doubt been unintentionally hidden by many reports which tell only of "net effects."

Other instances of conversion will be cited in the pages that

follow. Those pages will, however, be devoted primarily to discussing factors which have been observed to be operative in conversion. Many of these factors will be recognized as old, familiar
friends. Oddly enough—or in terms of our present orientation,
reasonably enough—they will often be found to be the same factors which more typically abet reinforcement.

Mediating Factors in the Service of Conversion

SELECTIVE EXPOSURE, PERCEPTION, AND RETENTION

Selective exposure, selective perception, and selective retention have been shown in Chapter II to be typically the protectors
of predispositions and the handmaidens of reinforcement. As
there indicated, however, they do not function with 100 per cent
efficiency and, under certain conditions, they even help communications to produce change.

Several studies cite occasions on which the selective processes
appear to have been largely inactive. Thus Siebert, who studied
the "influence of television on the presidential elections of 1952,"
found that in a predominantly Republican Ohio area, the Republicans had, as might be expected, viewed more Republican-spon-
sored programs than Democrat-sponsored programs, but they had
nevertheless seen many Democrat-sponsored programs, and had, in
fact, outnumbered Democrats "among those who viewed over 70
per cent of Stevenson's speeches."[8] Berelson, Lazarsfeld, and
McPhee (1954) found some relationship which does not appear
to have been wholly selective between high general exposure to
media and recall of political items. The three authors do not, however, go so far as did Berelson in 1941 when he asserted a correlation between the emphasis accorded campaign arguments in
the media and the incidence of their recognition or of their occurrence in social chats. None of these data in themselves attest

to any conversion, but they do indicate that the fortress of selective exposure is far from impregnable.

The selective processes appear, furthermore, to be rendered relatively inactive, or to be set at cross-purposes, by certain specific conditions—as, for example, the conditions that obtain for persons who are under cross-pressures or who are compelled to play a role. Several such conditions and their possible effects on the selective processes are described below.[9]

It may additionally be contended that the selective processes may even sensitize an individual to communications preaching change, providing that he is, as it were, currently predisposed to change. The possibilities of such predisposition are multiple. They may stem, for example, from personality needs of the individual, from changes in his primary or reference groups, or from environmental changes which make previous habits of thought and behavior unrewarding or even impossible. The susceptibility to change of individuals in such situations is well known, and is discussed at various places below.[10] It seems a reasonable if not precisely documented conjecture that individuals already impelled toward change would selectively expose themselves to communications which offer a new point of view or which are sympathetic to their new outlook.

THE INFLUENCE OF PRIMARY GROUPS

Primary groups to which the individual belongs, or wishes to belong, have been shown to serve often as reinforcing influences and to hinder change. Under certain conditions, however, influences from such quarters may be relatively inactive, or may even serve, atypically, to abet change.

Katz and Lazarsfeld (1955) note various such conditions and emphasize their implications for the study of the effects of mass communications. Their own insights and documentations are derived almost exclusively from small group research but literature on mass communication provides various parallel findings.

We have already noted, for example, that persons who highly

value their group membership might logically be expected to be particularly resistant to communications opposing group norms, and that resistance might also be expected to be intensified in regard to issues which are particularly salient to the group. But there is an opposite side to this coin, viz., that conversion effects would be expected to be greater among those who *do not* greatly value their membership, and in regard to issues which *are not* particularly salient. Under such conditions, group influence is, almost by definition, likely to be reduced.

The Kelley and Volkart studies, described above in relation to increased resistance, are equally applicable here and the results of the studies are equally inconclusive. These two investigators, it will be recalled, found (1952) that Boy Scouts who did not greatly value their Scout membership and who were assured that their reactions would be kept confidential were more extensively converted by a communication attacking Scout norms than were their more highly valuing colleagues. Oddly enough, however, the same relationship did not appear among Scouts who were told their reactions would be made public. Kelley (1958) found that a communication attacking Catholic norms produced more conversion among Catholic high school students for whom the issues had been deliberately made more salient than it did among Catholics not so sensitized, or among non-Catholics. No similar findings were obtained, however, among college student subjects. As previously remarked, then, the proposed relationships seem extremely logical but, by virtue of the anomalous findings, they cannot be said to have been conclusively demonstrated.

Mass communication campaigns aimed at conversion have been observed to become suddenly effective for particular individuals when the bonds between that individual and some restraining group were broken. Shils and Janowitz (1948), for example, found that allied propaganda appeals to Nazi soldiers frequently became effective only after the military situation had led to the actual or imminent dissolution of the Wehrmacht primary groups to which the soldiers belonged. Schramm (1954)

tells, in somewhat similar vein, of North Koreans, who, when finding themselves cut off from the groups to which they belonged,
accepted and acted upon U.N. propaganda which had had no
effect upon them while they were members of cohesive units.
Analysis of such situations in the light of learning theory suggests
that while adherence to the norms of the original primary group
was "rewarding," communications opposing those norms were
resisted. When, however, adherence became unrewarding, or
positively dysfunctional,[11] the previously conditioned responses
were apparently extinguished, and the individual became newly
susceptible to the communication stimulus and its promise of new
reward. In our own more general terms, the restraining influence
of the group may be said to have become inoperative.

A somewhat similar phenomenon was noted in the course of
studies of the effect of Voice of America broadcasts to European
satellite countries.[12] Investigators who interviewed escapees within
a few days of their crossing the border were puzzled by the extreme anti-Communist and extensive pro-Western attitudes dis-
played by refugees who had lived for years under Communism,
and who were not therefore expected so suddenly to exhibit such
an extreme and extensive Western ideology. Detailed analyses of
interview protocols revealed that the change in such persons frequently stemmed from some specific incident, usually unrelated to
political ideology, which rendered their future relatively hopeless,
and caused them to look elsewhere. Some, for example, had been
discharged from managerial positions because of failure to
achieve set quotas; others had simply come face to face with the
draft. As their lot became suddenly unattractive, they had apparently turned their eyes to the West and their ears to the Free
World broadcasts. By the time they defected they had developed a
set of attitudes totally out of keeping with their previous orientation, but in accord with the reference groups they had newly
adopted. They had apparently undergone what Katz and Lazarsfeld (1955) call a "motivated move"[13] from one set of primary and
reference groups to another. The original group norms had ceased

to hinder the influence of communications designed to convert, while at the same time, the attractions of the new group norms served to abet and reinforce the influence of the same communications. As one set of group norms ceased to play a restricting influence, a new set served to impel change.

Groups may abet the converting influence of communications even among their loyal members. Communications may, for example, stimulate group discussions which render the norms more clear, and which thus encourage conversions among loyal members who had perceived the norm incorrectly. The previously cited study by McKeachie (1954) in which "changes" in attitudes occurred under precisely such conditions may include cases in point, but his data, as reported, do not distinguish between changes in intensity of point of view and actual conversion.[14]

Katz and Lazarsfeld (1955) note that group discussion may also encourage those inclining toward change by revealing the presence of unsuspected minority support. They note also that entire groups may occasionally be converted, possibly because the new point of view is in accord with a norm more basic than the one discarded. Much of the empirical data from which Katz and Lazarsfeld derive these propositions do not involve communication stimuli at all, and those that do involve such stimuli bear on the greater efficiency of discussion as compared to lectures or individual instruction. The present author has encountered no data which demonstrate mass communication effecting conversions under these precise conditions.

OPINION LEADERSHIP AND PERSONAL INFLUENCE

Opinion leadership and personal influence have been shown by research to play a tremendously important role in the process of decision-making. We have already postulated that these phenomena may also frequently exercise a reinforcing influence. We have also noted that to date these processes have been studied mainly within the context of accomplished change, and it is their influence in that regard, rather than in accomplishing any reinforcement, which has been most extensively documented.

Katz and Lazarsfeld (1955) report on an elaborate study which assessed the relative impact of personal influence and various selected media in leading women to attend particular movies, to change their food purchasing habits, their habits of dress, or their opinions on public issues. The study design involved the interviewing and re-interviewing of a panel of 800 women to locate such changes, and the additional interviewing of persons mentioned by the respondents as having influenced them. A total of 1,549 "influentials" were identified, and 634 of them were actually reached and interviewed.

It is important to note—and it is a point which commentators are prone to overlook—that personal influence could not be established as having played a role in anywhere near all of the decisions and changes. Fully 58 per cent of the changes in opinion regarding public issues, for example, "were apparently made without involving any remembered personal contact, and were, very often, dependent upon the mass media."[15] What influences other than mass media and personal contact may have been operating is not known, nor can introspective reports be taken as necessarily wholly accurate. It would appear, however, that personal influence is not essential to the process of opinion change, and that mass communication may at times be a sufficient cause.

Where personal influence did play a role, however, it typically exercised a more crucial influence than any of the media with which it was compared. In regard to all four areas of change and decision covered by this study, it was reported to be the single most effective influence more often than newspapers, radio, magazines, or books.[16]

These findings are in accord with those of other studies, none of which are, however, precisely comparable in method or in regard to the topics about which decisions were made. In Erie County, Ohio, in 1940, persons who changed their vote intention during the election campaign cited personal influence as a contributary cause more frequently than they cited mass communication.[17] Among physicians who had adopted a new drug, "detail men" (drug house representatives) were found to be far the most common source of original information about the drug, and medical colleagues were found to be the most common final source prior to actual adoption; media (commercial mail and technical journals) were found to have played a far lesser role.[18] A series of laboratory experiments accomplished during the 1930's and 1940's indicate that face-to-face contact is a more effective means of persuasion and instruction than is radio, recorded voice, or print.[19]

The degree of advantage which personal influence has over media, and the relative positions of the several media, vary widely among the topics of decision studied. In reference to selecting a movie, for example, Katz and Lazarsfeld (1955) found that personal influence had been five and one-half times as effective as its nearest competitor, the newspapers. Fashion changes, however, were impelled by personal influence only two times as often as by magazines. No characteristic order of influence was observed by Katz and Lazarsfeld, but the influence which was reported to have occurred first was found likely to be the same one reported as most effective.

The several studies of personal influence, despite their high technical caliber and their frequently exhaustive nature, are differentially focused, and much of the data has yet defied any attempt at generalization. Our current knowledge of the subject is not only aptly summarized in Katz (1957), but is there equally aptly sub-titled, "An Up-to-Date Report on an Hypothesis."[20] The role of personal influence relative to mass communication is particularly unready for any definitive evaluation. Such conclusions as may tentatively be drawn must be qualified, and our ignorance currently far outweighs our knowledge.

Thus, it may be said with considerable assurance that when personal influence is present it appears to be more effective than persuasive mass communication. On the other hand, personal influence is clearly not always present, and it cannot, therefore, be regarded as necessary to successful persuasion.

Personal influence, furthermore, has been studied for the most part in the context of accomplished change. Its role in such change has been shown to be considerable, but there are indications that it may also function to hinder change.[21] As yet, little is known of the actual relative incidence of these two possible functions or of the conditions under which one or the other is more likely to obtain.

In addition, the relative superiority of personal influence over mass communication is known to vary widely from one topic to another. Nothing is known, however, about the relative importance of personal influence in relation to issues which vary in other than topical dimensions. We do not yet know, for example, whether personal influence becomes more or less important as the issue in question becomes more ego-involved and more closely related to group norms.

Above all, and surprisingly enough, very little is known of the role played by personal influence vis-à-vis mass communication in the actual process of decision-making. Selective perception has been shown to produce specific distortions in specific communications. Particular group norms have likewise been shown to mediate the effects of particular communications in particular ways. But precisely how personal influence affects the potential of particular communications has been only barely investigated. Opinion leaders who serve as "gate keepers" for followers otherwise inaccessible to the media have been shown to exercise a selective control over what communications do or do not get through the gate.[22] But within the United States, gate-keeping is a relatively uncommon form of opinion leadership. Studies of opinion change indicate that the more usual form in this society is far more subtly exercised, frequently by people quite unconscious of the power they are wielding. Of the dynamic interplay between mass communication and personal influence in this more subtle process we know little indeed.

Finally, and perhaps reassuringly, our current state of knowledge suggests that there is no simple way in which opinion leadership and personal influence might be surreptitiously marshaled to engineer popular consent.[23] Men of both good will and bad have held that to reach opinion leaders is to reach the masses. The proposition may be true, but the identity of opinion leaders in reference to any specific topic can be discovered only by expensive and elaborate research. Unless such research is accomplished before the campaign is instituted, there appears to be only one way, and that quite public, of directing a message to opinion leaders. The effective influentials appear to be distributed widely throughout the population, and to be almost indistinguishable from their followers. As noted before, they are likely to be somewhat more competent in reference to the matter at hand, and to be somewhat more accessible to outside sources of pertinent information, such as the mass media. While they appear to be insusceptible of identification before a campaign, except by elaborate research, they also appear to be, of all people, the most easily and automatically accessible. Personal influence may be more effective than persuasive mass communication, but at present mass communication seems the most effective means of stimulating personal influence.

"PERSUASIBILITY"[24]

Recent research strongly indicates that some persons are in general more persuasible than others and, correlatively, that some are less persuasible than others. The high or low "persuasibility" of such persons appears to be "topic-free"[25]—i.e., to persist regardless of the topic of persuasion.

The possibility that topic-free persuasibility existed as a personality characteristic was proposed by Hovland, Janis, and Kelley (1953), in the course of their report on a series of experiments dealing with persuasion by quasi-mass communications.[26] Subsequent research has been pursued almost exclusively by the same authors and their colleagues, and is reported in

detail in Janis *et al.* (1959). The experiments there described do
not deal exclusively with persuasion by communication, as the
term "communication" is used in this volume. Several of the
studies, for example, deal with the susceptibility of individuals
to mere expressions of majority or individual preferences, and
others deal with the psychological components of persuasibility
and the development of persuasibility in young children. We shall
here restrict ourselves almost entirely to those studies which deal
with persuasibility in relation to communications possessing some
text or substance.

Existence of topic-free persuasibility.—The fact that some persons *are*, at least at a given time, consistently more (or less) persuasible than others was apparently first demonstrated by Janis
(1954). In this study, 78 male college students were subjected
to attitude tests before and after exposure to persuasive communications (alleged magazine articles and editorials) bearing on
the possibility of curing the common cold, the future of the U.S.
movie industry, and the future supply of meat. "None of the
opinion estimates originally given by any of the subjects agreed
with the extreme . . . estimates advocated by the communications."[27] Forty-one per cent (32) of the subjects "were influenced by all three communications," and 32 per cent
(25) were influenced by only one, or by none at all.[28] Janis inquired
also into the personality characteristics of these "high" and "low"
persuasibles as will be noted below.[29]

Generally similar findings are reported in a subsequent study
by Janis (1955) and by several of the studies reported in separate
chapters of Janis *et al* (1959)—in particular those by Janis and
Field (chap. ii), Janis and Rife, and Linton and Graham. In all
of these studies, certain subjects were found to be consistently
more (or less) susceptible than were other subjects to persuasive
communications on a variety of topics. Other studies reported in
the same volume found similar differences in general persuasibility, as manifested by sensitivity to the mere indication of group
or individual opinion.

Research to date accordingly indicates, with remarkable consistency, that individual differences in persuasibility exist, and that at any given time extremely high and extremely low persuasibility appears to be topic-free. As the experiments to date have involved only print or face-to-face communication, it cannot yet be said that persuasibility is "media-free,"[30] although one might reasonably expect that it would prove to be so.

Personality correlates of high and low persuasibility.—No consensus exists, however, regarding possible personality correlates of high or low persuasibility. Except with regard to two characteristics, intelligence and self-esteem, the findings are either inconsistent or are too limited to be regarded as anything more than suggestive.

The weight of existing evidence indicates that there is no relationship "between persuasibility and level of general intelligence."[31] A series of early experiments reviewed by Hovland, Lumsdaine, and Sheffield (1949) led these authors to conclude that, despite the occasional appearance of a positive or negative correlation in specific experimental situations, there appeared to be no consistent relationship between the two variables. The same views were again expressed by Hovland, Janis, and Kelley (1953). Four studies reported in Janis *et al* (1959),[32] again investigated the problem, but in none of the four was any relationship discovered.

Feelings of inadequacy, or low self-esteem, appear to be positively correlated with persuasibility, at least among males. Such a relationship was found by Janis (1954), and confirmed by Janis (1955) and by two studies reported in Janis *et al* (1959), viz., Janis and Field (chap iii), and Janis and Rife. All of these experiments involved printed communications and used male subjects exclusively. Some additional evidence of such a relationship is suggested by some of the findings of Cohen and of Lester and Abelson (Janis *et al*, 1959), but neither of these studies involved communications in the sense in which the term is used in this volume.

A quasi-pertinent datum is provided by the literature on mass communication research in naturalistic situations. In the course of their analysis of the effects of the 1940 election campaign, Lazarsfeld, Berelson, and Gaudet (1948) had interviewers rate respondents who had been interviewed four times before

> on a graphic rating scale covering ten personality characteristics readily observed during interviews . . . Constants [those who never wavered in party preference] were reported to be more self-assured, better informed, more cooperative, and broader in their interests. . . . Waverers seemed to suffer somewhat more from emotional maladjustment as evidenced in more unhappiness and lack of self-assurance.[33]

The findings clearly support the relationship between low self-esteem and high persuasibility demonstrated in the experiments by Janis and his colleagues. They bear, however, on the effects of a specific campaign, and are not known to be topic-free. Virtually no other even quasi-pertinent data appear to exist in the literature on mass communication research in naturalistic situations.

In reference to the possible relationships between persuasibility by communications and other personality characteristics, the findings reported in Janis *et al* (1959) are either conflicting, unclear, or extremely limited. Contradictory findings by two or more studies are reported in regard to "hypothesized relation(s)"[34] between persuasibility by communications and "neurotic defensiveness,"[35] and between such persuasibility and "hostility and aggressiveness."[36] Adult females were found in two experiments to be significantly more persuasible by communications than were adult males,[37] but no such sex-linked difference was found in a third study in which the subjects consisted exclusively of young children;[38] numerous and marked differences were found between the sexes in reference to specific "personality correlates of general persuasibility."[39] A positive correlation between persuasibility by communications and "richness of fantasy"[40] was found in two studies.[41] A single study found positive correlations between persuasibility and "perceptual dependence,"[42] and between persuasibility and other-directedness, and the same study obtained conflicting findings regarding a possible relationship between persuasibility and authoritarianism.

Janis and Hovland, in a concluding chapter of Janis *et al* (1959), are careful to point out that there is no reason to believe that personality correlates of persuasibility are "determinants of persuasibility."[43] It is possible, they note, that the personality factors may produce the persuasibility, that persuasibility may produce the personality correlates, or that both persuasibility and personality correlates may be the products of as yet unidentified causes.

The entire concept of topic-free persuasibility and its personality correlates clearly requires further research. The limits of topic freedom, for example, have not yet been thoroughly tested, for none of the studies have involved topics which are likely to be highly ego-involved. The known personality correlates of persuasibility are still few. Virtually no inquiry has been made into the possible existence of socio-economic correlates, nor have the determinants of persuasibility been systematically sought. All of the literature to date, furthermore, bears upon experimental situations involving laboratory approximations of mass communications. No study has investigated persuasibility either in a naturalistic as opposed to a laboratory setting, or in a situation involving true mass media of communication as opposed to laboratory approximations.

Persuasibility, in short, is a phenomenon about which we have much to learn. Insofar as it exists, however, it would appear to be another of the several factors which mediate the effect of communications upon their audience.

Related Effect Phenomena

Certain aspects of the effects of mass communication, and in particular certain aspects of conversion effects, seem susceptible of at least partial explanation in terms of the activity of factors such as the selective processes, group pressures, and the like. The play of such factors seems particularly relevant to: (1) the susceptibility to conversion of persons under cross pressures; (2) the effect of "role playing"; (3) the communication of facts without consonant opinion change; and (4) the alleged success of "side attacks" on target attitudes. In the following pages, each of these phenomena will be objectively described and documented, and thereafter conjecturally explained. The explanations will reflect the theoretical orientation which the author has set forth in the introductory chapter.

THE SUSCEPTIBILITY TO CONVERSION OF PERSONS UNDER CROSS-PRESSURES

Persons under cross-pressures have been observed to be particularly susceptible to conversion by mass communication as well as by personal influence. They are also likely, however, to withdraw from the ideological arena altogether and to decline to take sides.

In their elaborate study of the effects of the 1940 election campaign, Lazarsfeld, Berelson, and Gaudet (1948) took special note of respondents who were subject to any of six cross-pressures upon their voting behavior. Two of these six situations involved personal characteristics of the respondent himself, two involved lack of political homogeneity among his family and close associates, and two involved his own basic attitudes on certain politically relevant issues. Respondents subject to *any one* of these cross-pressures tended to make their final decision considerably later in the campaign than did those who were not so plagued, with the most marked delays occurring among those whose family and primary-type groups lacked political homogeneity. Persons subject to two or more cross-pressures were, furthermore, particularly likely to change their vote intentions; they constituted only 21 per cent of the "constants" (i.e., those whose party adherence never wavered), but they accounted for

38 per cent of those who wavered between a given party and neutrality, and 64 per cent of those who were actually converted from one party to another.[44] Changers of any sort, furthermore, were highly likely to be repeaters: persons who were found during any interview to have made a change since the last interview proved three times as likely as those who had not made a change to change again before the next interview. The data, as reported, do not indicate how much of this repeated changing involved wavering between one party and neutrality, and how much involved complete reconversion. Some amount of recrossing of party lines can probably be safely assumed.

These findings on the one hand echo the widely observed susceptibility of "waverers" to conversion by propaganda, and on the other hand raise a question as to the possible impermanence of such conversion. Herz (1949), for example, considers the persuasibility of waverers to be one of the important "lessons [to be gleaned] from leaflet propaganda in World War II."[45] More recent studies performed by or for the U.S. Information Agency likewise suggest that Voice of America broadcasts and other Western propaganda are not so likely to convert confirmed Communists as they are to win over those who are already wavering in their allegiance.[46] It is of course to be expected that persons who already doubt will be more susceptible to conversion than those who are firmly committed. But the question arises as to how many such waverers are subject to cross-pressures and are likely to sway back and forth between the two camps in a repeating process of conversion and reconversion.

The tensions and multiple stimuli of cross-pressures do *not* appear, however, to render their victims peculiarly interested in the issue involved. Research in fact indicates that the opposite is more likely to be the case. Lazarsfeld, Berelson, and Gaudet (1948), for example, found that "many voters subject to cross-pressures tended to belittle the whole affair." "Great interest" in the election, exhibited by 44 per cent of voters not subject to cross-pressures, was found among only 31 per cent of those sub-

ject to one cross-pressure, and among only 27 per cent of those
subject to two or more. The investigators suggest that this loss
of interest is due to

> . . . a basic pattern of human adjustment. When people desire and
> shun a course of action in about equal degree, they often do not de-
> cide for or against it but rather change the subject or avoid the
> matter altogether. For many clashes of interest, the easy way to get
> out of the uncomfortable situation is simply to discount its impor-
> tance and to give up the conflict as not worth the bother.[47]

The degree to which such withdrawal may go is suggested by
Kriesberg (1949). As noted above,[48] he found that a considerable
number of Catholic members of a somewhat Communist-oriented
union were not even conscious of the cross-pressures to which
they were being subjected, and could not consistently defend the
point of view they individually held against the common opposition arguments.

Rationale.—The susceptibility to conversion of persons under
cross-pressures may be simply if conjecturally explained. Such
luckless souls have a foot in each of two conflicting soils. The
extra-communication mediating forces, which normally favor
reinforcement, are in some ways nullified and in other ways
working busily to reinforce two opposing opinions. Selective exposure and selective perception, for example, may well be largely
cancelled out. Divided family or primary groups may exert no
decisive pull, while undivided but conflicting groups pull both
ways at once. The sum total of personal influence to which the
individual is exposed may be assumed to do likewise. Mass communication on either side of the fence thus falls on relatively
fertile soil. The protective nets of resistance are partially down,
but sympathetic influences in both directions remain. Under
such circumstances conversion is hardly unlikely.

But conversion is likely to leave the situation basically un-
altered and the individual unrelieved. Influences in favor of the
position he has ostensibly deserted are unlikely to abate, and his
own feelings of guilt, insecurity, or nostalgia may in fact increase

their potency. Unless the victim of this tug of war loses all interest in the matter, and so remains where he is, he seems likely to change again, and possibly again.

ROLE-PLAYING

The conversion potential of persuasive communication appears to be intensified under conditions of audience participation and particularly among persons who are required, regardless of their actual feelings, to assume a role sympathetic to the point of view expressed. The phenomenon has thus far been explicitly demonstrated only in highly contrived laboratory situations, but the findings are obviously highly implicative for more normal social situations and additionally throw some light on the apparent successes of the "brainwashing" techniques employed by the Communists during the Korean War.

Two of the most pertinent studies were performed by Janis and King. In the first of these (1954), male college students were exposed to three communications which took very extreme views regarding the future of the U.S. movie industry, the future availability of meat in the U.S., and the likelihood of finding a cure for the common cold. The students were divided into groups of three, and each student was required to deliver a speech on one of the topics while his two colleagues listened and read outlines. Before and after tests revealed that in the case of the first two topics the net percentage of sizeable opinion shift was far greater among the speakers than among the listeners. In reference to the third topic, no significant difference was observed.

Speculation on the inconsistency of the results led the investigators to suspect that the "amount of opinion change occurring with active participation may depend upon the amount of improvisation" required of a speaker, and upon "the degree to which . . . [he] feels satisfied with his performance."[49] A second experiment (King and Janis, 1953) was designed to test these possibilities, using the more ego-involved topic of the likelihood of an early draft and long military service. In this instance, some

 . . . subjects were required to present the talk without a script, after having read it silently, while others were permitted to read directly from the script. Experimental variations were introduced in order to produce varying degrees of satisfaction and dissatisfaction with respect to the individual's speaking performance. The results consistently indicate that the amount of opinion change produced through active participation is dependent upon the amount of improvisation but is not related to the amount of satisfaction.[50]

Confirmatory findings were obtained by Kelman (1953) in the course of a study of incentives to conformity. Some 250 seventh grade students were required to listen to a talk on the relative worth of different types of comics and were then asked to write essays on this topic. The

 . . . control group was offered no special incentive . . . [for] conforming to the communicator's position; . . . a second group . . . was told that every student who conformed would receive a prize; a third group . . . was told that every student who conformed would be eligible for the prize, but that only a few would receive it. The results showed the control group to have the lowest and the [second or] high incentive group the highest degree of conformity. The amount of opinion change, however, did not vary directly with the degree of conformity: significantly more change was found in the low incentive group than in either of the other two groups. The essays produced under the low incentive condition were found to be of superior quality and to contain a higher frequency of new arguments. The findings provide additional support for the improvisation hypothesis.[51]

Closely related findings are reported by Zimmerman and Bauer (1956) in the course of a pioneering report on the influence of audiences upon communicators. They exposed groups of adults to one of two speeches, favoring or opposing salary increases for teachers. Half of the subjects who heard each speech were told that they might later be invited to talk on the same topic to a sympathetic audience, and half were told that they might be invited to speak to an unsympathetic audience. The subjects were found a week later to have selectively retained and improvised arguments in accord with the audience they expected to address, although no actual attitude shifts were observed. The study was later replicated by Schramm (1958) using a different topic and different types of subjects.

The ability of role-playing or improvisation to increase the conversion potential of communication has implications far beyond the laboratory situations in which it has been demonstrated. As Hovland, Janis, and Kelley (1953) point out, it "frequently happens [in the course of normal life] that an individual is induced to conform overtly before he has come to accept a norm or belief as his own."[52] Such situations occur not only in the course of socialization, but in reference to specific issues in everyday life. An individual may, for example, be exposed to persuasive mass communication to which he is personally unsympathetic while he is among people whom he knows to be sympathetic to the view expressed and among whom he dare not reveal his true position. The research findings we have cited suggest that overt agreement, conjured up for the specific occasion, may contribute to his ultimate actual conversion.

Other writers have advanced a similar hypothesis. Cooper and Jahoda (1947) noted, for example, that an individual's overt response to propaganda may vary depending upon whether he is among people who believe as he does, or among those he believes to be in disagreement with him, and that his overt response may influence his attitude. More recently, Glock (1953) has suggested that the effect of propaganda encountered in public may, for the same reasons, differ from the effect of the same propaganda encountered in private: an Arab listening to a Voice of America broadcast in a public coffee house, Glock points out, may react quite differently from the way he would were he alone. The findings of Janis and King, of Kelman, and of Zimmerman and Bauer lend considerable credence to these suggested possibilities and underscore the need of further research focused specifically on these problems.

Role-playing and improvisation seem, furthermore, to resemble techniques integral to the process which has become known as "brainwashing." During the Korean War, American prisoners were apparently required or urged by their Communist captors to give set responses, in accordance with Communist ideology, to various questions, and to produce essays and speeches expressing various Communistic points of view. Some of the Americans, to the consternation of their countrymen, apparently came to believe at least some of the material which they were forced to parrot or improvise. The research findings we have cited seem to confirm the sufficiency of such a technique for producing at least partial conversions. On the other hand, the situation in the laboratories of New England colleges can hardly be regarded as scientifically comparable to the situation in North Korean and Chinese prison camps. The role of primary groups in the latter situation, and the magnitude of the anticipated rewards and punishments, are surely without parallel within the ivied walls of the American experimental laboratory.

Rationale.—The effects of role-playing and improvisation upon opinion change are only partially explicable in terms of the play of such mediating influences as selective perception, group norms, and the like. It is clear that when a person is *required* to defend and elaborate a point of view which he does not believe, his tendency towards selective perception and retention in the other direction may well be at least temporarily reduced. Zimmerman and Bauer (1956), in fact, found selective retention to be working in favor of the position the individual was required to assume, even if that position was contrary to his original views. It may also be postulated that during the course of the King and Janis and the Kelman experiments, the group which was physically present served for the time being as a reference group in which the improviser sought status by excelling at the common task. Bauer (1958) postulates that the imaginary audiences in the Zimmerman and Bauer experiment functioned in a somewhat similar way. But these hypotheses fail to account entirely for the internalization of the overt behavior, and they are additionally

hard to reconcile with the apparent lack of relationship between
the degree of opinion change which the speaker undergoes and
the degree of his satisfaction with his own performance. The entire phenomenon seems to the present author more fully susceptible of explanation in terms of learning theory than in terms
of the generalizations which he has himself advanced. For an explanation in such terms, he defers to Hovland, Janis, and Kelley
(1953),[53] and to Bauer (1958).

THE COMMUNICATION OF FACTS WITHOUT
CONSONANT OPINION CHANGE

Reference has already been made to the fact that persuasive
mass communication has been often observed to communicate
facts, or even to change opinions on certain factual matters, without creating the more basic attitude changes that the facts were
expected to produce. Most of the pertinent findings are, however,
interwoven with the question of whether explicit coverage or
implication is more persuasively effective.

As early as 1948, Wilson found that the impressive informa-
tive successes of certain documentary radio broadcasts were in
no way paralleled by the changes of attitude which the information was intended to produce. Among a test audience for a broadcast on atomic energy, for example, 71 per cent learned "much"
and 24 per cent learned "some," but nowhere near 95 per cent
of the audience showed any appreciable *attitude* changes.

Similar findings in regard to an anti-discrimination film,
Don't Be A Sucker, were reported by Cooper and Dinerman
(1951) on the basis of an elaborate and multi-faceted study which
included the testing of approximately 1,000 high school students
divided into control and experimental groups. The producers of
the film "apparently believed that a good way to discourage
people from prejudiced attitudes and behavior is to show, implicitly or explicitly, that those who practice discrimination meet
disaster."[54] They accordingly provided a detailed portrayal of how
Hitler had set one minority group against another, to the eventual

detriment of all, and "hoped that the audience would see the moral of the tale and recognize the parallel between the German scene and the American scene."[55] Tests revealed that "although a notable proportion of the experimental group accepted these messages about Nazi Germany, the attitudes of the group as a whole were apparently not influenced."[56] Prejudice remained as common among the test audiences as among the control group which had not seen the picture, and as common among those who accepted the messages as among those who did not.

Cooper and Dinerman also observed certain relationships between the form of the message and the likelihood of its acceptance. Thus "less explicit messages . . . were not accepted by the less intelligent members of the audience,"[57] although some of them were accepted by some of the more intelligent members of the audience. Messages presented in a specific form, furthermore, stood more chance of acceptance than did the same message in more generalized form: for example, the

> . . . generalized message that 'There are no master races' was not accepted, despite its having been explicitly stated; while the less explicit but specific message that 'Negroes are not lazier than other people' was accepted to some degree.[58]

Despite some acceptance of such particular messages, the film, as noted above, did not achieve its ultimate aim of reducing anti-minority prejudice among its audiences.

The most detailed demonstration of the communication of facts without consonant opinion changes is provided by Hovland, Lumsdaine, and Sheffield (1949), who report on a series of studies of the effects of various communications on American soldiers during World War II. Their methodological procedure typically involved rigorously disciplined controlled experiments, with control and experimental groups numbering between 500 and 1,000 soldiers representative of the Army as a whole or of special sub-groups under intensive study.

One of the communications so studied was a film entitled *The Battle of Britain,* which was part of a larger series entitled

Why We Fight. Hovland, Lumsdaine, and Sheffield conceived the
purpose of these films as involving three steps: (1) the communication of certain facts about the background of the war,
which were intended (2) to induce in the soldiers more favorable
opinions and attitudes relative to American participation, which
opinions and attitudes, in turn, were intended (3) to increase the
soldiers' motivation and willingness to serve.

The films proved highly effective, as did various other communication devices, in imparting various objective facts. Knowledge of how the British managed to safeguard ground-parked
planes from German bombing, for example, was found to be almost four times as common (78 per cent) among the soldiers
who had seen *The Battle of Britain* as it was (21 per cent) among
those who had not. The films were also highly if less dramatically
successful in communicating facts about events leading up to the
war.

The Battle of Britain also succeeded, though to a markedly
lesser degree, in eliciting agreement with certain essentially
factual but partly interpretive points of view regarding the
British war effort *for which grounds were explicitly provided
by the film*. Percentage differences of up to 27 per cent between
the control and experimental group were observed in regard
to such matters as whether "there was an actual 'Battle of Britain,'" in which "heroic British resistance" was manifest and was
aided by the great "contribution of the Royal Air Force." A
notable portion of the audience was convinced by the picture that
"British resistance gave us [the United States] time to prepare."[59]

The film was almost entirely ineffective, however, in changing "general attitudes toward the British"[60] or toward American
participation in the war. Such topics were not explicitly treated
in the film, but the facts presented were expected to influence
such opinions. However, differences of only 3 per cent or less,
most of which were not statistically significant, were observed in
regard to pertinent test items "which were considered the criteria

for determining the effectiveness of the films at achieving their orientation objectives."[61]

Finally, the films appeared to be totally ineffective in changing "the men's motivation to serve as soldiers, which was considered the ultimate objective of the orientation program."[62]

In sum, the success of the films decreased steadily as the effect sought became less a matter of communicating objective facts and more a matter of changing attitudes. The films communicated information, but they accomplished little or no conversion.

In both of the two studies cited above—i.e., in Cooper and Dinerman (1951) and in Hovland, Lumsdaine, and Sheffield (1949)—several variables may have been at work. Material which was successfully communicated, but presumably only preparative to the ultimate ends of the communication, was explicitly covered and not particularly affective. The ultimate ends, which were not achieved, were *not* explicitly covered and *were* highly affective. But degree of explicitness, while probably an influencing variable, does not appear to be the crucial variable. Both purely objective facts and quasi-interpretive points were presented explicitly, but the quasi-interpretive material was not nearly as successfully communicated.

The findings of Cooper and Dinerman (1951) and Hovland, Lumsdaine, and Sheffield (1949) are in general accord, if not precisely similar, to those of Wiese and Cole (1946) and Rosenthal (1934). They are wholly out of accord, however, with those of Thistlewaite, deHaan, and Kamenetzky (1955). These experimenters exposed over 700 U.S. Air Force recruits to taped recordings designed to convince hearers that the United States was right to participate in the Korean War. In two versions of the communication explicit conclusions were drawn, and in two versions they were not. Clarity of organization was also used as an experimental variable. All versions of the communication were found equally effective in producing opinion change, although those with explicit conclusions and clearly defined organization were better comprehended, particularly by relatively low I.Q. subjects. The methodology employed appears to be valid, and the findings cannot be reconciled with those of the earlier studies. Replication would seem indicated, and pending its occurrence, it can only be said that the great weight of evidence to date favors explicitness over implicitness in attempts at attitude conversion.

Several studies of the relative effectiveness of explicit vs. implicit treatment in regard to non-affective material seem, on the whole, to give the palm to explicitness. Because these deal with such non-affective matters, they appear hardly related to conversion phenomena and will be treated in Chapter V, in the course of the discussion of contextual devices which facilitate persuasion.

The weight of pertinent mass communications research to date thus points to two general conclusions:

(1) facts may be successfully communicated without producing the opinion changes which they are intended or expected to produce;

(2) in regard to affective matters, explicit material is more likely to be communicated, especially among the less intelligent, than is implicit material.

There is some evidence that these variables are independent of one another, and that facts can be more easily communicated than attitudes can be changed, even when explicitness is held constant. Further research is needed, however, completely to disentangle the effects of these two variables.

Rationale.—There is perhaps no need to account for the fact that explicit material is more widely communicated than implicit material, especially among the less intelligent. As Cooper and Dinerman (1951) suggest, "implicit . . . messages may well [be] . . . actually inaccessible to this less intelligent group."[63]

The communication of facts without consonant opinion change is less obviously and only conjecturally explicable. Cooper and Dinerman advance several possible explanations for this

"lack of transfer," most of which are related to possible contextual shortcomings of the specific film they tested, or to the
position of non-convertees within the then current climate of
opinion. Hovland, Lumsdaine, and Sheffield (1949) advance an
essentially similar hypothesis regarding the resistance of a deviant minority. This hypothesis bears more on the general relation
of the climate of opinion to persuasion than it does to the specific
phenomenon here under discussion, and it will accordingly be
treated below among miscellaneous conditions related to persuasion by communication.[64] Hovland, Lumsdaine, and Sheffield
also conjecture upon the effect of explicitness vs. implicitness
and upon the possible "need for a 'sinking in' period." [65] Any or
all of these hypotheses may well be valid, but none have been
conclusively shown to account for the phenomenon.

The phenomenon may also be viewed as a manifestation of
the relative inactivity of the extra-communication mediating
forces which, we have proposed, ordinarily mediate the effects of
mass communication in favor of reinforcement. The facts which
are communicated may simply not be recognized as pertinent
to the attitudes they are intended to change. Such lack of recognition may reflect the honest inability of the audience to perceive
the relationship, or may be in part a product of selective perception. In either case the facts per se are regarded as innocuous, and
the forces which might otherwise mediate against their communication are not called into play. Selective perception does not
hinder their acceptance, nor does the influence of group norms or
opinion leaders exercise any restraining effect. The audience
member is accordingly directly affected by the factual aspects of
the communication. But since these facts are not recognized as
pertinent to the attitudes, no change in attitude occurs. The attitude is, in fact, never under attack.

The question arises as to whether the facts would be so readily
accepted if their implications for attitude change were made
explicit. Various studies have compared the relative degree to
which explicit and implicit conclusions are communicated, but

none has compared the incidence of communication of the facts on which the conclusions are based.[66] In line with our present interpretation, we would hypothesize that persons who did not accept the explicit conclusion would be more likely to reject the facts as well. The mediating forces, we hypothesize, would be alerted and active.

"SIDE ATTACK" AND PERSONAL CONFLICT

The literature of some twenty years ago often asserted that conversion could be far more easily accomplished by "side attack," i.e., by building a new opinion, than by direct frontal attack on existing opinion. Thus Albig (1939) quotes Lowell's assertions that " 'opinions change by making exceptions to general rules until the rule itself is broken down' and 'opinions have this in common with intrenchments that they offer an obstinate resistance to a frontal attack, but not to a turning movement.' "[67] Waples, Berelson, and Bradshaw (1940) found, after a review of the then existing literature, that in conversions attributed to reading, the change

> . . . generally results from the reinforcement of an associated but subordinate attitude, which causes it to dominate the matrix of conflicting attitudes and interests . . . Conversion is most likely to occur either when the counterappeal is made in terms which promise the reader the satisfaction of his personal interests (if nothing more tangible, simply the prestige of being converted) or when it elevates a previously subordinate attitude to a superordinate position, usually by supporting one loyalty or one part of the conscience against another.[68]

Recent literature does not deal specifically with this concept. It may be noted, however, that side attack involves, at least at the outset, the creation of a new opinion, a task at which the media have been shown to be quite effective, rather than an attack on existing opinion, at which the media are considerably less effective. Thus, Lazarsfeld, Berelson, and Gaudet (1948) observed that

. . . insofar as mass media of communications led to conversion at all, it was through a redefinition of the issues . . . issues about which people had previously thought very little or had been little concerned, took on a new importance as they were accented by campaign propaganda.[69]

In terms of our current orientation, side attack, which consists of creating a *new* opinion, may be said to be a procedure in which the extra-communication forces, which normally hinder change, are not likely to be operative. Direct frontal attack, on the other hand, is likely to stimulate them to immediate and effective activity.

When and if the new attitude develops sufficiently to challenge the old, conflict is likely to occur, and may be resolved by conversion. Waples, Berelson, and Bradshaw (1940) noted that

The larger changes can seldom be ascribed to a single reading experience. Typical case studies of conversion to communism, for example, have the following steps in common; first, the reader chances on a liberal publication, which slightly increases his tolerance for that type of writing and his interest in reading more of it; second, the reader begins an eager search for publications which will meet his more serious objections to the doctrine; third, the readers say, 'after much reading, I gradually came to see the wisdom of communism.' The case study evidence supports the conclusions of group studies in explaining the predispositions favorable to such conversions. The explanation is that a change of attitude in the direction of the reading is facilitated by a sharp conflict of attitudes. The reading offers relief from the emotional disturbances caused by the conflict.[70]

To the best knowledge of the author, the relative efficiency of side attacks, as compared with direct frontal attacks, has not been a subject of recent research.

Theoretical Considerations

It is proposed that the data presented in this chapter are in the main illustrative of the third of the five generalizations advanced in the introduction. That generalization was formulated on the basis of precisely such considerations as have been here advanced.

By way of review, the first of the five generalizations proposed that mass communication rarely functions as the sole agent in the process of effect, but rather works amid a nexus of other extra-communication mediating forces. The second generalization proposed that these forces normally rendered mass communication a contributory agent in the service of reinforcement.

The third generalization, with which we are here primarily concerned, proposed that when mass communication serves as an agent of change, one of two conditions will usually be found to exist: either (1) the mediating forces will be found to be inoperative, and the effect of the communication upon its audience will be found to be direct; or (2) the mediating forces will be found to be themselves, atypically, favoring change.

Our discussion of reinforcement in Chapter II identified several such mediating factors and forces. These included the selective processes (selective exposure, perception, and retention), the influence of groups and group norms, the exercise of opinion leadership and personal influence, and inter-personal dissemination of the content of communications.

Extra-communication factors found by objective studies to be operative in *conversion* effects have included all but one of the same factors and forces, and have added "persuasibility," which apparently plays a role in reinforcement effects as well. All of these factors have been observed in various studies of conversion to be, for one reason or another, impelling toward changes. The author has additionally pointed out that all except persuasibility may, under certain conditions, be inoperative and so cease to hinder the communication stimulus to change. On the basis of these considerations, the author proposes that the third generalization is largely supported by existing data.

Certain objectively observed aspects of conversion effects have been shown susceptible of explanation—conjectural and incomplete explanation, of course—in terms of the same generalization. It has been suggested that for persons under cross-pressures, some of the mediating forces may function at reduced efficiency while others work in both directions at once, impelling both change and inconstancy. In role-playing, it has been suggested, the same forces impel toward change. The communication of facts without consonant opinion change and the successfulness of "side attacks" have been shown to be at least partially explicable on the basis of the mediating forces being inoperative.

Accordingly, the generalizations as a whole appear to be continuing to serve the kind of organizational and theoretical functions outlined at the end of Chapter II. More specifically:

(1) They provide a concept of the process of effect in accord with which reinforcement and conversion need not be viewed as mysteriously contradictory phenomena, but can rather be viewed as related and understandable outcomes of the same general dynamic processes. The same forces appear to be involved, and the outcome appears to depend on the degree and direction of their activity.

(2) They continue to suggest a relationship between the relative *incidence* of certain gross effects (reinforcement, minor attitude change, attitude creation, and conversion) and the *process* of effect. To whatever degree our concept of the process is correct, reinforcement may be viewed as the more normal or normative effect and conversion as the outcome to be expected under certain more or less atypical conditions.

(3) The fact that the same mediating forces are involved strengthens the concept that these factors belong to a special "class . . . as yet only hazily defined, but clearly distinct from such other factors as the textual characteristics of the communication itself, or the nature of its source."[71]

(4) The generalizations continue to help us bring together and relate various bits of knowledge regarding the effects of communication. Generalization 3, for example, helps to "account for" the susceptibility to change and the inconstancy of people

under cross-pressure, the communication of facts without consonant opinion change, and, to a lesser degree, the effects of roleplaying.

(5) The generalizations continue to promote "certain predictive formulations and hypotheses, and so indicate logical avenues for further cumulative research."[72] For example, generalization 3 suggests that if the attitude implications of specific facts are made explicit, the facts themselves might be less readily accepted.

Withal, the author reasserts his freedom from commitment to these particular generalizations, which are obviously gross and demand refinement. He also reasserts, however, his belief that the time is overripe for *some* exploratory generalization, and that exploration is a necessary prelude to the fashioning of accurate maps.

Summary

1. Although relatively infrequent in comparison to reinforcement effects, conversions in which mass communication plays a role do occur and have occasionally been quite widespread.

2. Various extra-communication factors and conditions which ordinarily make for reinforcement appear to be less active, and occasionally to function in an atypical direction, in processes of conversion which involve mass communication.

a. *The selective processes* (selective exposure, selective perception, and selective retention) which normally aid reinforcement are imperfect. Further, when an individual is impelled ("predisposed") toward change by extra-communication conditions, the selective processes may sensitize him to communications suggesting change.

b. *Groups and group norms,* which often abet reinforcement, may well be less influential in regard to issues not salient to the group and among persons who do not greatly value their group membership; empirical evidence on these points is, however, inconclusive. Groups and group norms may also cease to exert any influence at all because the group has itself ceased to exist, because its norms have become unrewarding, or, in the case of a specific individual, because he has changed reference groups. Group discussion of communications may render the norms more conspicuous and thus reconvert drifters, and group norms may themselves change, as, for example, in the interests of a more basic norm.

c. *Personal influence* appears to exercise a more crucial influence toward change than does mass communication when both such influences are present. However, personal influence does not appear to be a necessary factor in conversion, and its relative superiority over the media differs markedly from one topic of decision to another. Personal influence appears also to function as an agent of reinforcement, but the relative incidence of these two functions is not clear. The mass media seem to offer the most practicable way to reaching opinion leaders.

d. *"Persuasibility."*[73] Recent experiments, performed under laboratory conditions and employing approximations of mass communication, indicate that some persons are considerably more persuasible than others and that some are considerably less persuasible. Such extremes of persuasibility appear to be "topic-free,"[74] i.e., to persist regardless of the topic of persuasion, Persuasibility appears to be correlated with feelings of inadequacy, and to be unrelated to intelligence. In reference to other possible personality correlates, the evidence to date is either conflicting or extremely limited. Virtually nothing is known regarding the causal relationship, if any, between persuasibility and its personality correlates.

3. Certain aspects of mass communication effects, and in particular certain aspects of conversion effects, seem susceptible of at least partial explanation in terms of the play of such factors as are cited immediately above.

a. Persons under cross-pressures have been found to be peculiarly susceptible to conversion, to be unstable in opinion and thus susceptible to reconversion, and to tend on occasion to lose interest in the issue altogether. This may be due to the mediating forces working continually in both directions, rather than to their sensitizing the individual to one or the other side of the issue.

b. Persons who are required to parrot—and, even more, those who are required to supplement—the arguments of a communication with which they initially disagree often tend to accept the arguments. Selective retention has been shown in such cases to work *against* reinforcement, and actual or anticipated audiences, sympathetic to the original communication, seem to function as reference groups. Additional factors, as yet unidentified, are probably also at work. These findings offer a partial explanation of the persuasive efficiency of "brainwashing."

c. Various studies indicate that facts may be successfully communicated without producing the opinion changes which they are expected to produce. Most of the pertinent studies involve communications in which the facts are stated explicitly, while the opinion to which they are supposed to lead is not, thus evoking an additional variable. The communication of facts without consonant opinion change is conjecturally explicable in terms of our present theoretical orientation. Selective perception may deter the audience member from seeing the facts as pertinent to the attitude in question. The facts, thus rendered innocuous, are accepted, but not attitude change follows.

d. The literature of a decade ago commonly asserted, with little documentation, that conversion could be more easily accomplished by "side attack" than by frontal attack—i.e., that communications could create a new attitude on a quasi-pertinent issue, and this attitude could grow to the point of overwhelming the old attitude. If this is true, it may be regarded as a phenomenon more akin to the creation of new attitudes, at which the media are known to be effective, than to conversion, at which the media are known to be less effective.

4. *Theoretical Considerations.* The data adduced in relation to conversion are proposed to be illustrative of the third of the five generalizations advanced in the Introduction. The generalization, in turn, is held to be generally supported by the data. It is proposed that the set of five generalizations is continuing to serve the kind of organizational and theoretical functions outlined in Chapter II.

Contributory Aspects of the Communication and the Communication Situation

Introduction

$\mathcal{V}$ARIOUS ASPECTS of mass communications themselves and of the situations in which communications occur have been found to be related to the effectiveness of persuasion. In reference to most such variables, existing data do not permit valid distinctions to be drawn between their contribution to processes of reinforcement and their contribution to processes of conversion. They have simply been found to render persuasion generally more (or less) effective. They may thus be said to increase somewhat the ease of reinforcing existing opinion, and to reduce somewhat the difficulty of achieving conversion.

We will here make no attempt to define the "communication situation," but will regard it from a broad point of view as including: (1) the immediate source of communication; (2) the medium through which it is transmitted; (3) the content of the communication itself; and (4) certain miscellaneous aspects of the social situation in which the communication is received.

The effects of some of these variables will be found to be explicable, to some degree, in terms of the extra-communication mediating factors, such as predispositions, group norms, and the like, which have already been discussed. But this theoretical orientation does not seem capable of wholly explaining their power. Rather than indulge in long and undocumented conjecture, the author has elected to regard them, at least for the time being, as residual variables, whose processes of effect are not yet wholly clear or classifiable. Their existence is acknowledged in generalizations numbers 4 and 5—particularly number 5—which frankly serve, in the present tentative state of the generalizations, to take note of residual phenomena. All of the communication and situation variables to be discussed will, however, be recognized as constituting an order or class obviously unlike the extra-communication factors to which generalizations 1 through 3 refer.

The Source

AUDIENCE IMAGE OF THE SOURCE

The source of a communication, or, to be more exact, the source as conceived by the audience, has been shown to influence the persuasive efficacy of the communication itself. In general, sources which the audience holds in high esteem appear to facilitate persuasion, while sources which the audience holds in low esteem appear to constitute at least a temporary handicap. The possible bases of such esteem are perhaps infinitely variable. Audiences have been shown, for example, to respond particularly well to specific sources because they considered them of high prestige, highly credible, expert, trustworthy, close to themselves, or just plain likable.

The influence of sources which the audience considers highly credible or less credible, trustworthy or untrustworthy, and the like, has been extensively investigated by the Yale Communication Research Program.[1] Hovland and Weiss (1951), for example, presented college students with a series of four articles dealing respectively with the sale of anti-histamine drugs, the possibility of building atomic-powered submarines, the causes of a steel shortage, and the future of the motion picture industry. Each of the articles was attributed for one half of the group to a source previously established as having "high credibility," and for the other half to a source established as having "low credibility."

Communications attributed to high credibility sources were more often considered "fair" than were the same communications when attributed to low credibility sources, and their conclusions were more often considered "justified." The major differential, however, occurred in regard to opinion change. Net change in the direction intended by the communication was found, directly after exposure, to be three and one-half times as great among those who read the communications attributed to the high credibility sources as it was among those who read the same communications attributed to low credibility sources.

This differential does not, however, appear to be permanent. Opinion tests administered a month later showed no significant difference between the groups. The amount of change in the high credibility group had decreased, while the amount in the low credibility group had *increased*.

Investigating this phenomenon further, Kelman and Hovland (1953) pursued a study generally similar to that of Hovland and Weiss (1951), except that the topic involved treatment of juvenile delinquents and the source was varied in reference to apparent competence and fairness (versus bias) as well as mere credibility. Immediate differences of the same general order were observed, and the same drift toward similarity occurred over a space of three weeks. At that time, Kelman and Hovland "reinstated" the source in the course of an opinion test. The differences between the two groups immediately reappeared, although the amount of opinion change did not rise to quite its original level among those for whom the communication had been attributed to a "high credibility" source.

These phenomena are not easy to explain. The drift, including the upward drift of the "low credibility" group, is not due to their simply forgetting the source. Hovland and Weiss in fact found that the two groups could name the source equally well a month after the exposure. They suggest that persons "must be less likely with the passage of time to *associate spontaneously* the content with the source and that . . . the passage of time serves to remove recall of the source as a mediating cue that leads to rejection."[2] This hypothesis, however, has yet to be validated.

A single discrepant note among these findings is provided by Mandell and Hovland (1952). They exposed two groups to a communication advocating devaluating the currency, ascribed in the case of one group to a "suspect" source, and in the case of the other to a "non-suspect" source. No significant difference was found between the two groups in terms of immediate opinion change. Hovland, Janis, and Kelley (1953) suggest that this discrepant finding may manifest the differing importance of various *components* of credibility, such as "intention, expertness, and trustworthiness."[3]

Despite this one discrepant note, and despite the still hazy knowledge of the causes of the shift over time, the weight of evidence from the Yale studies is quite consistent. It indicates that sources regarded as credible, trustworthy, and the like facilitate persuasion, while sources which the audience regards negatively confer a handicap which is partially overcome by the passage of time.

The findings of the Yale Communication Research Program are in general accord with those of various less exhaustive or less precisely focused studies. Bettelheim and Janowitz (1950), for example, mailed anti-Semitic literature attributed to various sources to 50 Gentile males. They found the propaganda was more likely to be effective if ascribed to a known Jew; the readers apparently regarded such authorship as "objective." Freeman and Weeks (1955) found that experimental subjects who liked Drew Pearson to begin with were more apt than those who did not to assume opinions or to modify their existing opinions in the direction of his "predictions" after hearing a tape of one of his broadcasts. Kishler (1950) found that the degree to which subjects held Catholic priests in high esteem was crucially related to the amount they learned from the film *Keys of the Kingdom* and to the extent to which their opinions were modified in the direction of religious tolerance. His findings underline the importance of the *audience's image* of the source, as opposed to the actual source. The film was in fact a commercial production which dealt with a Catholic priest, who was, of course, portrayed by a professional actor.

The power of prestige sources to assist persuasive communication appears to be manifest in the peculiar sales ability of some of the more luminous stars in mass media's galaxy. At least part of their audiences apparently regard the stars as sources (rather than as transmission belts), and apparently additionally regard them as parent surrogates, as love objects, or, in extreme cases, as persons approaching omniscience. At the height of her career, for example, Kate Smith succeeded in obtaining "thirty-nine million dollars of [war] bond pledges in the course" of an 18-hour radio marathon.[4] Some of the purchasers apparently bought their bonds merely because Kate Smith advised it. Queried as to what they thought of her, such persons replied that

> "She talk how the mother talk to the children."
> "You know what she says is true. Next to God
> she comes when she tells it to you."[5]

There is some evidence and much reputable conjecture that even lesser luminaries achieve considerable audience prestige from the mere fact of their being carried by the media. The un-realistic audience concepts of such celebrities as Smith, Arthur Godfrey, and various others are similarly believed to be, in part, a *product* of their position on the media. Both of these points will be discussed below in reference to the effects of the mass media themselves upon the persuasive power of the communications they disseminate. For the moment, it need merely be noted that prestige sources facilitate persuasion, and that being featured by the media may very well increase prestige.

SPECIALIZED SOURCES

Highly specialized sources, directed to special interest, occupation, or age groups, and thus not in a true sense mass media, have been observed to be especially persuasive for their particular audiences. Most such appeals are made in print since the expense of radio, television, or screen production for small audiences is ordinarily prohibitive.

The audiences for such specialized publications apparently regard the publication as voicing their own personal interests and they are thus more likely to accept its advice. Lazarsfeld, Berelson, and Gaudet (1948), for example, found that in

> Erie County in 1940, the *Farm Journal* was mentioned as a concrete influence upon changes in vote intention as frequently as *Collier's*, despite their great difference in circulation, and the Townsend publication as frequently as *Life* or the *Saturday Evening Post*.[6]

The effectiveness of such specialized publications is probably increased by the fact that exposure to them is likely to be highly selective and in accord with group norms and interests. It is quite possible that persuasiveness may even be correlated with degree of specialization, i.e., that very highly specialized publications are still more persuasive than the ordinary run of specialized publications. A recent study of how doctors came to adopt a new drug, for example, found some indications that learned journals devoted to special branches of medicine were more influential among such specialized practitioners than were the journals directed to the profession as a whole.[7] Such highly specialized publications are probably regarded by their readers as peculiarly "expert" sources.

The Media Per Se

AUDIENCE IMAGE OF THE MEDIA

The mass media are themselves invested with an aura of prestige by a large portion of their audience. The process involved can no longer be traced in detail, nor has it been explicitly documented by attitude studies. But it is a matter of common observation that the media are regarded by many in their audience with considerable awe, and that media recognition or espousal *ipso facto* confers a degree of prestige upon the concept, person, or agency so recognized. Lazarsfeld and Merton (1948) are particularly cogent on the topic. They observe that

> The mass media *confer* status on public issues, persons, organizations, and social movements.
>
> Common experience as well as research testifies that the social standing of persons or social policies is raised when these command favorable attention in the mass media. In many quarters, for example, the support of a political candidate or a public policy by *The Times* is taken as significant, and this support is regarded as a distinct asset for the candidate or the policy. Why?
>
> For some, the editorial views of *The Times* represent the considered judgment of a group of experts, thus calling for the respect of laymen. But this is only one element in the status conferral function of the mass media, for enhanced status accrues to those who merely receive attention in the media, quite apart from any editorial support.
>
> The mass media bestow prestige and enhance the authority of individuals and groups by *legitimizing their status*. Recognition by the press or radio or magazines or newsreels testifies that one has arrived, that one is important enough to have been singled out from the large anonymous masses, that one's behavior and opinions are significant enough to require public notice. The operation of this status conferral function may be witnessed most vividly in the adver-

tising pattern of testimonials to a product by "prominent people." Within wide circles of the population (though not within certain selected social strata), such testimonials not only enhance the prestige of the product but also reflect prestige on the person who provides the testimonials. They give public notice that the large and powerful world of commerce regards him as possessing sufficiently high status for his opinion to count with many people. In a word, his testimonial is a testimonial to his own status. . . . The audiences of mass media apparently subscribe to the circular belief: "If you really matter, you will be at the focus of mass attention and, if you *are* at the focus of mass attention, then surely you must really matter."[8]

Hovland (1954) has also remarked upon this "halo" effect of media prestige and called for further research on its processes and components.

The prestige of media transmission apparently acts, among other ways, to increase the persuasion potential of communications. Waples, Berelson, and Bradshaw (1940), for example, concluded from a study of case histories that "an attitude frequently changes from a subordinate to a dominant position when it is justified by the authority of print,"[9] and we would probably be justified in ascribing similar power to the other media. One might postulate that the broadcast media and films have some degree of similar authority.

The prestige native to the media, some writers believe, is sufficient to allow them to build media personalities into the kind of "prestige sources" which are in themselves aids to persuasion. Merton has shown, for example, that Kate Smith's phenomenal success in selling war bonds was due in no small measure to her having been variously built up as a "symbol of sincerity, [and] of truth" and a person "competent in public affairs,"[10] whose advice was *ipso facto* to be trusted. Arthur Godfrey, Walter Winchell, and various other luminaries, current or faded, may probably be assumed, despite the lack of precise documentation, to be or to have been similarly persuasive for at least parts of their audience. Mr. Winchell's advices, for example, have been credited with causing major stock market fluctuations and with hindering the national campaign for anti-polio inoculations.

DIFFERENTIAL PERSUASIVE POWER OF THE SEVERAL MEDIA

Considerable research on the relative persuasive power of the several media bears out the widespread belief that they are in fact differentially persuasive. Although some generalizations may be hesitantly drawn, the data more clearly indicate that the relative powers of the media differ markedly from one persuasive task to another.

A series of laboratory studies, pursued for the most part in the pre-television years before 1935, indicated rather consistently that formal face-to-face contact (e.g. lecture) was more efficiently persuasive than radio (or such approximations as tapes), and that radio was more efficiently persuasive than print. The typical procedure and findings are exemplified in the work of Wilkie (1934) who exposed three matched groups of university students to texts on war, religion, birth control, and economic issues. The identical material was presented to one group by a lecturer, to another group via a wired speaker, and to the third group in printed form. The lecturer was found to be the most effective in modifying opinions, the wired speaker next most effective, and the printed material least effective. Similar findings were obtained by Knower (1935, 1936) under roughly similar circumstances. Cantril and Allport (1935), after reviewing a number of experiments, also lend their support to the apparently unanimous opinion that personal address is superior in persuasive power to mechanical aural appeal, which is in turn superior to printed appeal.[11]

Experiments that compared the effects of single and multiple media exposure typically found multiple media exposure to be more persuasively effective. Rose (1948), for example, cites several much earlier studies in justification of his stand that religious and racial prejudice can be more effectively fought by combined media appeal than by a campaign using a single medium.

The findings of such laboratory experiments cannot, however, be automatically generalized to real life situations. Laboratory subjects are ordinarily artificially motivated to pay attention to communications, and the material to which they are exposed is typically controlled with regard to length, content, etc. Insofar as possible, all conditions but one, viz., the medium, are held constant. Under normal conditions, however, no such constancy obtains. The audience may set down the newspaper or switch off the radio or TV set at will. Some may be exposed to one brief communication by radio, while their neighbors are exposed to six, two, or none by print or television. In short, the conditions under which the persuasive powers of the media are compared in the laboratory cannot be assumed to obtain in the work-a-day world.

Despite these different conditions, findings generally similar to those of the laboratory experiments were obtained by Lazarsfeld, Berelson, and Gaudet (1948) in their study of the effects of the 1940 election campaign among voters of Erie County, Ohio. Personal influence—here informal, as opposed to the formal lectures of the laboratory studies—was observed to be more effective than radio, which was in turn observed to be more effective than print. The investigators advance various conjectural bases for this hierarchy, most of which concern the degree to which the audience member is personally involved, or feels himself to be personally involved, in the communication situation. Such conditions, the authors believe, are at their height in personal contact, are reduced in radio listening, and are still lower in reading. If personal involvement is really critical, television might be expected to be more persuasive than radio, and second only to personal influence. Oddly enough, no studies of the relative persuasive efficiency of radio and television have reached the public domain.[12]

Stouffer (1940) has suggested, and others have echoed,

another reason for the apparent persuasive superiority of radio over newspapers. Print, he notes, reaches an audience with a somewhat higher education level than the overall audience for radio. The less educated, he suggests, may also be less critical and more suggestible.

A very different picture of the relative persuasive powers of the media emerges from the exhaustive study reported by Katz and Lazarsfeld (1955). These investigators, as previously noted, identified changes that had taken place among 800 women over a period of some months in regard to food purchasing habits, personal fashion preferences, and opinions on public issues. They also inquired into how respondents had come to attend particular movies.

Although the study was specifically focused on the role of personal influence, many such changes and decisions were found to have taken place without any recollected personal influence whatever. In approximately 60 per cent of the opinion changes in reference to public issues, for example, no personal influence could be discovered.[13]

Where personal influence did play a part, however, it was typically found to be more effective than any of the mass media, although the degree of its superiority varied from one topic of decision to another. The relative influence of the other media was found to vary so widely among the several topics as to defy any attempt at generalization. The study clearly suggests that personal influence is more persuasive than mass communication, but that no mass medium can be assumed to be generally or always more persuasive than any other mass medium. The nature of the topic must be taken into account, and to do so properly ordinarily involves extensive research.

The earlier findings of the laboratory studies and the later findings of Katz and Lazarsfeld are not easy to reconcile. We would seem, however, to be justified in concluding that:

(1) *All other conditions being equal, as they are in the laboratory*, face-to-face contact is more efficiently persuasive than

radio, which, in turn, is more efficient than print. TV and films probably rank between face-to-face contact and radio, but this latter point has not been empirically demonstrated.

(2) *All other conditions are, however, rarely equal outside of the laboratory.* The media are, to begin with, differentially attended. Some topics, furthermore, may be susceptible of better presentation by visual rather than oral means, or by print rather than by film, while for other topics no such differences exist. The relative persuasive power of the several media is thus, in real-life situations, likely to vary from one topic to another. Personal influence, however, appears to be generally more persuasive than any of the mass media.

MULTI-MEDIA USAGE SUPPLEMENTED BY FACE-TO-FACE CONTACT

The combined use of several media plus face-to-face contact, formal or informal, is believed by both master propagandists and by social scientists to be a peculiarly effective technique of persuasion.

Comparative studies of this technique as opposed to appeal through more limited channels are sparse indeed. Staudohar and Smith (1956) found that the film *Twelve O'Clock High* produced more favorable attitudes toward discipline among Air Force trainees when it was preceded or supplemented by a lecture than when it was presented alone. More or less similar findings are reported by a few other studies, but these latter typically employed such poor methodology as to inspire little or no confidence in their findings. The problem is, in short, almost untouched by disciplined research. Combined appeal has, however, characterized various highly successful propaganda campaigns. The Nazis, for example, supplemented their domestic media campaigns by local discussion groups, and the same technique is typically employed by Communist governments whenever they come to power.[14] The singular persuasive successes of Father Coughlin in this country in the 1940's likewise followed upon his simultaneous use of newspapers, pamphlets, radio, and local discussion groups.

Such multi-media usage, supplemented by face-to-face contact, not only places the propaganda before the somewhat different audiences of the several media, but probably derives extra persuasive power from two other sources. The mere presence of the message on mass media probably confers status on the speaker, on the movement as a whole, and on the local group, whose members may come to regard themselves as part and parcel of a national enterprise.[15] In addition, the local organization may function as a primary type group, whose norms are tailored to the goals of the communications.

UNIQUE ADVANTAGES ATTRIBUTED TO THE SEVERAL MEDIA

Certain characteristics of each medium are believed by various social scientists to provide that medium with unique capabilities as a persuasive instrument. Some of these characteristics are patently obvious, others have been documented, and some remain purely conjectural. *None has been explicitly shown to contribute to persuasion,* but because all have been thought to do so by careful observers, they seem worthy of at least brief mention.

Print, alone among the media, allows the reader to control the occasion, the pace, and the direction of his exposure, and permits him easy re-exposure. More easily than other media, print allows a topic to be developed to whatever length and with whatever complexity seems desirable. A series of laboratory experiments, mostly conducted during or before the 1930's, suggests, but does not conclusively prove, that print produces superior retention of *complex* factual material than does oral presentation, but that the same advantage does not obtain in regard to simple material.[16] As noted before, print may be readily used to reach small and specialized audiences for which other media would be prohibitively expensive. It is traditionally associated with culture, and may carry a higher prestige for some people than do the other media. In addition, print is believed by some observers to demand a more active, creative participation on the part of the reader than is demanded of the audiences of other media, because the communication is less "structured"; it does not confront the reader with a visible or audible speaker, as do film, radio, and TV, and therefore permits him greater freedom to assign or imagine nuances, interpretations, and the like. The reader is thought to be *less* personally involved than is the radio listener or screen viewer in the sense that he does not feel that he is being personally addressed, but, at the same time, to be *more* involved in the sense that he is forced to participate creatively in this more impersonal type of communication. Such creative participation is supposed by some observers to be persuasively advantageous,[17] but the hypothesis has never been tested. It may be added that creative participation, if it exists, seems not unlikely to produce at least occasional critical reactions and at least at such times, to hinder persuasion.

The broadcasting media, i.e., radio and television, and particularly television, are able to provide their audiences with a sense of participation, personal access, and "reality" which approximate face-to-face contact. In addition, the two media reach virtually the entire population, including certain groups such as the very old, the very young, and the less educated, who are not so easily accessible to the other media, and who may be more suggestible. Radio (or other types of purely oral presentation) was found by the experiments cited above to produce greater retention of *simple* material than does print, especially among the less educated and less intelligent. Radio is believed by some writers to allow greater "structuring" or creative participation than does the concrete imagery of TV. It is perhaps the most easily used of all the media, but it is also the most casually attended and seems now to serve more typically as a source of background entertainment than as a target of concentrated attention.[18]

The visual media, i.e., television and film, are widely believed to be uniquely effective simply because they are visual. Both media have been observed to command more complete attention from their audiences than do the other media and to be at times completely preoccupying, especially for children. A group of related studies published in 1933 revealed that most children and many adults tend to accept unquestioningly all presumably factual information in films, and to retain such information peculiarly well. A series of later studies, taken as a whole, provides contradictory findings in regard to whether material presented over television is or is not better retained than comparable material presented by lecture, print, or radio.[19]

Face-to-face contact may be carried out on a more personal basis than media contact, and may be tailored continually to the specific resistances and sensitivities of the listener. It is frequently part and parcel of the process of opinion leadership, and is commonly the channel through which the impressive power of group norms is brought to bear.[20]

TECHNICAL MEDIA USAGE

Any medium may, of course, be used well or poorly, and the manner in which it is used may obviously affect the degree to which its persuasive messages are effective. Format, volume, pace, camera angles, and a thousand other variables similarly associated with production techniques have been found to affect the overall effectiveness of given communications. The vast literature on the topic cannot conceivably be reviewed within the scope of a single volume, nor is the present author qualified to review it. The appropriate specialized journals and certain summaries of long-term research programs may serve as points of departure for interested readers.[21]

Content Characteristics

Various characteristics, devices, and techniques of content have been found to be related to the persuasiveness of communications. We will here consider six of the more widely discussed devices and techniques. Specifically, we will survey the data relative to the effects of: (1) presenting only one side of an argument, as compared with presenting both sides; (2) drawing explicit conclusions, as compared to leaving the conclusions implicit; (3) "threat" appeals; (4) repetition and cumulative exposure; (5) "canalization" and providing release from tension; and (6) order, emphasis, organization, and the like.

ONE SIDE VERSUS TWO SIDES

Communication research has been almost perennially concerned with the question of whether persuasion is more effective when it presents only one side of an argument or when it also cites opposing arguments.

A series of experiments on the topic was conducted during the war years by the Information and Education Division of the War Department and reported by Hovland, Lumsdaine, and Sheffield (1949). In general, the investigators found that presentation of "both sides" was more effective in converting the highly educated, but that one-sidedness was more effective in converting the poorly educated. One-sidedness also proved generally more effective among men originally favoring the advocated view, i.e., as a technique of reinforcement.

Presenting both sides in apparent but illusory impartiality was also found to be likely to boomerang for either of two reasons. If the pretense to impartiality is in any way suspect, the two-sidedness becomes peculiarly ineffective; omission "of one relevant argument against the stand taken by the programs was more noticeable in the presentation using arguments on both sides than in the presentation in which only one side was discussed."[22] On the other hand, if the impartiality is too nearly complete, the propaganda may become a truly balanced presentation, in which case it will tend to be without effect. Waples, Berelson, and Bradshaw (1940) noted long ago that when "readers are confronted with arguments both for and against an issue, the effects tend to cancel out."[23]

Confirmatory findings are provided by Thistlewaite and Kaminetzky (1955), who exposed 750 United States Air Force cadets and 400 high school students to various versions of a taped communication favoring United States participation in the Korean War. Some of the tapes included refutations of known counter-arguments, others elaborated upon those counter-arguments before refuting them, and others did not mention the counter-arguments at all. The last were found to be generally most effective in inducing attitude changes in the intended direction. Versions containing refutations, furthermore, were found likely to be "discounted" by the audience; their suspicions were apparently aroused by such a nod toward impartiality.

Two-sided communications appear, however, to be more efficient "inoculators" than are one-sided communications. Lumsdaine and Janis (1953) subjected groups of college students to one-sided and two-sided versions of an alleged radio program to the effect that the Soviet Union would not soon be able to produce atomic arms in quantity. Both versions produced a net change in the desired direction in excess of 60 per cent.[24] All subjects were then exposed to a communication expressing the opposite point of view. Net change in the direction of the original communication was thereafter found to have dropped to 2 per cent among the group originally exposed to the one-sided communication, but to have remained above 60 per cent for those who originally heard the two-sided communication. Being made aware of counterarguments had apparently inoculated the group against their subsequent use.

It must be noted, however, that one-sided communications seem able to serve as efficient inoculators *provided that audience members are required to commit themselves publicly after being exposed to the communication.* In two experiments reported by Hovland *et al* (1957), high school students were divided into control and experimental groups, both of which were exposed to communications relative to lowering the draft age.[25] The experimental groups were then asked to write out their own views for a publication to be distributed among their schoolmates, while the control group simply filled out anonymous questionnaires. Both groups were then exposed to a second communication which opposed the views expressed in the original one. Net change in the direction of the *second* communication was four times as common (25 per cent: 6 per cent) among the control group as it was among the experimental group in one experiment, and more than ten times as common (32 per cent: 3 per cent) in a second experiment in which the strength of the commitment procedure was increased. Put another way, the committed experimental group resisted the second communication far more than did the uncommitted control group. There were also some indications, which were not, however, statistically significant, that the commitment demand reduced the persuasive effect of the *first* communication. Opinion changes in the direction of the *first* communication were more common among the control groups than among the experimental groups in both experiments, although, as previously indicated, such changes were far less stable than were the changes in the committed group.

Whether one-sided presentation and required audience commitment is a more or less effective inoculator than two-sided presentation without commitment is not yet known.

The relative value of one-sided and two-sided communications, as indicated by studies to date, is succinctly summarized by Hovland, Janis, and Kelley (1953), who note that

1. A two-sided presentation is *more* effective in the long run than a one-sided one (a) when, regardless of initial opinion, the audience is *exposed* to subsequent counterpropaganda [except as indicated below], or (b) when, regardless of subsequent exposure to counterpropaganda, the audience initially *disagrees* with the commentator's position.

2. A two-sided presentation is *less* effective than a one-sided if the audience initially *agrees* with the commentator's position and *is not exposed* to later counterpropaganda.[26]

It may be added that two-sided presentations are generally less effective than one-sided presentations for persons of lesser education and are particularly susceptible of boomeranging. It is also to be noted that a one-sided presentation is an efficient "inoculator" among persons who are thereupon required publicly to commit themselves on the issue; whether this procedure is a more efficient inoculator than a two-sided presentation without commitment has not yet been tested.

EXPLICITNESS VERSUS IMPLICITNESS

Research evidence strongly indicates that persuasion is likely to be more effective if the communication draws explicit conclusions, rather than allowing audience members to draw the conclusions themselves.

As noted at some length above, a considerable number of studies have found that communications designed to produce attitude conversions may succeed in communicating facts without producing the attitude changes which are expected to follow. In such instances, the explicit material, i.e., the facts, are successfully communicated, whereas the implicit goal of the communication is not attained. But, as we have pointed out, another variable is involved in many such studies. The explicit material is typically relatively objective, whereas the implicit goal usually involves overcoming existing attitudes, which are, to varying degrees, ego-involved. It is not possible on the basis of existing data wholly to disentangle the effects of these two variables, and it seems probable that both are actively at work.

One single study on this general topic involves material which is not likely to be ego-involved, and on which the audience is unlikely to have strong pre-existing opinions. Mandell and Hovland (1952) exposed students to tape recordings of an alleged radio program dealing with the advisability of devaluating currency. The two versions employed were identical, except that conclusions were explicitly drawn in one and not in the other. Net change in the direction intended was 47.9 per cent for the group hearing the explicit version as compared with only 19.3 per cent for those hearing the implicit version. Boomerang effects, futhermore, occurred among 11.4 per cent of the audience for the non-explicit version, but only among 3.3 per cent of the audience for the explicit version.

Action in accord with the recommendations of the communication likewise seems to become more probable as the suggestion for action becomes more explicit. Cartwright (1949) concluded, after a study of war bond appeals, that "the more specifically defined the path of action to a goal,"[27] the more likely it is that the path will be followed. Katz and Lazarsfeld (1955) likewise found that the "more specific the suggestion which a personal contact makes, the more likely it is that his or her advice will be followed."[28]

Wiebe (1951) has pointed out at some length that it is easier to sell commodities over TV than it is to sell good citizenship, because specific action may be more easily suggested and action outlets more easily provided. These considerations go beyond the simple question of explicitness versus implicitness, but in a sense they take root in that distinction.

EXTREME "THREAT APPEALS"[29]

A series of fairly recent studies presents remarkably consistent findings to the effect that persuasive communications which employ threat appeals are likely to be *less* effective as the threat becomes more extreme. An audience whose anxieties have been too highly stimulated apparently tends to recoil, rather than to learn or to consider.

A now classic study on the topic was performed by Janis and Feshbach (1953). They presented three groups of high school students with three versions of an illustrated lecture on dental hygiene. All versions cited the dangers of dental neglect and recommended specific procedures of tooth care. The three versions differed, however, in the degree to which they emphasized the possible dire consequences of dental neglect. Tests administered a week before and a week after the lecture revealed that the recommended procedures were adopted most widely by the group exposed to the minimum threat version (36 per cent net change), next most widely by the group exposed to the moderate threat (22 per cent net change), and least widely by the group which was most strongly threatened (8 per cent net change). Differences between the groups were still apparent a full year later.

A second and somewhat similar study by Janis and Milholland (1954) suggests that a strong threat is in itself preoccupying and may thus hinder learning of other material in the communication. Hovland, Janis, and Kelley (1953) discuss both of these studies and conclude that "when fear is strongly aroused but not fully relieved by the reassurances contained in a persuasive communication, the audience will become motivated to ignore or minimize the importance of the threat."[30] They caution against over-generalization of the findings, suggesting that they might not hold, for example, when the threat is immediate and certain, and the communication suggests a mode of escape.

Related findings are provided by various other studies. Bettelheim and Janowitz (1950), for example, found that anti-semitic propaganda was less likely to be effective when it attacked such pillars of society as Felix Frankfurter and Bernard Baruch. By suggesting that such "symbols" were not to be trusted, the propaganda created anxiety and became more likely to be rejected; some of the respondents in fact tore up the pamphlets. Cannell and MacDonald (1956) see threat-avoidance as a possible explanation for their findings that smokers read fewer articles about cigarettes and cancer, and were far less often persuaded that a causative connection existed, than were non-smokers.[31]

Kaufmann (1952) has pointed out the considerable implications of these various findings for civil defense programs and for international propaganda. Emphasis on the horrors of possible bombing may be a peculiarly ineffective way to stimulate the populace to civil defense efforts. Voice of America and Radio Free Europe emphasis on the horrors of Communism may be a similarly inefficient way to induce listeners in free countries to take active measures against the threat.

REPETITION, VARIATION, AND CUMULATIVE EXPOSURE

Belief that repetition in itself helps to make persuasion successful is manifested by current advertising techniques, often asserted by public opinion experts, and, to a lesser extent, attested by communications research. A campaign designed to improve the public's attitude toward the oil industry, for example, was found to have produced the greatest attitude changes in regard to those points of view which were most often reasserted.[32] Rose (1948), reviewing various earlier studies, concluded that repetition, particularly repetition at intervals, increased the persuasive effectiveness of pro-tolerance propaganda themes. His general position is in accord with the views of such psychologists as Thorndike and such practitioners as Joseph Goebbels.[33]

Analyses of the more successful campaigns of persuasion suggest, however, that although repetition is of value, sheer parrot-like reiteration may begin to irritate the audience. Repetition with variation, on the other hand, serves both constantly to remind the listener or reader of the goal of the persuasion, and, simultaneously, to appeal to several of his needs and drives. Thus Bartlett (1940) proposed, without citing supporting data, that

> It is not sheer repetition that is influential, but repetition with variations . . . so . . . some new welcoming tendency stands a chance of being brought into play.[34]

Research generally supports Bartlett's stand. Repetition with variation is believed by Merton (1946), for example, to have contributed heavily to the success of Kate Smith's war bond marathon. Merton identifies some 60 appeals, each to some degree distinct from any of its fellows, and all aimed at the same goals: the creation and reinforcement of the desire to buy a war bond and the intensification of that desire to the point of actual purchase or pledge. "Each new entreaty sought out a new vulnerability in some listeners," and repeated exposure to these varying appeals reinforced the growing response-tendency in individual listeners.[35] Lazarsfeld, Berelson, and Gaudet (1948) not only found that varying appeals were peculiarly successful in campaign propaganda, but also that a certain degree of ambiguity apparently increased the effectiveness of appeals by rendering them susceptible of various interpretations. Cartwright (1949), summarizing the findings of research on war bond sales, concluded that "the more goals which are seen [by an individual] as attainable by a single path, the more likely it is that a person will take that path."[36] Thus persons given more than one type of reason to buy bonds were found more likely actually to do so.

The data on effectiveness of repetition are considerably more conclusive than are the data on the seemingly related topic of cumulative exposure to propaganda. Annis and Meier (1934) found exposure to seven editorials precisely as effective as exposure to fifteen; and Hovland, Lumsdaine, and Sheffield (1949) found that exposure to two Army orientation films produced no consistently greater results than exposure to a single (but different) film in the same series. On the other hand, Peterson and Thurstone (1933) found the effect of cumulative exposure to films on the same topic to be in all respects greater than the effect of single exposure, and the findings of these investigators are in part substantiated, in reference to other media, by Lazarsfeld, Berelson, and Gaudet (1948) and by Merton (1946). These contradictory findings regarding cumulative exposure are difficult to reconcile with the more consistent findings regarding repetition with variation—particularly since repetition with variation is, after all, built into cumulative exposure.

"CANALIZATION" AND RELEASE FROM TENSION

Social scientists, public relations experts, and the like have commonly observed that persons are far more amenable to having their existing needs implemented than they are to developing entirely new needs. Communication research generally confirms this view, strongly suggesting that persuasion is more likely to be effective when it can make the opinion or behavior it espouses appear to the audience to be a mode of satisfying their existing needs. To create new needs and to impel the audience to a particular mode of satisfying them appears a far more difficult task.

Thus Cartwright (1949), reporting on a series of studies on mass persuasion in the interests of the Treasury Department, considers it unlikely that such campaigns can create new needs. "To induce a given action by mass persuasion," he believes, "this action must be seen by the person as a path to some goal that he has."[37] Likert (1954) takes essentially the same position on a somewhat more abstract plane in proposing that appeals must be related to what Lewin called the "life space" of the audience. A manuscript "ostensibly dictated" by Joseph Goebbels suggests that existing audience attitudes may be directed toward new objects by the use of words which are associated with the existing attitudes;[38] such symbol transference is, of course, part of the conscious or unconscious stock in trade of virtually all successful propagandists.

The efficacy of advertising, with which, however, we are not here primarily concerned, is believed by some observers to be largely due to its almost exclusive concern with such canalization. Even before the days of formalized motivation research, which in effect identifies semi-conscious or unconscious consumer needs and suggests modes of partially sating them, Lazarsfeld and Merton (1948) observed that

> Advertising is typically directed toward the canalizing of pre-existing behavior patterns or attitudes. It seldom seeks to instill new attitudes or to create significantly new behavior patterns.[39]

The same authors caution, however, that

> . . . the leap from efficacy of advertising to the assumed efficacy of propaganda . . . is as unwarranted as it is dangerous . . . mass propaganda typically meets a more complex situation. It may seek objectives which are at odds with deep lying attitudes. It may seek to reshape rather than to canalize current systems of values.[40]

Wiebe (1951) draws a similar if more detailed distinction between "merchandising commodities and citizenship on television."[41]

Nevertheless, various successful propaganda campaigns have wittingly or unwittingly assumed for a time the cloak of canalizers. Some of the success of Kate Smith's marathon broadcast in the interest of war bond sales was due, Merton (1946) believes, to her providing a handy way in which people who were just about ready to buy anyway could implement their intentions. "Her drive was perceived [by such persons] as an immediate and convenient opportunity for removing any lingering doubts . . . [as a way] to convert an intention into a commitment."[42] Smith furthermore made the act of purchase a mode of releasing a whole range of existing needs and tensions, many of which she first further stimulated. She reminded her audience of the sacrifices being made by servicemen, by other purchasers, and by herself, eliciting a feeling of guilt from which relief could now be attained. By couching "her appeal . . . in terms of 'we,' 'our' and 'us' . . . [she] provided surcease from individuated, self-centered activity and from the sense that the war is too big for the individual's effort to count."[43] She related bond purchasing to bringing the boys back home, and, finally, she communicated, at least to her more avid fans, the feeling that buying a bond would involve personally assisting their idol.

The needs which a communication may offer to implement are, of course, boundless, and cannot here be listed. The essential point is that communications which seem to the audience to promise relief from such existing needs are more likely to be widely persuasive than those which are faced with the task of creating needs to begin with.

ORDER, EMPHASIS, ORGANIZATION, AND THE LIKE

Virtually hundreds of studies have investigated the influence upon both instruction and persuasion of an almost endless list of variables related to the organization of content and to techniques of presentation. Included among such variables are the number of topics treated;[44] the position (first, last, or intermediate) of the topic, and the order of arguments (strong before weak, or weak before strong);[45] the form of the presentation (monologue versus dialogue; documentary with "visuals" versus straight-forward presentation; etc.);[46] clearly defined organization versus poorly defined organization;[47] and a host of technical matters pertaining to size of print, position of pictures, radio montages, television camera angles, duration of shots, and the like.

Numerous studies of such matters have been performed in the course of a continuing research program which has been pursued at Pennsylvania State University for more than a decade.[48] Almost equally extensive programs have been pursued by or for the various armed services, and the Yale Communication Research Program has recently focused its intensive light on the same general area.[49] Many of these investigations are educationally oriented, aimed at maximizing the pedagogical efficiency of the media. Recently burgeoning studies of educational broadcasting and television have added to the already copious literature.

No attempt can be made here to survey or cite the findings of this vast literature. To collect and digest the studies, to identify and compare those that are comparable, to take into account those that are not comparable, and to present the sum of it all is a task which would necessarily occupy a considerable staff for several years. The compilation would obviously be tremendously useful, and it is to be hoped that the necessary human and financial resources will be somehow brought to bear before the literature becomes so vast that it can no longer be surveyed at all.

Caution should perhaps be sounded, however, against generalizing the results of any such individual studies with which the reader may come in contact. In reference to many topics, the findings are almost infinitely variable. The history of investigation of "order" provides a superb example of such variability. In 1925 Lund, on the basis of an experiment, formulated his "law of primacy in persuasion." Specifically, he proposed that the first point of view on a given issue to which an audience was exposed was likely to be more persuasively effective, and remain more persuasively effective, than any later counter-arguments on the same subject. The notion has persisted and is still occasionally expressed today, although in point of fact Lund's findings did not remained long unchallenged. During the next twenty-odd years a considerable literature appeared dealing with the relative effectiveness of first versus last position, and of climactic (weak argument first) versus anti-climactic order. Hovland (1954) ably reviews this literature and points out that virtually all possible orders of effectiveness have been observed in various studies.

Hovland *et al* (1957) again review the literature and report as well on a considerable series of similarly focused studies recently pursued at Yale University. According to Hovland

The general picture which emerges from the experiments in which both sides of an issue are presented successively is that concern as to the danger of first impressions becoming lasting impressions is probably exaggerated, at least for situations where representatives of both sides have an opportunity to present their views. The public is not necessarily permanently swayed by the view to which it first lends an ear, or biased by the man who first captures its attention.

The present group of experiments indicate the conditions under which the danger of the first side's prevailing is likely to be pronounced and also permit some specification of procedures which minimize such a danger. The combined findings from all of the different studies reported suggest that the side of an issue presented first is likely to have a disproportionate influence on opinion under the following conditions: (1) when cues as to the incompatibility of different items of information are absent, (2) when the contradictory information is presented by the same communicator, (3) when committing actions [of a public nature] are taken [by the audience] after only one side of the issue has been presented, (4) when the issue is an unfamiliar one, and (5) when the recipient has only a superficial interest in the issue (low cognitive need). When one deals with situations in which exposure to both sides cannot be assumed, but where the recipient himself controls whether he will expose himself to the second side after hearing the first, additional factors [such as the selective processes] favoring primacy become involved.

Under conditions other than those enumerated above, "the law of primacy" does not seem to be particularly valid. Thus, the findings about order of presentation remain variable, and as yet so tied to specific situation factors as to be susceptible of little generalization.

Similar, if in some cases less exhaustive, variety exists regarding the findings of many of the other variables pertaining to organization and presentation. Other bodies of findings, though more consistent, pertain to such topically or technically specific situations that they can hardly be generalized without further replicative but varied research. Above all, however, the literature is so vast, and much of it is so specifically focused, that it cannot be surveyed or summarized within the scope of this volume, nor, very possibly, within any other single volume.

Climate of Opinion

The persuasive success of a communication may be affected by the climate of opinion in which it is received. In general, a communication in accord with the prevailing climate of opinion seems more likely to attract other people to its position than does a communication which echoes a minority point of view. This general statement, however, is subject to various qualifications.

THE BANDWAGON EFFECT

A vast body of research has demonstrated that people will adopt opinions simply because they believe those opinions to be in accord with the majority view. The classic studies by Sherif (1936) and Asch (1952) deal with judgments about moving lights, relative length of lines, and the like, and are pertinent though they are topically irrelevant to the present volume. Wheeler and Jordan (1929) modified student opinion on campus issues simply by making the majority view known. Sorokin and

Baldyreff (1932) played two identical records of a symphony to a group of listeners previously informed that one record was "unanimously judged" by a group of music critics to be the better; 96 per cent of the subjects thought one superior to the other, and 59 per cent agreed with the alleged choice of the experts; only 4 per cent recognized that the records were identical.

The same desire to stay with the larger crowd has been widely observed to affect opinions outside the laboratory and has become familiarly known as "the bandwagon effect." Lazarsfeld, Berelson, and Gaudet (1948), for example, found numerous persons in Erie County whose vote decision was based entirely and consciously on this single criterion. One respondent reported, for example, that

> "Just before the election it looked like Roosevelt would win so I went with the crowd. Didn't make any difference to me who won, but *I wanted to vote for the winner.*"[51]

Hovland (1954) has suggested that to persons who board the bandwagon, the majority view serves as a "cue for the anticipated reward of social approbation."[52]

THE RESISTANCE OF SMALL MINORITIES

As attractive as the bandwagon may be, it is not likely to lure members of small, deviant minorities, who seem to be *ipso facto* peculiarly resistant to change. Cooper and Dinerman (1951), for example, ranked various messages in the anti-prejudice film *Don't Be A Sucker* according to how widely they were accepted by persons who had not seen the film. Before-and-after tests of persons exposed to the film revealed that those messages with which a bare majority originally agreed were accepted relatively widely among the large minority which originally disagreed. *But messages with which a very large majority originally agreed had little or no effect on the small minority which originally disagreed.* Cooper and Dinerman suggest that when deviant minorities are very small they are likely to consist of people who are particularly firm in their beliefs, and who have already withstood the arguments which have convinced most others. Hovland, Lumsdaine, and Sheffield (1949) advance the same explanation to account for the resistance of soldiers who were totally unaffected by the film *Battle of Britain*, which favored U.S. aid to England during the early war years. The population as a whole, they point out, favored aid to Britain; those who still opposed it were not likely to be converted by the arguments of the film. Coleman, Katz, and Menzel (1960) noted a similar phenomenon among physicians adopting a new drug; after the great majority in a given town had adopted the drug, there remained a small, highly resistant minority whose members either adopted the drug much later, or never adopted it at all.

Studies which are not primarily concerned with mass communication suggest that members of such deviant minorities derive considerable strength from each other, i.e., from the knowledge that there is at least some support for their opinion. Asch (1952), for example, found that individuals were far more likely to maintain their own opinions, in the face of contrary group opinion, if they were supported by even one other member of the group. Coleman, Katz, and Menzel (1960) found that doctors who are friends are more apt to follow similar therapeutic practices when such practices are still a matter of controversy than they are when the practices have the general sanction of the medical community; during the period when majority support is unobtainable, the friends seem to provide support for each other.

Theoretical Considerations

Various aspects and characteristics of communications and of the communication situation have been treated in this chapter. In general, these variables are not particularly related to the relative likelihood that communications will reinforce or change the existing opinions of their audiences. All are, however, related to the general ability of communications to persuade, whatever their task or goal may be vis-à-vis particular audience members. Put another way, judicious exploitation of the devices and techniques cited in this chapter is likely to increase somewhat the ease with which a given communication reinforces sympathetic views and simultaneously to reduce somewhat the difficulty it faces in converting persons holding opposite opinions.

These several factors and characteristics are covered by the last of the five generalizations proposed in the Introduction. That generalization proposes that "the efficacy of mass communication, either as a contributory agent or as an agent of direct effect, is affected by various aspects of the media themselves or of the communication situation (including, for example, aspects of textual organization, the nature of the source and medium, the existing climate of public opinion, and the like)."

This generalization, unlike the preceding four, serves to *note* that such variables exist, rather than conjecturally to *explain* their process of influence and effect. The sole point which the generalization makes regarding that process is that it differs from the process of mediation cited in the first three generalizations.

Generalization number 5 is accordingly of only very limited organizational and theoretical helpfulness. It serves to underscore generalizations 1 through 3, and that in two ways:

(1) It removes from the province of those generalizations a group of factors which pertain to the communication itself or to the communication situation;

(2) It thus underscores the propositions that the forces cited in the earlier generalizations are external to the communication, that they *mediate* the effect of the communication upon its audience, and that they in fact constitute a class of factors as yet only hazily defined, but clearly distinct from such other factors as the textual characteristics of the communication itself, or the nature of its source.

The present author has repeatedly asserted that he considers all of the generalizations exploratory, and that he considers their emendation to be both inevitable and desirable. Generalization number 5, which is essentially an acknowledgement of what the other generalizations do not cover, is particularly in need of such refinement.

Summary

Various aspects of the communication itself and of the communication situation appear to be related to the persuasive efficacy of mass communications.

1. Sources, or, more precisely, the audience's image of sources, affects the audience's interpretation of the communication and its persuasive effectiveness. Sources regarded as credible, trustworthy, or high in prestige apparently abet persuasion; while sources inspiring more negative images apparently hinder persuasion. The differential effect tends, however, to disappear with the passage of time. Highly specialized sources appear to be more persuasive for their own specialized audiences than are more general sources for the same audiences.

2. The mass media are themselves widely regarded with awe and apparently confer status on the persons and concepts for which they are vehicles.

3. The several media appear to be in themselves differentially effective as channels for persuasive communication, over and above the fact that they normally draw on somewhat different audiences.

a. In laboratory experiments, wherein all conditions other than the media are kept constant, formal personal appeal is typically found more effective than radio, which is in turn found more effective than print. Television and films may be hypothesized to fall between personal appeal and radio.

b. In real life situations, informal personal appeal has been consistently found to be more effective than any mass medium, but it is nevertheless not essential to successful persuasion. The relative efficacy of the mass media varies so widely from one topical area to another as to defy generalization. Multi-media usage supplemented by face-to-face contact is believed to be peculiarly effective and has characterized various highly successful propaganda campaigns.

c. Each of the media has been ascribed various advantages which are believed, but rarely demonstrated, to be related to that medium's persuasive capabilities. These include such characteristics as the unique ability of print to permit the audience member to govern his rate of exposure, and the ability of the broadcast media to provide the audience member with some sense of personal participation. Other such characteristics are cited above too briefly to be susceptible of further summary.

d. The degree of technical efficiency with which a medium is used may obviously affect its persuasive efficiency. Variables pertaining to presentation techniques (pace, camera angles, etc.) are discussed in a literature far too vast to be here reviewed.

4. Various content characteristics and devices appear to be related to the ability of mass communications to persuade.

a. Two-sided presentation (i.e., citation of arguments on both sides of the question) is more effective than one-sided presentation as a device for converting the highly educated, and as a safeguard against later counter-propaganda. One-sided presentation, however, is more effective in converting the less educated, is generally more effective as a reinforcing device, and is less likely to boomerang. It is an efficient inoculator against later counter-propaganda provided that the audience members are required publicly to commit themselves; whether it is *more* effective under these conditions than two-sided presentation is not yet known.

b. Persuasive communications which explicitly state conclusions are more likely to be effective than those which allow audience members to draw their own conclusions. Action recommendations, also, seem more likely to be followed as they are the more specific and explicit.

c. Communications which evoke extreme fear are *less* likely to persuade the audience to take precautionary actions than are communications which do not so strongly emphasize the threat.

d. Repetition, particularly repetition with variation, has been consistently found to increase the efficacy of persuasion. Cumulative exposure to propaganda, however, has on some occasions been found to be more effective and on other occasions has been found to be no more effective than single exposure.

e. Communications which offer ways of implementing ("canalizing") the existing needs of their audiences are more likely to be successfully persuasive than communications which undertake to arouse new needs and then suggest ways of satisfying them. This distinction is peculiarly pertinent to the difference between "merchandising commodities and [merchandising] citizenship"[53] or other attitudes.

f. Hundreds of studies have investigated the effects of variables pertaining to organization and presentation, such as the order of topics and of arguments, montages as opposed to no montages, camera angles, etc. The literature on these topics is so vast and the findings so varied and often so specifically focused that years of collation would be prerequisite to any general summary.

5. Persuasive communications in accord with majority opinion, or which are believed by their audience to be in accord with majority opinion, are likely therefore to be effective among members of the minority who do not share the opinion. If, however, the minority is extremely small, it is likely to be composed of persons who are particularly resistant to conversion. The resistance of such deviants appears to be intensified when they are aware that other people, or even one other person, think as they do.

6. *Theoretical Considerations.* The topics of this chapter are covered by the fifth of the five generalizations proposed in the

Introduction. That generalization serves to note that certain phenomena and processes are not covered by the preceding generalizations. It is less helpful in regard to the topics to which it refers than it is in underscoring the characteristic identity and processes of the factors to which it does *not* refer—i.e., those covered by the preceding generalizations.

Part Two

THE EFFECTS OF
SPECIFIC TYPES OF
MEDIA MATERIAL

Introductory Note

Part Two is devoted to the effects of certain specific types of media material. Chapters VI, VII, and VIII deal, respectively, with the effects of media depictions of crime and violence, the effects of "escapist" material, and the effects of adult TV fare on child audiences. Chapter IX deals with "passivity," an effect alleged to accrue from media fare in general, or even from mere attendance upon the media.

In reference to each of these topics, the precise nature and incidence of the concern is first made clear; reputable conjecture on the topic is summarized; and, finally, the findings of pertinent research are presented and considered. As in the case of Part One, each chapter contains a final section on "Theoretical Considerations," and concludes with a relatively detailed summary.

The Effects of Crime
and Violence in the Media

Incidence of the Concern

*A*MONG THE MOST PREVALENT of social concerns
regarding the effects of mass communication is a brooding worry
about the possible effects upon audience members—particularly
upon young members—of the media's abundant depictions of
crime and violence.

The fear is less frequently expressed by disciplined communication researchers than it is by parents, educators, and free-
lance writers, but among these latter groups it is a matter of
continual comment and concern. Bogart (1956) reports, for
example, that a 1954 Gallup survey found that 70 per cent of the
interviewed adults placed "at least part of the blame for the
'upsurge in juvenile delinquency' on crime-type comic books and
on mystery and crime programs on television and radio."[1] Among
New Haven families interviewed by Smythe (1955) regarding
children's TV habits, crime and violence was the subject of 57

per cent of all objections specific enough to classify. In a survey of prevalent concerns regarding children and TV, conducted by the present author in 1953, all network continuity acceptance and public relations personnel among the respondents, as well as all persons professionally concerned with children's programs, agreed "that the incidence . . . of crime and violence . . . [was] the most frequent topic of written complaint or concern."[2] Popular literature[3] was found in the same survey to be more concerned with the effects of crime and violence than with the effects of any other aspect of television content.

Incidence of Crime and Violence in the Media

DOCUMENTATION

The abundance of crime and violence in media content is attested often and in statistical detail by elaborate studies, individual researchers, and by lay groups organized for that express purpose. Logan, for example, until recently provided annual counts of murders, holdups, kidnappings, and other crimes within a selected sample of TV programs.[4] Mirams (1951) tallied the violence in films imported into New Zealand and found the incidence twice as high among the 70 U.S. products as among the 30 made elsewhere. Head (1954) performed a content analysis of 209 TV network programs and found homicide to be 22 times as common as it was in real life, although, interestingly enough, certain small crimes were underrepresented.

The most elaborate of all tallies of violence were provided in three successive annual reports published by the National Association of Educational Broadcasters.[5] For these studies, monitors tallied every act or threat of violence depicted on TV entertainment programs visible in New York during a full week period. The number increased from year to year, and the final count, made in 1954, noted 6,868 incidents during the 1954 test week, as compared with 3,350 during a comparable week in 1953.[6] In all three years "the frequency of violence . . . [was found to be] higher during the children's hours than in other time periods."[7]

Abundant violence in children's program hours is apparently not peculiar to the United States. Himmelweit, Oppenheim, and Vince (1958) found that about 20 per cent of British TV programs shown during children's peak viewing hours featured violence and aggression; they note that this figure is approximately equal to one reported by a U.S. Senate sub-committee on the basis of a monitoring study performed in Washington, D.C. in 1954.[8]

CRITIQUE

There can be no doubt that violence is frequently depicted in the media. However, the precise significance, and in some cases the validity, of these testimonies of abundance is somewhat difficult to define.

Protests may be entered, for example, against some of the more alarmistic reports which include outright pornography among their source materials. Thus Wertham (1954), the *Report of the New York State Joint Legislative Committee to Study the Publication of Comics* (1955),[9] and various other reports draw upon publications and, in some cases, privately made films which are not mass media, nor, because of their price and *sub rosa* distribution, are they ordinarily available to children. The mass media undoubtedly portray crime and violence, and some comic books do contain almost pathologically weird material. Sheer pornography, however, very rarely appears in comic books, and is unheard of in the other mass media. It is undoubtedly true, as the critics claim, that some easily available comic books do or did deal with "murder, mayhem, robbery, . . . carnage, . . . and sadism," but the present author has yet to be convinced that they "offer short courses" in these subjects, let alone in "rape, cannibalism, . . . and necrophilia."[10] In short, it seems patently unjust to hold mass media culpable for either the existence or effects of esoteric erotica.

Even among those reports which hew to mass media proper, the significance of the statistics themselves is hard to define, and that for at least three reasons.

(1) Some of the counts define violence so broadly that the psychological validity of the category seems open to question. The studies performed for the National Association of Educational Broadcasters, for example, tally both violence and "threats" of violence, and "violence" is so defined as to include any "physical or psychological injury, hurt, or death addressed to living things."[11] The over-all category includes "sham . . . or humorous violence, such as the comedian's fall," "legal" violence, "verbal" violence, and violence resulting from "act of nature" or "accident."[12] Tallied incidents were, in one or more of the studies, classified and cross-classified according to such categories as source stations, types of program, whether occurring in humorous or non-humorous context, whether committed in the course of upholding the law, and the "means used" (a category divided into thirty-five subcategories in the 1953 report but reduced to nine subcategories by 1954).[13] It is hardly a wonder that with so broad a definition the monitors noted 6,868 incidents during the 1954 test week.

The present author has long wondered what significance could be attached to so inclusive a definition of violence or to the single total of incidents covered by such a definition. Recent research, performed after these counts had been accomplished, indicates—as might have been expected—that audiences do not react similarly to these various forms of violence.[14] The summation of this wide variety of incidents in a single total thus appears to be methodologically unwarranted and in fact misleading.

(2) The significance of the statistics and their presumed relationship to audience reaction are further obscured by the peculiar fact that objections to violence and tallies of its occurrence bear almost exclusively on violence which occurs in fiction.

Real violence is not statistically observed and its vehicles, far from being castigated, are typically commended as educational. The studies performed for the National Association of Educational Broadcasters, for example, carefully tally fictional evidence resulting from "act of nature" and "accident" but ignore "because of special problems in definition and . . . methods, violence found in sports, news, weather, public issues and public events programs."[15] Documentaries bearing on war, strikes, riots, nuclear fission, or fall-out were mentioned in this context by only one single respondent and by none of the fifty-odd pieces of literature encountered by the present author in his 1953 survey of socially prevalent concerns regarding children and TV. Bogart (1956) reports that audience objections to the violence in a particular TV series were replaced by letters of praise when the shows were fitted out with introductions which gave the impression that the incidents depicted were part of Indian lore;[16] this quasi-documentary cloak was apparently enough to win over previously critical adults.

A recent study by Himmelweit, Oppenheim, and Vince (1958), whose findings are discussed in detail below, indicates that child TV audiences do react differently to real and fictional violence. The differences, however, are not consistent and appear to stem from aspects of the depiction which are only spuriously related to its real or fictional nature. The whole matter is quite complex and has not yet been wholly clarified. There appears, however, to be no real justification for the assumption implicit in popular literature and in audience mail that depictions of real violence are somehow less psychologically dangerous than depictions of fictional violence.

(3) Finally, and perhaps basically, nothing is known about the relationship, if any, between the incidence of violence in media programs, and the likelihood that it will produce effects. What effects such fare produces is in itself a matter of controversy which will be treated below. But even if it is granted, for the sake of the argument, that some effects occur, absolutely nothing is known

regarding the relative potential of varying amounts of stimuli. The statistics of violence shine conspicuously in a standardless void. Their increasing size may attest a trend in media content, but it does not indicate that any particular effects are therefore more or less likely to occur.

None of this, however, is to gainsay that crime and violence are abundantly depicted in the mass media. It is only to suggest that existing tallies of its precise incidence are occasionally unfair, occasionally slightly hysterical, and of indefinable significance. The crucial question is not the exact number of violent acts, but the effect which they have upon their audiences.

Popularly Feared Effects

The effects which media depictions of crime and violence are feared capable of producing are varied. At least six separate, if somewhat related, concerns are discernible in the literature:

(1) Some of those who fear the effects of violence in the media seem unsure of what specific consequences might follow. They are merely convinced that *the consequences are undesirable.* "Common sense," says Logan (1950), "tells us crime is not for children . . . we should protect children from these crime programs just as we protect them from physical danger."[17]

(2) Other writers express more specific fears, including the belief that *such material elicits direct, imitative behavior.* Cousins (1949), for example, believes, or then believed, that "terror comic strips" and television were "prime movers in juvenile misconduct and delinquency." He tells of children led by the media to commit heinous acts:

> In a Boston suburb, a nine-year-old reluctantly showed his father a report card heavily decorated with red marks, then proposed one way of getting at the heart of the matter: they could give the teacher a box of poisoned chocolates for Christmas. "It's easy, Dad, they did it on television last week. A man wanted to kill his wife, so he gave her candy with poison in it and she didn't know who did it."

In Brooklyn, New York, a six-year-old son of a policeman asked his father for real bullets because his little sister "doesn't die for real when I shoot her like they do when Hopalong Cassidy kills 'em."

In Los Angeles, a housemaid caught a seven-year-old boy in the act of sprinkling ground glass into the family's lamb stew. There was no malice behind the act. It was purely experimental, having been inspired by curiosity to learn whether it would really work as well as it did on television.[18]

Many such reports seem to imply, if only by default, that such acts are, at least occasionally, committed by otherwise normal children who saw them depicted in the mass media and were thereby impelled to perform them themselves. The *Report of the New York State Joint Legislative Committee to Study the Publication of Comics,* for example, quotes as "additional evidence of the link between juvenile delinquency and the publication, distribution, and sale"[19] of crime and horror literature, a probation officer's statement that

This boy had no previous record, but he said he got the idea of accosting this woman from reading a pocket book and had driven to Mankato Sunday night with that specific purpose in mind.[20]

Other statements imputing a similarly immediate cause-and-effect influence to media depictions of violence abound in the popular literature. The mass communication industry itself recognizes the belief that the media are capable of provoking direct imitation, and forbids exercise of the capability; the Code of the Comic Magazine Association of America, for example, prohibits the presentation of crime "in such a way as . . . to inspire . . . a desire to imitate criminals."[21] The codes of the Motion Picture Association and the National Association of Broadcasters contain essentially similar statements.

(3) A variation of the theme just discussed, and one frequently voiced by the same authors, is the fear that media depictions of crime and violence constitute *a school for delinquency.* In this version of the concern, media violence is not seen so likely to produce immediate, irrational imitation, as rather to slowly de-

velop in its juvenile audience a constellation of deviant desires and a tendency to delinquent and heinous behavior. This view was, in fact, espoused by an early piece of communications research. Blumer and Hauser (1933) concluded, after interviewing and otherwise studying convicted criminals, that movies often contributed significantly to their downfall, and that

> Through the display of crime techniques and criminal patterns of behavior; by arousing desires for easy money and luxury, and by suggesting questionable methods for their achievement; by inducing a spirit of bravado, toughness, and adventurousness; by arousing intense sexual desires; and by invoking daydreaming of criminal roles, motion pictures may create attitudes and furnish techniques conducive, quite unwittingly, to delinquent or criminal behavior.[22]

Documents such as the *Report of the New York State Joint Legislative Committee to Study the Publication of Comics* are filled with allegations of this sort of effect, typically quoted from statements by police officers, jurists, the clergy, and officials of the PTA and similar organizations. An essentially similar view has been expressed by some psychiatrists.[23]

Soviet critics of the American scene seem to go along with the school of delinquency theory. Jordan (1956) reports that they consider that delinquency must inevitably prevail "in the U.S. where from their earliest years, children are bred on comics, horror stories, or robberies perpetrated by gangster supermen."

(4) Many persons fear that *crime in the media will have a kind of trigger effect which will become operative among persons in situations of reduced moral resistance*. Mirams (1951), for example, feels that the media's "reiteration of assault might create a behavior pattern which might, in certain circumstances (say, too much to drink), become a sort of conditioned reflex with some types of individuals."[24] Bloch and Flynn (1956) note that a considerable number of reputable social scientists believe that the media's emphasis upon violence might elicit violent behavior from normal individuals in emotionally critical situations.

(5) Many writers feel that media depictions of violence are not so likely to produce imitative violent behavior as rather to

create an undesirable general value orientation. Thus Muhlen
(1949) wonders if children may, under the tutelage of the media,
acquire a view of crime and violence as normal and common to
the adult world, or fail to develop due regard for the sanctity of
life. Essentially similar fears are voiced by Seldes (1950) and
Smythe (1955), both of whom also consider that such orientations are essentially totalitarian rather than democratic. Several
psychiatrists have spoken in similar vein at Senate committee
hearings.[25]

(6) Media depictions of crime and violence are also believed
by some observers to have *beneficial social effects.* A considerable
number of psychiatrists and psychologists, interviewed by the
present author in 1953, held that vicarious identification with the
media characters might serve children as an outlet for aggression
which might otherwise be asocially manifested. Similar views
have been expressed by various writers.

All of these fears and hopes, and various others less frequently expressed, are, however, essentially conjectural. Those
who voice them typically cite no documentation, or refer to a
few specific cases in which media-depicted violence seems
clearly to have played some kind of role. Precisely what role it
played, and amid what other forces, is in most such cases unknown. In ascribing crucial powers to the media, the great majority of the fearful are thus in fact speaking conjecturally. They
are stating what they think may be occurring, and, in so doing,
they are posing questions for communications research.

Definitive Research Findings

Definitive research findings regarding the actual effects of
crime and violence upon media audiences are unfortunately
sparse. Such data as there are, however, can best be presented
under two heads. We shall first consider those findings which

bear upon the question of the immediate emotional reactions of children to depictions of violence. Thereafter, we shall turn to findings which deal with the effect of such depictions upon children's attitudes, values, and behavior. There appear to be no studies whatever which deal with the reactions of adults to crime and violence in the media, except to note that adults are concerned about the influence of such material upon children.

IMMEDIATE EMOTIONAL EFFECTS OF DIFFERENT TYPES OF VIOLENCE

Despite long and widespread concern, few data have been accumulated regarding the immediate reactions of children to different types of violent media content. A few studies of physical reactions, made for the most part more than twenty-five years ago, indicated that the nervous systems of children were at least temporarily affected by some motion picture content,[26] but virtually no systematic refinement of these relatively gross data followed.

A recent study performed in England by Himmelweit, Oppenheim, and Vince (1958) provides what are therefore pioneer findings on the subject. The investigators did not restrict their inquiry to the effects of crime and violence, but rather performed a broad and unusually elaborate "empirical study of the effect of television on the young."[27] The study will be cited frequently throughout the rest of this volume, and a brief description of the rather elaborate study design is therefore in order.

In what they call their "*main survey*,"[28] Himmelweit, Oppenheim, and Vince (1958) studied 1,854 children, aged ten-to-eleven and thirteen-to-fourteen, who were divided into "*viewers*, who had television at home" and "controls," who "had no television at home and were also not regular guest viewers." Members of the two groups were individually matched in reference to "sex, age, intelligence, and social background," and, "as far as possible, they were selected from the same classroom."[29] To determine whether observed differences between the groups were the product of viewing or were pre-existing, the investigators supplemented their "main survey" with an ingenious before-after study. Almost all students in the ten-to-eleven and thirteen-to-fourteen age groups in Norwich were tested prior to the introduction of television in that area, and a year later a group of those who had since acquired a set were compared with a matched group of those who had not (total N=370). In both the "main survey" and the "Norwich study" the investigators employed a series of research instruments including diaries, and questionnaires, both completed by the children, and "ratings by the teachers of the children's behavior and personality characteristics." The investigators also carried out eleven "special studies . . . to examine groups not covered by the survey, and to investigate problems for which other techniques were needed." These typically involved smaller groups, and in some cases "relied more on the qualitative data . . . obtained through observational methods or through long, informal interviews."[30] An extremely wide range of possible effects of television were investigated in the course of these two surveys and eleven special studies.

In reference to the immediate effects of crime and violence, Himmelweit, Oppenheim, and Vince (1958) found that a minority, but a fairly sizeable minority, were apparently "frightened" by such fare. "In direct questioning . . . one boy in four and one girl in three . . . admitted to fear of things seen on television." Older children were, "if anything, . . . more often frightened than the younger ones." The reasons for this are not completely clear, but the authors "suggest that the greater maturity of the older children [may have] enabled them to become identified with more situations, to respond to motives as well as to actions."[31] When asked if they thought there were "things on television" which are "bad for children to see," slightly less than one-fifth of the children said that there were. Most mentioned murder, horror plays, and thrillers which, they said, "frighten you and give you bad dreams."[32]

Inquiring more closely into precisely what sort of violence frightens children, Himmelweit, Oppenheim, and Vince (1958) discovered that "some of the common stereotyped ideas" on the subject "have little foundation in fact."[33] The "number of shots fired or the number of aggressive episodes contained in any one programme," for example, turned out to be considerably less important than "the setting in which the violence occurs, . . . the manner of its presentation, and . . . the complexity of the characterization of the two sides in the struggle."[34]

Four specific findings pertinent to this point may be culled from the detailed report of the authors:

(1) The degree to which children are disturbed appears to be related to the means by which injury is done.

> Shooting is not very disturbing, nor fighting on the ground, but injury by knife or dagger is far more so; swords and other weapons occupy an intermediate position.[35]

(2) Violence which follows a conventional pattern, the outcome of which is predictable, apparently disturbs very few children. Only "seven children out of a thousand mentioned a Western when asked *'Have you ever been frightened by anything you have seen on television?'* "[36] and five of these were girls of below average intelligence. Crime and detective programs were likewise found to be rarely and minimally disturbing. In reference to all three of these program types, "the format has [apparently] been learnt sufficiently for tension not to mount too much . . . Because the children know that the ending will be happy, with no harm done to the hero, the violence does not matter."[37] Such programs accordingly proved less disturbing than did televised versions of *Jane Eyre, 1984,* and two science-fiction programs, in all of which the violence followed no pattern known to the young viewers.

The conventional pattern of Westerns is also believed by the authors to be responsible for the paucity of residual tension among children who have just seen such a film, and for the ease with which even that tension is worked off.

Observations, made on a group of 6–10 year olds during the showing of an episode from *Cisco Kid*, illustrate children's reactions to
Westerns; intense involvement during the showing of the programme
with complete release of tension at the end . . . Any residual tension . . . tends to be worked off in play . . . These are not games of
uncontrolled aggression, but are only versions of chasing and being
chased—of cowboys and Indians, of cops and robbers—the oldest
of childhood games, which were, of course, played long before television was thought of. They express the child's ingrained fondness
for rules and for a clear differentiation between good and evil.[38]

It is characteristic . . . that when children were asked whether there
was a programme which they "could not get out of their minds"
they would mention adult plays or thrillers, but not Westerns. These
made no lasting impact.[39]

(3) Children are apparently "more sensitive about acts of
verbal than of physical aggression."[40] Asked which acts of violence they "dislike" on television, 6 per cent or less of the children
mentioned shooting, and from 19 per cent to 23 per cent mentioned "fighting with other weapons," but 23 per cent to 30 per
cent mentioned such things as "when the sheriff tells the good
cowboy off because he is not catching the bad man quickly
enough," when "someone is told off when it is not really his
fault," and "when grown-ups are angry with one another and
shout."[41] This finding will doubtless come as a considerable sur-
prise to persons who have for long speculated upon the effects of
violent media content. The possibility that children are more
sensitive to verbal than to physical aggression has never to the
author's knowledge even been suggested in the speculative literature.

(4) Real violence is less likely to frighten children than is
violence in fictional programs, but, on the other hand, real violence is more widely disliked.

Asked whether they had seen anything on television which frightened
them, only 14 children mentioned non-fiction programmes; some referred to floods and fires seen on newsreels, others to hospital scenes;
a small response rate when set against the 200 or so who had been
frightened by fictional programmes.[42]

When, however, the children were asked whether they "like" or "dislike" various sorts of content, a quite different picture emerged. Only 9 per cent and 6 per cent, for example, disliked "fighting with fists" in Westerns or detective stories, whereas 25 per cent disliked it in newsreels. From 18 to 21 per cent disliked seeing disasters "in plays" whereas 23 to 39 per cent disliked seeing them in newsreels.[43] In reference to "verbal aggression . . . the strongest dislike occurred in connexion with anger or rudeness shown in panel games."[44]

The precise significance of these findings is not yet clear. Himmelweit, Oppenheim, and Vince (1958) themselves remark that the technique they employed "fails to distinguish between degrees of dislike; . . . does not go into the many reasons behind dislike or ambivalence; . . . [and] equates dislike with unease or disturbance."[45] The authors suggest that "whether an incident will disturb [i.e., be disliked] depends less on whether it is fictional or real than on whether it comes within the child's experience and is one with which he can identify himself."[46] A far deeper analysis of the components of "dislike" is, however, clearly necessary if the significance and implications of these pioneer findings are to be made clear.

Further inquiry into the nature of media-inspired fright is also necessary before much can be said about the importance of the phenomenon. Virtually nothing is known, for example, regarding the duration of such fright or the ways, if any, in which it may affect children's concepts or behavior. Neither Himmelweit, Oppenheim, and Vince nor the early studies of children's reactions to movies[47] inquired into such matters. The manifest effects which these studies cite—disturbed sleep, nightmares, and the like—would seem likely to be evanescent, but there are no hard data to indicate that they are or are not, or that they do or do not contribute to less obvious long-range disturbances. Occasional case histories in psychiatric literature attest to long-term traumas connected with specific media experiences, but these seem to be very few and far between, and to involve children who were, prior to the incident, already deeply disturbed.[48] Extreme effects have also been observed to accrue, even among normal children, from highly individualistic interpretations of content which is manifestly innocuous.[49]

The sparse data available on the immediate emotional effects of violent media content thus present a picture which is as yet incomplete and whose social significance cannot yet be assayed. It appears that most children are not frightened by violent media content, but that about one-fifth occasionally are frightened. A larger number "dislike" certain forms of violence or aggression. Some sorts of violent content are more often disturbing or disliked than are others, but data are as yet available on the relative effects of only a few of the almost infinite variations of form and content. Finally, as we have just noted, nothing is known about the duration or psychological significance of such immediate effects as have been observed.

INFLUENTIAL ASPECTS OF THE COMMUNICATION AND THE COMMUNICATION SITUATION

Himmelweit, Oppenheim, and Vince (1958) provide two more or less isolated data which bear upon the relationship of non-content variables to fright. On the basis of wholly "qualitative, not quantitative material,"[50] including direct observation, discussions, and reports in parental diaries, the investigators made the not very surprising discoveries that a child is likely to be more easily frightened when viewing "alone or with children of his own age" than when viewing with adults present, and that he is more easily frightened when viewing in a totally dark room.[51] On the basis of similar data, the authors also made the more interesting discovery that sound effects are about equally as frightening as are visual effects. Not only were "sound effects . . . often mentioned" in reference to television experiences, but, in addition, as many non-viewers "were frightened by murder plays on the radio as were viewers by murder plays on television."[52]

Aside from the study of Himmelweit, Oppenheim, and Vince (1958), which bears exclusively on television, no disciplined research of any scope seems to have been directed upon character-istics of the communication, the medium, or the communication situation which might increase or decrease the effects which vio-lent media content produces among its audiences. One single systematic survey of non-verbal presentational techniques em-ployed by horror comics has been accomplished by Graalfs (1954), but the present author knows of no attempt to assay the differential effectiveness of such devices. No parallel study of movies or radio seems ever to have reached the public domain.

MEDIA VIOLENCE, PERSONAL VALUES, AND DELINQUENT BEHAVIOR

Definitive research findings regarding the effects of depicted crime and violence upon the values and behavior of media audi-ences are not much less sparse than are the findings on immediate emotional reactions. The present author is inclined to believe that this paucity of hard data, and in fact of pertinent research, derives from the way in which the concern is typically formulated, for most of those who fear the effects of the media, and many of those who scoff, talk primarily in terms of direct effects. The media material is regarded much as the serum in a hypodermic needle. It is presumed to have observable and direct effects on values and behavior, or to be capable of being shown to have no effects.

We have previously suggested, in discussing the effect of mass communication on opinions and attitudes, that the media rarely serve in this way as the sole and sufficient agents of attitude effects. Such research as is relevant suggests that they are no more likely to do so in relation to crime and violence.

The results of several studies indicate that exposure to crime and violence in the media is not a crucial determinant of behavior nor of attitudes which might be manifested in behavior. On the other hand, there are indications that such fare may serve special functions for those who are already socially maladjusted.

Thrasher (1949) cites two earlier studies by Cressey to the effect that "thousands of observations under controlled conditions, showed that the movies did not have any significant effect in producing delinquency in the crime breeding area in which the study [sic] was made."[53]

Several studies compare the attitudes and behavior patterns of persons who are heavily exposed to violent media fare with the attitudes and behavior patterns of those not so heavily exposed.

Ricutti (1951), for example, studied the radio listening habits of 3,125 elementary and junior high school children in Waterbury, Connecticut, and also investigated their individual scholastic achievements, personal and social adjustments, and attitudes toward law. Those who particularly liked anti-crime programs (wherein violence typically abounds) were found to have a somewhat lower average I.Q. and scholastic achievement score than their colleagues and to be somewhat more aggressive; while those who particularly liked daily adventure programs (which are also a prime source of violence) were found to be slightly below average in general happiness, personal and social adjustment, and scholastic achievement. A 30 per cent sub-sample was additionally intensively studied regarding nervous habits, fears, daydreams, and frustration reactions. No significant difference in these regards was found between those who did and those who did not listen to crime, anti-crime, and daily adventure stories. The results suggest that violence in media content does not determine attitudes or behavior, although certain types of theme and format (anti-crime and daily adventure) may serve some undefined function for particular personality types.

Ricutti's findings are in part confirmed by Lewin (1953), who classified 260 twelve- to thirteen-year-old New York City boys of average intelligence according to their interest in comic books. The twenty-five boys who were most interested in comics were compared with the twenty-five least interested regarding their tendencies towards delinquency, their school attendance, school achievement, and conduct. No significant differences were found between the two groups at the time nor on the occasion of a retest eighteen months later.

Himmelweit, Oppenheim, and Vince (1958), whose elaborate study has been described above, generally support Ricutti and Lewin. They "found no more aggressive, maladjusted, or delinquent behavior among [British child TV] viewers than among controls [i.e., non-viewers]."[54]

Bailyn (1959) performed an elaborate study of "mass media . . . exposure habits and cognitive effects"[55] among 626 children in the fifth and sixth grades of the public schools in a Boston suburb. Questionnaires, interviews, and experimental techniques were employed to investigate the relationship between the extent of the children's exposure, certain sociological and psychological characteristics, and certain habits of thinking. The study is focused primarily upon the children's habits relative to the "pictorial media—television, movies, and comic books," and for the most part upon their habits relative to "aggressive hero . . . material" in those media,—i.e., material in which the heroes defend themselves and others, often by means of force, "against elements that threaten *them* by force."[56] Such content, Bailyn found, was a "particular preference" of boys (but not girls) who were highly exposed to the pictorial media in general, and who exhibited certain psychological characteristics, specifically, numerous problems relative to themselves, their families, and their peers; a tendency to place blame for difficulties on others rather than themselves; and some measure of what Bailyn regards as "rebellious independence."[57] Bailyn considers that all of these factors antedate the children's partiality for "aggressive hero" material. High exposure, she found, was primarily associated with lack of parental restriction on media usage and with low I.Q. The psychological characteristics, in Bailyn's opinion, "would not logically be thought of as effects of exposure,"[58] and were in any case also found to exist among children with low exposure. As will be noted below, Bailyn found certain other correlates of high exposure to aggressive hero material which she considers may be effects of such exposure, but she does not consider the characteristics cited above to be effects.

Bailyn also notes that the psychological characteristics of the boys who particularly liked aggressive hero material are very similar to traits which were previously found by Glueck and Glueck "to play a role in the 'causal complex' of delinquency."[59] She points out, however, that these characteristics do not in themselves differentiate between high and low exposure, and that it is only those boys who are highly exposed *and* possess these characteristics who are especially partial to aggressive hero material.

In short, research which compares persons who are and who are not habitually exposed to violent media content usually finds no significant differences between the two groups, and most of such differences as are found (e.g., by Ricutti and Bailyn) do not seem likely to be the *result* of differential exposure. The media do not appear, therefore, to be a crucial or primary determinant of behavioral tendencies.

Two studies which addressed themselves to persons with criminal records did find that such persons exhibited a particular fondness for violent media material. Thus Blumer and Hauser (1933) found crime movies to be peculiarly popular among persons convicted of crimes. More recently Hoult (1949) compared the comic book reading habits of 235 boys and girls, aged ten to seventeen, who had been arrested for delinquency, with a group of non-delinquents matched for sex, age, school grade, and socio-economic status. The delinquents read a tremendously greater number of comic books dealing with crime, violence, and thrilling adventure, although they did not significantly differ from the non-deliquents matched for sex, age, school grade, and socio-eco-other types.

Hoult is careful to disclaim any implication that the crime comics played a causal role in the delinquency of his subjects. He notes that the course of influence could theoretically have functioned in either direction, i.e., that while crime comics might create an appetite for crime, such an appetite might equally as well lead to a diet of crime comics. We have previously cited studies, however, which indicate, at the very least, that media fare is not the crucial or primary determinant of delinquent behavior. We are accordingly led to suspect that the course of influence is in the other direction, i.e., that the existing psychological orientation of audience members determines their reactions to violent media fare.

Expert opinion and the findings of research in closely related fields lend considerable credence to this belief. The findings of three studies seem particularly pertinent.

Maccoby submitted a group of fifth and sixth grade Boston school children to a spelling test consisting of easy words, and submitted a similar group to a spelling test consisting of extremely difficult words.[60] Directly thereafter both groups were exposed to films which contained depictions of aggressive conduct. The presumably unfrustrated control group "remembered the general content of the films somewhat better than did the frustrated children. However, the frustrated children remembered more of the aggressive content and less of the neutral material."[61] What function this selective retention may have served is not wholly clear, but it appears that the frustration, relatively superficial as it was, sensitized the children to aggressive content. Put another way, the existing orientation of the audience members determined their selective retention of violent media content.

Riley and Riley (1951) performed an elaborate study, employing as subjects 400 children from the fifth, sixth, and seventh grades of certain public and private schools in New York and New Jersey. On the basis of sociometric investigations, the children were divided into those who were members of peer groups and those who were not. Radio and TV programs "characterized by violence, action and aggression" were found to be considerably more popular among the children who were members of family groups only than among those who were also members of peer groups: 47 per cent of the boys and 34 per cent of the girls among the peer group members liked such fare, as compared with 55 per cent of the boys and 47 per cent of the girls who were not members of peer groups.[62] The more specific radio preferences and the uses to which the two types of children characteristically put the material also differed significantly. Peer group members preferred anti-crime stories and material dealing with normal people or with nature. They typically exploited the "social utility" of such material as, for example, by using it as a basis of group games. Children who were not members of peer groups, on the other hand, preferred material about the Lone Ranger and similar extraordinary characters, and tended to use the material as stimulants for eerie and escapist fantasies.

Riley and Riley pursued their investigation further by dividing the older peer group members into those who also used the peer group as a reference group (i.e., who shared the values of their peers), and those who used their family as a reference group. Children in the latter category—i.e., those who were members of peer groups but shared the values of their families— were found to be much more apt to like action and violence than were children who shared the values of their peers. They were also more likely than the other children to believe that they were falling short of their parents' expectations. In short, action and violence were most popular among the children who were apparently most frustrated.

Riley and Riley hew rather closely to their data, rather than speculating at length upon its implications. They do point out, in regard to the first set of findings, that family demands are likely to be more intense and frustrating than peer group demands, and that if this is so, then frustration apparently correlates, at least in some degree, with an appetite for media violence. The precise function which the action and violence serves is not, in their opinion, very clearly defined by the data. The present author additionally suggests that peer group membership or non-membership probably reflects personal adjustment as well as social habits, and that if this is true, the data suggest that action and violence are probably more popular among the emotionally disturbed than they are among the well adjusted.

Additional suggestions in this direction are provided by Wolf and Fiske (1949) who subjected children to depth interviews designed to explore the functions served by comic book reading. The study was primarily focused upon developing tastes, and the content categories employed do not definitively separate violent content from other types of content. The observed patterns of taste development are, however, suggestive. Well-adjusted children were found typically to give prime preference to *Superman, Batman,* and similar superhero-vs.-criminal comics only during their early teens, after which they graduated to a preference for "true" and "classic" comics. The more neurotic children, on the other hand, frequently did not make this transition. In addition, they were given to fantasy in which they themselves revealed super powers before a hitherto unappreciative world, or in which Superman himself took their parts against parents and other human sources of frustration. In short, as in the Riley and Riley study, the more frustrated children used the more active heroes as stimuli to aggressive or escapist fantasy.

Himmelweit, Oppenheim, and Vince (1958) come to conclusions which are less detailed but generally in accord with the findings of Maccoby, Riley and Riley, and Wolf and Fiske. On the basis of various sources of qualitative data, they propose that

. . . the child's preferences in mass media reflect not only his age, sex, and intelligence, but also his general outlook, spare-time interests, anxieties, and needs.[63]

They feel, furthermore, that children are on the whole most *unlikely* to

. . . translate television experience into action. It may happen in extreme cases where children [already] have a strong desire to be aggressive or to perform a delinquent act, and for whom constant watching of programmes with an explosive content may be the last straw. . . . [But] even in extreme cases, the influence of television is small. The child's emotional make-up and the total of his environmental influences determine his behavior. . . . Our findings and those of Maccoby suggest . . . that these programmes do not initiate aggressive, maladjusted, or delinquent behavior, but may aid its expression.[64]

Bailyn (1959) is similarly careful to disclaim any concept of violent media material serving as the sole cause of overt behavioral tendencies. She found, as did Riley and Riley (1951) and Wolf and Fiske (1949), that devotees of such fare were likely to react to it in ways she considers escapist (a point more fully developed in the chapter on escapism).[65] She found also that such children were more inclined than others to believe that events of the sort depicted really did occur, and that they were more inclined to judge real people in stereotyped terms (a point which is also more fully developed in a later chapter).[66] She makes no mention of the possibility that violent behavior may be elicited by such material, and, even in regard to escapism, she is careful to note that the tendency exists as a mode of thought only when habitual exposure is accompanied by psychological problems, and "that any connection between the mass media and the overt behavior will be indirect, mediated by . . . [a considerable variety of] factors."[67]

Thus, communications research strongly indicates that media depictions of crime and violence are not prime movers toward such conduct. The content seems rather to reinforce or implement existing and otherwise induced behavioral tendencies. For the well adjusted, it appears to be innocuous or even to be selectively perceived as socially useful. For the maladjusted, particularly the aggressively inclined and the frustrated, it appears to serve, at the very least, as a stimulant to escapist and possibly aggressive fantasy, and probably to serve other functions as yet unidentified.

This same general point of view was espoused by a considerable number, although by no means all, of the various psychologists, psychiatrists, and criminologists who testified in person or by proxy during the 1955 hearings of the Senate Subcommittee to

Investigate Juvenile Delinquency. Most such persons expressed their professional judgment rather than adducing actual evidence and, as previously noted, other equally well qualified experts echoed most of the fears which characterize popular literature.[68] A considerable number, however, voiced one or another aspect of the general position that the media help to develop personality tendencies which are themselves otherwise determined, and that the effect of crime and violence in the media therefore depends largely on the individual child. Surveys of similarly professional opinion typically find that the great majority of these experts believe that media violence is not a direct cause of juvenile delinquency, but that it may, on the other hand, advance delinquent tendencies or channel the frustrations of the disturbed toward violence.[69]

Research—as opposed to professional opinion and intelligent conjecture—tends, as we have seen, to document this point of view. But although research has thus contributed greatly to our knowledge of the effects of media depictions of crime and violence, it has in a sense evaded the socially important question of whether such material is in an overall sense socially harmful or socially innocuous. Research has, in effect, found that for some children the material *is* innocuous, while for others it stimulates undesirable and in some cases pathological habits of thought and behavior. But the relative incidence of these effects is not yet known. Bailyn (1959) does point out that boys who were highly exposed to pictorial media and had one or more of the psychological characteristics associated with a strong preference for violent content amounted to only 12 per cent of all boys in her sample (6 per cent of the total sample) and that only 3 per cent of the boys (1.5 per cent of the total sample) were highly exposed and possessed *all* the psychological characteristics. But such statements of incidence are extremely rare and refer only to the particular set of characteristics discussed in the particular study.

We may hope that those for whom violent media material is

not innocuous comprise only a minority of the nation's children. But we do not know that they are a minority and, in any case, their absolute number is not likely to be insignificant. Our present and very limited knowledge suggests that the group may include a notable proportion of those children who are not peer group oriented, of those children who are for one reason or another often frustrated, and of those children who are maladjusted in various and some as yet unspecified ways. The total number of such children cannot be small, and, even if it were, any influence contributing to the continuance or intensification of their difficulties can hardly be dismissed as socially unimportant. If depictions of crime and violence have an unhealthy effect upon even 1 per cent of the nation's children, it becomes socially important to inquire whether and how the situation can be rectified.

That question will not be discussed in this volume, which is essentially a report of research findings. The findings themselves indicate, however, that the mass media are by no means the sole nor the basic cause of the problem, and that therefore, although their co-operation may legitimately be sought in any campaign designed to ameliorate the situation, the problem as a whole must be attacked on more basic levels. Remedies, if they can be defined at all, seem likely to involve the family, the school, and virtually all institutions and forces that are active in the socialization of the American child.

Theoretical Considerations

The author submits that both the findings of communications research and the professional judgment of experts suggest that media depictions of crime and violence function in ways described by the generalizations proposed in the introductory chapter of this book.

More specifically, the media appear, as proposed in generalization 1, ordinarily to function not "as a necessary and sufficient cause of audience effects, but rather . . . [to work] among and through a nexus of mediating factors and influences." The outcome of the process, as proposed in generalization 2, appears to be the reinforcement of the existing attitude or behavioral tendencies of the individual audience member, be these socially good or ill.

Some violent and particularly some horror content appears to frighten at least some children. Although what does and what does not frighten appears to be determined, at least in part, by the personal experiences of the audience member, it seems logical to assume that some content is in and of itself frightening to some audience members—i.e., that, as proposed in generalization 4, it produces direct and immediate, if possibly evanescent, psychophysical effects. As generalization 5 indicates, various aspects of the communication itself and of the communication situation appear to be related to the likelihood or intensity of such efforts.

The data thus support generalizations 1, 2, 4, and 5. Some thoughts relevant to the third generalization will be presented shortly.

The author proposes that the generalizations have again been organizationally and theoretically helpful. They have been *organizationally* helpful in suggesting, as they did in reference to persuasive communications, the existence of a class of factors which mediate the effects of communications but which are external to the communication itself. Neither the identity of the mediating factors nor the dynamics of their mediation is by any means as clear in the case of violent media content as it is in the case of persuasive communication. Research has thus far merely identified a few variables which seem to be related to the functions which the media fare serves. Existing pre-dispositions toward aggression, including immediately induced frustration and other psychological characteristics appear to be included among such variables, and to function, at the outset, through the familiar channels of selective exposure and retention. The nature of the audience member's group orientation likewise appears to be such a variable, but may turn out, after further research, to be largely an index of his level of frustration. The relationship of the actual group norms to the effect of the media fare has not been directly investigated.

These identified variables are, of course, strongly reminiscent of, although not precisely similar to, those which have been demonstrated to be operative in reference to the effects of mass communication on opinions and attitudes regarding specific issues. The hypothesis inevitably follows that those previously identified mediating factors serve similar roles in regard to the effect of media-depicted violence. Should the similarity be borne out by further research, the hypothesized class of mediating factors would be established as cross-topically effective.

The generalizations have been *theoretically* helpful in that they have in fact provided a kind of primitive theoretic framework which suggests avenues for new and logically cumulative research.

If, for example, generalizations 1 and 2 are valid, and they appear to be, then generalization 3 becomes a logical, in fact an inevitable, hypothesis. Generalization 3 proposes, in part, that mediating forces which normally abet reinforcement may, on atypical occasions, reverse the direction of their influence and assist communications which stimulate change. Further investigation would seem to be indicated, and our general orientation suggests two lines of approach. One procedure would involve identifying individuals for whom the mediating factors, or the variables known to be pertinent, had changed: it would be helpful to know, for example, whether any of Riley and Riley's subjects later changed the nature of their group orientations and *whether the change was accompanied by predictable changes in their reaction to violent media content.* Another and more broadly based approach would involve case studies in depth of non-delinquent persons who became delinquent, or vice versa; such studies would seek to identify changes in the extra-communication situation of such persons which were accompanied by changes in their use of and reaction to violent media content. Maccoby's findings that children who are deliberately, if superficially, frustrated are at least temporarily more affected by aggressive media content, are, of course, suggestive in this connection.

It seems relatively clear, in any case, that the functions served by violent media fare are complex, and that the dynamic which results in the audience member's pursuing or avoiding delinquent behavior is at least equally complex. Neither topic seems likely to be further illuminated by inquiries which assume that the media exert a hypodermic effect. The more fruitful path of research would rather seem to lie through a study of the variables known to be associated with reaction to violent media content, and through what we have called "the phenomenistic approach," —pursued, of course, with the cautions we have suggested in describing the approach itself.

The phenomenistic approach, in reference to the topic in hand, would first require the determination of phenomenistic criteria—the commission of a crime, the display of particular psychological syndromes, or the like—and, secondly, an attempt to retrace the road which led individuals to the point of conforming to such criteria. This is in effect to say that further information on the role of mass communication in the development of delinquency is more likely to come from the study of delinquency than from the study of mass communication. Such an approach is also likely to define the other factors in the process and the way in which these mediate the effects of mass communication.

Criminologists, psychiatrists, and case workers already know a good deal about juvenile delinquency; and communications researchers, freed of the concept of hypodermic communication effect, will do well to take the findings of such experts into account. All the researchers will perhaps do even better to form interdisciplinary teams.

Such a team, however, if it is to fulfill its social as well as its academic responsibilities, must consider questions of incidence as well as questions of process. As we have noted above, knowledge of the conditions under which violent media content has definable effects must be supplemented by inquiry into the relative incidence of these conditions and effects. Until knowledge on both of these matters is available, communications research will not have provided a socially meaningful answer to the question of whether violence in the media is or is not harmful.

Summary

1. Parents, educators, social observers, and occasional researchers have been perennially and widely concerned about the possible effects of mass media's abundant depiction of crime and violence.

2. Crime and violence have been shown by objective tallying techniques to be in fact abundantly depicted in virtually all media.

3. These elaborate counts and reports may be criticized on at least three grounds:

a. Some draw upon esoteric material which is not in fact mass distributed.

b. Almost all deal exclusively with violence in fiction, while ignoring, and in some instances condoning, portrayals of real violence (as, for example, in TV news pictures and in documentaries). No valid basis for such a distinction is apparent.

c. The counts imply that any ill effects which may accrue from depicted violence are intensified by more abundant depictions. In point of fact, no relationship is known to exist between the quantity of such stimuli and any effects which they may produce.

None of these criticisms, however, are to gainsay the fact that depictions of crime and violence are abundant in all media.

4. Media fare of this nature is variously and popularly believed to:

a. be harmful, in some unspecified way.

b. evoke direct, imitative behavior.

c. serve as a training school in delinquency.

d. be capable of triggering violent or criminal behavior among normal people in situations of stress.

e. reduce the value its audience attaches to human life.

f. serve as a vicarious outlet for aggression, and thus to be psychologically and socially desirable.

These various allegations are typically undocumented or are based on a very small number of specific individual cases.

5. Few objective data are available on the immediate emotional reactions of audience members to violent media content.

a. Studies performed more than twenty-five years ago indicate the media content stimulates the cardio-vascular and nervous systems of some children. The types of content involved are not precisely specified.

b. A recent study of British children and television indicates that somewhat less than a quarter of these children are occasionally frightened by violence on TV. The amount of such violence seems less important than its form or context. Violence which follows a conventional pattern of known outcome (e.g., Westerns) frightens practically no one. Verbal aggression is more widely "disliked" than physical aggression. Violence in fiction is more often "frightening" than is real violence, but the latter is more widely "disliked." Further inquiry into the components and significance of "disliked" is obviously desirable.

c. Certain technical aspects of the communication (e.g., the nature of the sound track) and of the communication situation (e.g., whether the child is among peers or adults) are related to the likelihood and intensity of immediate emotional effects.

6. Communications research has also provided some data relative to the effects of media-depicted crime and violence on values, attitudes, and behavior.

a. Heavy exposure to such fare is apparently not a sufficient or crucial cause of delinquency. In at least five major studies, heavy consumers were found no more likely to be delinquent than were light users or non-users. Two studies do indicate that persons who already have criminal records are likely to be heavy consumers of violent media material, but neither study demonstrates the direction of causation.

b. Children who are not members of peer groups, or who are in one or another way neurotic or frustrated, have been found to have heavier appetites for violent media fare and to employ it as a basis for asocial, escapist, hostile, and occasionally pathological fantasy. Their more normal colleagues have been found to have lesser or less lasting appetites for the material, and to react to it in socially wholesome ways.

In combination, these various findings strongly suggest that crime and violence in the media are not likely to be prime movers toward delinquency, but that such fare is likely instead to reinforce the existing behavioral tendencies, *good or ill,* of individual audience members.

7. The findings of research, as interpreted above, are echoed, although not unanimously, by psychiatric and criminological opinion.

8. Research has not yet provided data on the relative incidence of conditions such as are described in paragraph 6-b, above. Until such knowledge is available, it can only be said that violence in the media is innocuous for some—probably for the majority—and unhealthy for others. Research has thus not yet provided a socially meaningful answer to the question of whether violent media fare is socially undesirable to any significant extent.

9. *Theoretical Considerations.* The data adduced in this chapter directly support the first, second, fourth, and fifth of the five generalizations proposed in the Introduction to the volume, and suggest that the third generalization may also be valid in this context. The generalizations as a whole are helpful in organizing the data, in providing a primitive theoretical framework, and in suggesting certain avenues for new and logically cumulative research.

The Effects of
Escapist Media Material

$\mathcal{B}$OTH LAY CRITICS and social researchers have been long concerned with the great abundance of escapist material in the mass media. Such fare has, on the one hand, been accused of promoting an unreal picture of the world, of diverting its audience from real problems, of rendering them unable to face life as it is or of misinstructing them in how to do so, and of promoting social apathy. The same fare, on the other hand, has been held not only to provide desirable relaxation, but to perform virtually therapeutic and adjustive functions, rendering more bearable the life and self-image of the average person, and in fact serving to bolster the entire social system.

We shall here first clarify the kind of material which is under discussion, and then note some of the effects which some writers *believe* it may produce. We shall then examine, in some detail, the findings of disciplined research regarding the actual nature of the material and what it apparently does to and for the audiences of mass communication.

The Fare and the Fear

WHAT IS "ESCAPIST" COMMUNICATION?

The common use of the term "escapist" in connection with various alleged effects of mass communication is somewhat unfortunate and possibly misleading. For the accepted meaning of the word describes neither the kind of material to which the critics object, nor yet the effects which they fear may ensue.

The dictionary defines "escapist" as

> Offering or intended to offer relief from unpleasant or monotonous realities of life; as escapist drama, escapist novels.[1]

This definition is obviously based not on the content of the material, but upon the effect it produces. Virtually any material might, by these criteria, be escapist for at least part of its audience. The most serious music, for example, might serve such functions for a physician or even for a social researcher. A technological account of bridge-building might provide relief from the "unpleasant or monotonous realities" of an accountant's life, and a mathematical treatise might provide similar escape for a dentist or manufacturer. Thus Mott (1947) inquires

> What is this crime of escapism? Escape from what? Apparently it is escape from work and worry. Escape to what? Apparently to play and fun. Now the difference between work and play is that the one consists of activities performed under the compulsion of duty after the freshness and novelty have worn off, while the other is activity which is not compulsory but is engaged in because its novelty is not exhausted to the point of boredom. Thus big game hunting is still play despite its fatigue and hardship, but professional baseball is work for the "player" because the sport has, for him, passed from the status of an activity enjoyed for its own rewards to that of a job required by duties under a contract. And so reading, if required

and onerous (as professional study may often be) becomes work; but if done for pleasure, as most of our reading is, it is play— whether it is the light literature of romance and adventure or in the heaviest dissertations in science and philosophy. In other words, all general reading is escapism.[2]

Such escapism, however, is not what the social critics fear. They are rather concerned with the possible effect of a very particular sort of material. Specifically, they are concerned with the effects of content which presents a picture of life and the world which is not in accord with reality. Included in such fare is not only frank fantasy, but—and as far as the critics are concerned, more importantly—material which purports to depict, or may be taken as depicting, life as it really is. Typically included in this genre are family comedy, as exemplified in virtually all media; musical variety shows on radio, TV, and the screen; the daytime serials of radio and TV; much light fiction, including the more serious comic strips; adventure stories; and a good deal of what the mass media consider serious drama.

CONJECTURED EFFECTS

Escapist mass communication has been accused, often bitterly, of producing a variety of undesirable effects. Siepmann (1948), for example, finds

> Small wonder . . . that most of us prefer escape from, rather than concern with, reality. There is an indolence in each of us which is resistant both to growth and change. As radio indulges us in this respect it retards rather than advances our growth. Herein lies its danger. . . . It can make of this potential instrument a drug rather than a stimulant.[3]

Seldes (1950) inveighs against the "myth world" of mass communications and fears that

> . . . adults who remain fervent patrons have perhaps not reached the phase of reality or have retreated from it. They may find consolation in the bright lies that the movies tell about love, as they may find it in the low pitched and agonized falsifications of the daytime serial.[4]

Such material, Seldes believes, actually renders its devotees less able to face reality, which is unlike and less attractive than the movie world, is thus experienced as a shock, and avoided. He believes that the media not only "divert, but . . . deceive. . . . They prevent the community from raising mature and responsible citizens."[5] Demant (1955) expresses similar fears regarding the effects of British TV programs. Maccoby (1951 and 1954) and Lewin (1953), writing respectively on American TV and on comic books, feel that fantasy may temporarily reduce its audience's tensions, but, since the real source of tension remains unaffected, these writers fear that the ultimate result may be a tendency on the part of audience members to avoid real problems or to seek their solution by fantastic or violent means. The possibility that such material may result in individual or collective social apathy is advanced by the writers cited above, by Dollard (1945), Lazarsfeld and Merton (1948), and by various other observers.

Precisely the same kind of material, on the other hand, has been held to serve highly desirable functions. Maccoby (1954), for example, notes that such content is said to provide helpful relaxation and diversion, to permit vicarious trial of depicted behaviors, and to permit vicarious and socially innocuous release of aggressions. Similar views were earlier reported by Waples, Berelson, and Bradshaw (1940), and by various other writers.

But we have been talking only of allegations, of the considered conjectures of acute observers regarding both the escapist nature of mass media offerings and the effects of these offerings. Disciplined research has much to say on both these topics.

THE ACTUAL NATURE OF THE FARE

A considerable number of content analyses indicate that much mass media material does indeed depict a world which differs, in various ways, from the world around us.

Arnheim (1944) conducted an elaborate analysis of the content presented during three successive weeks by 43 different daytime radio serials. He found, among other things, that no unskilled laborer, miner, or factory worker played an important role in a single serial; that the disproportionately frequent wealthy characters pay "courtship to the attractiveness or efficiency, or both, of the middle class people";[6] that the characters are continually beset by gigantic problems, 47 per cent of which involved personal relations, and only 15 per cent of which were caused by nonpersonal forces; and that poetic justice almost always obtains, largely through *deus ex machina*.

Arnheim's findings are generally confirmed by Warner and Henry (1948) which, being essentially a study of effects, is described in detail below.

Saenger (1955) analyzed 156 comic strips appearing in New York City papers during October 1950. He found that approximately two-thirds of the characters of identifiable social class were white-collar workers, approximately a fifth were professionals, and only one-eighth were workers. "In keeping with middle class morality, there were practically no divorced or separated men and women."[7] Most characters strove to excel within the limits of their class, rather than to climb higher socially. A curious and provocative finding was that single males were generally depicted as larger, more masterful, and more aggressive than single women, but among married characters the women eclipsed the men in precisely the same respects.

Head (1954) analyzed 209 randomly selected TV dramas exhibited in 1952. As in the case of the daytime serials and comic strips, the middle and upper classes were found to be tremendously over-represented and the lower classes equally underrepresented. Head also noted that there was practically no mention of major illnesses, births, or *natural* deaths.

Elkin (1950) performed a qualitative analysis of old-style Western movies, many of which are, of course, current TV fare. Justice, he found, always prevailed. The typical hero of the time neither smoked nor drank, did not lose his temper, fought fair, and was a paragon of democratic social attitudes.

Smythe (1955), summing up a series of content analyses of TV programs as a whole, concludes that the population of the TV world consists largely of black and white stereotypes, and contains very few persons who are "motivated by the peculiarly human kaleidoscopic range of human emotions."[8]

Virtually all of the cited analyses bear upon media material of five or more years ago and cannot automatically be assumed to be wholly valid in reference to current offerings. The hero of the currently popular "adult Western," for example, is most unlike the Galahads observed by Elkin; today's hero may smoke, often holds his liquor better than does the villain, and is frequently more neurotic than democratic. But old-type Westerns remain, and, in general, it can probably be safely assumed that much of today's escapist material maintains many of the characteristics of the earlier material.

We have now to inquire into what research reveals regarding the effects of this depicted world upon the audiences of mass media.

Effect Studies: The Functional Orientation and the Simpler Functions

THE FUNCTIONAL ORIENTATION

Research on the "effects" of escapist fare has been somewhat atypical of communications research in general in that it has always concentrated on the functions which such material serves for its devotees, rather than on the occurrence or nonoccurrence of specific effects of which the media material was presumed to be the primary cause. It is hard to say why this should be so. But the fact is that from the very beginning, pertinent research seems, implicitly or explicitly, to expect no immediate effects from such content. To the best of the author's knowledge, no one ever conducted a before-and-after test or other controlled experiment on the assumption that exposure to a series of soap opera episodes would affect the experimental group's ability to face or solve problems. The research has rather addressed itself to known consumers of escapist material, inquiring into why they were devotees and how they differed from non-devotees, and thus emphasizing the functions which such material serves rather than its presumed direct and immediate effects.

This functional orientation, which is only now being "discovered" by research on persuasive communication, was clearly stated in regard to the daytime serial as early as 1944. At that time Herzog, attempting to define "what . . . we really know about daytime serial listeners," rejected any hope of formulating the effects in terms of "a simple conclusive result [such as might accrue from] . . . a single concerted campaign." Asserting that "the putative influences of the serial have developed through slow accretions," she proposed that a full answer to the question in hand required knowledge of the content of the serials, comparative studies of listeners and non-listeners, and, finally and essentially, "a close study of listeners themselves" to determine "what satisfactions . . . [they] say they derive,"[9] coupled with a psychological evaluation of such claims. Similar functional orientations are reflected in the titles and methodologies of various other pertinent studies, such as "The Radio Serial; a Symbolic Analysis" (Warner and Henry, 1948); "The Children Talk about Comics" (Wolf and Fiske, 1949); "The Psychological Appeal of the Hollywood Western" (Elkin, 1950), and, more recently, "Why Do Children Watch Television?" (Maccoby, 1954).

The findings of some of these studies have often been held to be mutually contradictory. To the present author, however, the variety seems more amenable to logical ordering than is the melange of findings in the area of effects of persuasive communications. In presenting these findings, we shall here simply note the various functions observed, proceeding from the simple to the complex. From time to time we shall point out that these findings are generally in accord with the theoretical orientation adopted in this volume. More specifically, we will propose that in reference to all but the simplest functions, the media do not serve as prime movers, but as sources of supply, whose escapist offerings are seized by a particular clientele as a result of extra-communication conditions. The fare, we will propose, serves those audience needs and functions accruing from such conditions, and, in so doing, seems more likely to reinforce existing attitude and behavior patterns than to produce any significant changes.

THE SIMPLE FUNCTIONS

The provision of relaxation.—Escapist communication has been often observed to be indeed escapist—i.e., to provide enter-tainment, relaxation, and surcease from care. This is obvious to the casual observer and has been documented by research. Waples, Berelson, and Bradshaw (1940), for example, after re-viewing the appropriate literature on reading, and after analyzing various case studies, noted the existence of the effect and pro-posed that it was of no social importance.

> The typical comments which characterize a broad respite effect are "doing something different," "forgetting worries," "having a good laugh," and "killing time." Such responses suggest an "effect" which tends to evaporate about as soon as the reader's eye leaves the page. Furthermore, the effect is confined to the reader himself; it seldom involves any attitude change, and it is almost never accompanied by any overt behavior.[10]

Herzog (1944) has noted that daytime serials provide a similar release for some listeners, and Lazarsfeld and Dinerman (1949) have noted parallel comments regarding the effects of quiz and variety shows. More recently, Maccoby (1954) has noted that fantasy programs on television have been alleged to serve a similar function for children. It is incidentally interesting, if not particularly startling, that Lazarsfeld and Dinerman also found that many women *avoid* daytime serials because these programs *increase* their tensions and *remind* them of their troubles: one man's respite appears to be another man's annoyance.

Particular media, or the way in which people use them, are believed by some writers to enhance this respite effect. Asheim (1951) notes, for example, that print has been held to be particularly capable of providing "liberation" by virtue of the fact that reading, unlike, say, television viewing, provides a "kind of unstructured situation which allows users to be part of the creative process."[11] Much the same claim has been made for radio. McPhee and Meyersohn (1955) additionally note that radio has, since the advent of TV, become particularly important as a source of respite and relaxation. It is now widely used as a source of background entertainment, which may be attended with one ear by persons engaged in routine or semi-routine tasks.[12]

Although there can be no doubt that respite and relaxation are both necessary and desirable, some social scientists have postulated a harmful social effect accruing as a result of over-indulgence in such escape from daily problems. The thesis of these writers will be more fully considered later in the chapter.

The stimulation of imagination.—It is occasionally suggested that fantasy may healthfully "stimulate the imagination" of the audience, particularly the younger audience.

Asheim (1951) reports, for example, that a group of social scientists and publishers, discussing the effects of reading upon children, thought there was "some reason to believe that books which stimulate the imagination and foster invention and fancy might in the long run be more desirable than the 'purely practical' works."[13] Similar comments about TV space drama were made by various teachers and free-lance psychologists interviewed by the present author in 1953. None of these persons, however, was able to specify the kind of thought or behavior which they expected of imagination so stimulated. Reported incidents of behavior typically involved creative play—such as the building of soap box space ships, or the pursuit of accurate information, as, for example, the reading of books on astronomy.

Such response to fantasy no doubt exists, but little is known regarding its extent or its value for the growth of young minds. The incidents reported, furthermore, could obviously be as easily evoked by realistic material. It would clearly be useful to know whether and how situations and characters peculiar to the fantasy world stimulate their young audience to creative imagination.

The provision of vicarious interaction.—There is considerable conjecture and some suggestive evidence that escapist media fare which involves people talking to people serves as a kind of substitute for real human contact among persons who are, for one reason or another, frequently alone.

The phenomenon has been often informally observed. Bogart (1956) reports, for example, that critic John Crosby

> . . . once asked a housewife why she listened to soap operas. He received the answer that soap operas were all she could get on the radio. "Then why not turn off the radio?" he asked. "It's a voice in the house," she said.[14]

Disciplined research suggests that escapist media material often serves a similar function. Katz and Lazarsfeld (1955), for example, found that the less gregarious women among their respondents in Decatur, Illinois, reported greater exposure to popular fiction (true story and movie magazines, radio serials, and the like) than did those who were more highly gregarious. The authors suggest that such material may "serve to some extent as a substitute for socializing activity."[15] McPhee and Meyersohn (1955), who interviewed 200 residents of TV cities regarding their use of radio, found that radio programs involving social interaction were more commonly heard by persons who were, at the time, in solitude. Such shows provided them with both a vicarious sense of participation and a feeling of kinship and concern. The listening often developed into what the authors call "a mild addiction"; the audience member wished to "live along" with his new friends and became upset when barred from his daily dose of vicarious participation.

It is to be noted that such use of media material is determined by extra-media factors—specifically, those social, physical, or personal characteristics which function to deprive individuals of adequate social participation. Thus predisposed or sensitized, the audience member selects from the vast supply of media fare the sort of material which serves his existing needs and he reacts to the material in accordance with those needs. That the material he chooses is largely escapist is in part an artifact. He is seeking interactional material, and at present much of that material on the radio and on TV screens during daylight hours *is* fictional and light. Realistic material would probably serve this particular function as well, so long as it remained simple and suitable for background listening by persons engaged in other chores.[16] But realistic material would probably not serve, with equal efficiency, the other functions which escapist fare serves for other audience members. The media, playing to the larger audience, provide a content which suits the widest number. Those for whom the interactional material serves the function of providing a substitute for social contact thus become, perforce, members of the audience for escapistic material.

The literature nowhere specifies any secondary or developmental effects which do or might accrue from using escapist material in this way. Those writers who believe that such content produces social withdrawal would probably consider the danger to be as likely to follow this type of exposure as any other. The case for and against social withdrawal is considered later in this chapter.

Providing a common ground for social intercourse.—Escapist fare apparently also serves to provide some people with topics of conversation and thus to supply a common ground for real social intercourse of a relatively superficial sort.

The sole research directly focused on this particular point was performed by Bogart (1955), who studied the role played by comic strips in the daily lives of 121 males of low income and relatively little education. Eighty-five per cent of the respondents read such strips and 65 per cent habitually discussed them, mostly with other men. The characters of the strips were frequently employed as descriptive archetypes, and plot developments were used as analogies for real life situations. A worker might, for example, describe a colleague as a "regular Dick Tracy" or sum up a situation as "just like in *Blondie*." In order to participate in such conversations, the men had to be familiar with the strips, and it can thus be said that they were under social pressure to read them. Group norms also prescribed a particular mode of reaction: the characters were typically discussed as though they were real, but to take the story seriously was considered "nuts," and such men as did take it seriously were at considerable if unconvincing pains to deny the fact. Bogart concludes that familiarity with the strips permits sociability without personal commitment or discussion of controversial matters.

Similar use of other escapist material has been incidentally observed in the course of other researches. Radio quiz programs and daytime serials were respectively found to serve as conversation pieces by Lazarsfeld (1940) and Herzog (1944). The same function is served by TV characters, program situations, and even commercials. Fan clubs devoted to a particular vocalist or movie star may perhaps be regarded as the ultimate development of the same function: the common ground for social intercourse becomes, in such cases, the very cement of group relations.

Precisely the same observations may here be made as were previously made with regard to the provision of vicarious interaction. Thus, reaction to the material is not determined primarily by the material itself, but by extra-communication factors. Specifically, the socio-structural and work-a-day situation of the audience member is such as to demand a ground for social intercourse without personal commitment. The vast and convenient supply of media material contains commodities—e.g., comic strips—which may be made to serve such a function. They are seized upon and made to serve. Insofar as the process is functional for the group as well as the individual, group norms come to dictate not only that the commodity be employed, but the manner of its employment as well.

Here again, the escapist nature of the material is at least in part an artifact. What is necessary is material comprehensible to all group members which does not involve issues either side of which violates group norms. For lesser educated and more varied groups, suitable material must be so devoid of the complex and the controversial that it is likely to be, by default, escapist. For a less varied, better educated group, more realistic material might serve equally well. The Kinsey reports and *Marjorie Morningstar*, for example, have served as conversation pieces in many group situations. The limits of realism probably correlate directly with the homogeneity of the group. Conversely, the more varied and less cohesive the group, the more unrealistic or escapist the material must necessarily be.[17]

Finally, as in the case of escapist fare supplying interactional needs, specific supplemental effects, if any, have not been a subject of either conjecture or research.

Effect Studies: The Complex Functions and the Question of Causation

Escapist material, in particular daytime serials, has been observed to serve various functions far more complex than those hitherto cited.

In a now classic study, Herzog (1944) drew on five different substudies to determine "what . . . we really know about daytime serial listeners."[18] Respondents in the various studies included a nation-wide sample of non-farm women; cross-sectional samples of the population of Iowa and of Erie County, Ohio; a sample of adult women in Syracuse, Memphis, and Minneapolis; and a supplementary sample of 150 known serial listeners in New York and Pittsburgh.

Herzog found that the serials provide a considerable array of gratifications for various listeners, or, in our current terminology, serve a variety of functions, virtually all of which have since been confirmed by other studies. Most of these functions can be grouped under two heads: the provision of emotional release, which is more complex and varied than one might at first suppose; and the provision of help and advice.

EMOTIONAL RELEASE

Many women found the stories "a means of emotional release. They like 'the chance to cry' which the serials provide; they enjoy 'the surprises, happy or sad,' " and in any of several ways, they "feel better to know that other people have troubles too."[19]

Some women, for example, are comforted merely by learning that they are not alone in their particular woes, and they gratefully adopt the attitudes of their heroines. One listener reported that

"In *Women in White* the brother was going off to war. She [the heroine] reconciled herself, that he was doing something for his country. When I listened it made me feel reconciled about my son— that mine is not the only one. In the story the brother is very attached to the family—he tells them not to worry, that he would be all right and would come back."[20]

For others, the serials provide the dream of what might have been, and the opportunity for vicarious participation. Thus

. . . a rather happily married woman whose husband happens to be chronically ill, listens to *Vic and Sade* mainly for the "funny episodes," pretending that they happen to herself and her husband. A woman whose daughter has run away from home to marry and whose husband "stays away five nights a week," lists *The Goldbergs* and *The O'Neills* as her favorites, each portraying a happy family life and a successful wife and mother.[21]

For still others, the emotional release is considerably more complex: the "sorrows of the serial characters are enjoyed as compensation for the listener's own troubles." Thus

> . . . a woman who had a hard time bringing up her two children after her husband's death mentions the heroine of *Hilltop House* as one of her favorites, feeling that she "ought not to get married ever in order to continue the wonderful work she is doing at the orphanage." This respondent compensates for her own resented fate by wishing a slightly worse one upon her favorite story character: preoccupied by her own husband's death she wants the heroine to have no husband at all and to sacrifice herself for orphan children, if she, the listener, must do so for her own.[22]

Herzog finds that in some of these cases the serials serve additionally to confer a certain prestige upon the listener. By

> . . . identifying themselves and their admittedly minor problems with the suffering heroes and heroines of the stories, the listeners find an opportunity to magnify their own woes. This is enjoyed if only because it expresses their "superiority" over others who have not had these profound emotional experiences.[23]

The serials, in short, provide emotional release in various diverse ways: by indicating that the listener is not alone in her woes, and supplying a more comfortable way of perceiving them; by providing the dream of what might have been; and by providing opportunity for a rather complex sort of compensation, which may involve self-punishment, aggression, or a kind of borrowed prestige.

Similar findings regarding the daytime serial are presented by Warner and Henry (1948), whose study is discussed in detail below. Similar views regarding the functions of other escapist material have been expressed by various writers, usually without benefit of such extensive documentation as Herzog (1944) provides. As early as 1939, for example, Albig suggested that motion pictures, unrealistic as they might be, "perform an important function in providing the material for compensation."[24] Waples, Berelson, and Bradshaw (1940) proposed, on the basis of case histories, that mass media products furnish compensation to the frustrated by providing "an opportunity for achievement through vicarious identifications with successful people."[25] More recently, Elkin (1950) proposed, in the course of a qualitative content analysis of Western movies, that such films permit children to identify with a confident and successful hero and thus symbolically to win the approval of their elders, while simultaneously relieving their feelings of guilt at not living up to the standards which the same elders have set for them.

THE SCHOOL OF LIFE FUNCTION

Another function of the serials, first documented by Herzog (1944), has since given rise to a considerable body of discussion and has been the basis of assertions both that the serials were socially unwholesome and that they were socially desirable.

Herzog discovered that a relatively large number of listeners regard the serials as sources of help and advice in meeting real life problems. Among 2,500 listeners in Iowa, for example, she found that

> . . . 41 per cent claimed to have been helped . . . to deal better with the problems . . . [of] everyday life . . . and only 28 per cent [claimed] not to have been helped. The remainder held that they had never thought about it that way or that they did not know, or refused to answer the question.[26]

In some cases, the allegation of having been helped seems to be in reality a cloak for what is instead a compensation effect of the vicarious participation variety. The asserted aid, in such instances, typically pertains to situations which the listeners are likely to encounter only in wishful dreams (or in daytime serials). Several respondents, for example, claimed they had been helped by stories involving the sudden acquisition of great wealth. One such respondent admitted that a parallel was unlikely to occur in her own life, but she nevertheless thought it "a good idea to know and to be prepared for what I would do with so much money."[27]

In other instances, however, some of the women seem actually to have learned something from some serials. Thus one woman felt that

> ". . . Papa David helped me to be more cheerful when Fred, my husband, comes home. I feel tired and instead of being grumpy, I keep on the cheerful side. *The Goldbergs* are another story like that. Mr. Goldberg comes home scolding and he never meant it. I sort of understand Fred better because of it. When he starts to shout, I call him Mr. Goldberg. He comes back and calls me Molly. Husbands do not really understand what a wife goes through. These stories have helped me to understand that husbands are like that. If women are tender, they are better off. I often feel that if my sister had had more tenderness she would not be divorced today. I saw a lot of good in that man."[28]

More often, however, the lesson is superficial, consisting simply of the provision of a formula. Thus one or another respondent remarked:

> "Bess Johnson shows you how to handle children. She handles all ages. Most mothers slap their children. She deprives them of something. That is better. I use what she does with my children."[29]

> "I like Helen Trent. She is a woman over 35. You never hear of her dyeing her hair! She uses charm and manners to entice men and she does. If she can do it, why can't I? I am fighting old age and having a terrible time. Sometimes I am tempted to go out and fix my hair. These stories give me courage and help me realize I have to accept it."[30]

> "When Clifford's wife died in childbirth the advice Paul gave him I used for my nephew when his wife died."[31]

Such women may call the attention of their friends to the fount of wisdom; in so doing, they may serve as advisers without shouldering any responsibility for the outcome.

> "I always tell the woman upstairs who wants my advice to listen to the people on the radio because they are smarter than I am. She is worried because she did not have any education and she figures that if her daughter grows up, she would be so much smarter than she was. I told her to listen to *Aunt Jenny* to learn good English. Also, you can learn refinement from *Our Gal Sunday*. I think if I told her to do something and something would happen, I would feel guilty. If it happens from the story, then it is nobody's fault."[32]

The one great lesson which seems to be most widely learned is to remain calm and do nothing, for things will surely turn out all right in the end.

> "It helps you to listen to these stories. When Helen Trent has serious trouble she takes it calmly. So you think you'd better be like her and not get upset."[33]

> "I learned that if anything is the matter, do not dwell on it or you go crazy."[34]

> "These stories teach you how things come out all right."[35]

THE QUESTION OF SOCIAL WHOLESOMENESS AND THE QUESTION OF CAUSALITY

Herzog (1944) goes on to comment, more by implication and question than by explicit judgment, on the psychological and social value of the serials' pedagogy. The respondents' testimonies, she feels, raise questions as to "the adequacy of the aid and comfort" afforded.[36] She notes, as we have reported, that the situations for which the women feel they have been prepared are often fanciful and unrealistic; that the preparation for real situations may consist more of good intentions than of any real behavioral change; that the alleged aid often consists of the adoption of a superficial and ready-made formula which is not truly generalizable; and that the major lesson seems to be to remain calm and do nothing, in the sure faith that somehow, some way, everything will turn out all right in the end. "Calmness in the face of crises," Herzog remarks, "is certainly a useful attitude. However, it is not always sufficient for a solution of the problems."[37]

The finding that escapist media material not only provides emotional release but also serves as a school of life has been confirmed by other researchers, including Warner and Henry (1948) and related findings are noted by Bailyn (1959).[38] Warner and Henry, however, propose that the functions so served by daytime serials are individually and socially supportive. The studies of

Herzog (1944) and Warner and Henry (1948) are, presumably for this reason, often said to be contradictory.

Such a statement is, however, an extreme oversimplification, for the evaluation of the functions is based, in the two studies, on different criteria, and these criteria are in turn bound up with the question of whether serials *produce* the *Weltanschauung* which apparently characterizes their listeners, or whether the listeners react to the serials as they do because they already possess such a *Weltanschauung*. Neither of the two studies poses this question explicitly, but it appears in both cases to be a matter of concern, and certain of the data which are sought and reported are clearly pertinent to the issue. These data are obtained by different techniques, and the emerging findings are very different.

Herzog (1944) undertakes a "comparative study of listeners and non-listeners." She notes that this is "a type of analysis which is often heir to fallacies" and which does not define the direction of causation, but she feels that "such comparisons are indispensable for a fuller understanding of the problem."[39]

Herzog postulates that listeners might be more socially isolated than non-listeners; that their "intellectual range" might be narrower; that they might be preoccupied with personal problems to the exclusion of public issues; that they might be "beset with anxieties and frustrations"; and that they might simply be more given to radio listening.[40] She accordingly compares listeners and non-listeners in regard to a wide variety of characteristics related to these hypotheses.

In reference to most of these characteristics, no significant differences were discovered. Listeners were found, for example, to engage as often as did non-listeners in various types of social gatherings, to read about the same amount, and to exhibit equal interest in current affairs. The two groups did not differ in regard to whether they thought they worried more or less than other women, and they were similarly distributed by interviewer ratings along rough scales of "talkativeness" and "emotionality."[41]

Small but statistically significant differences between the two groups were observed in regard to a few characteristics. The listeners included proportionately more women who had not gone beyond grade school. They were more likely than non-listeners to read mystery stories and magazines like *True Confession* and *Household,* and less likely to read historical novels and magazines like *Time* and *The New Yorker.* They were less apt to vote than were non-listeners, and participated less often in political campaigns. They listened to the radio more than non-serial listeners, both during daytime and evening hours, relied upon it more for certain types of news, and were less critical of commercials. They were somewhat more apt than non-listeners to be rated by interviewers as below average in "self-assurance" and above average in "energy."[42]

Not only are these differences slight, but in the light of the observed similarities, their significance is difficult to determine. It is hard to know, for example, what to make of the fact that listeners vote less, when one considers that they are as interested as non-listeners in current affairs and participate as frequently in social occasions. The data permit one to conclude only that listeners tend to be slightly less educated, tend to have less sophisticated reading tastes, use the radio more, and may tend to be slightly less self-assured.

There is thus no reason to suppose, on the basis of Herzog's data, that listeners become listeners or that they react to the serials as they do by virtue of a distinctive and presumably pre-existing pattern of personality and behavior. But, by the same token, there is no reason to suppose that they have *developed* any such pattern as a result of prolonged exposure to the serials. The comparative study, in short, in itself *reveals neither original differences nor effects.*

The critical researcher, such as Herzog herself, is therefore inevitably led to wonder whether the data sought might not have been in some way insufficient or inappropriate to provide a definitive answer to the question involved. The data which Herzog develops, for example, deal for the most part with overt behavior, rather than with the psychological significance of that behavior. The author herself repeatedly notes this limitation. She suggests that "it is possible that social relations have a different psychological significance for listeners and non-listeners";[43] that "interpretation of the marked differences in actual voting . . . should . . . be left pending until we know something more of the personality characteristics of the listeners;"[44] and that "more detailed investigation of the personality characteristics of listeners and non-listeners is clearly one of the most important lines for future research in this field."[45]

The small differences between serial listeners and non-listeners which were observed by Herzog (1944) were again observed by Lazarsfeld and Dinerman (1949) in the course of a study focused on other matters. The same slight difference in education was noted, and the listeners were again found to possess a narrower range of interests, to be less active voters, and to read somewhat less.

Considerable additional, if more qualitative, data regarding the personality characteristics of serial listeners and the functions which the serials serve for them are provided in an involved study by Warner and Henry (1948).

In brief, Warner and Henry employed interviews and projective devices to study the personalities of serial listeners and the functions which the serials served. They conclude that the serials serve functions in many respects similar to those earlier described by Herzog (1944), but they also propose that the life and *Weltanschauung* of the ardent serial listener is very similar to the kind of lives and *Weltanschauung* celebrated in the serials themselves, and that the serials are therefore individually and socially supportive.

More specifically, Warner and Henry focused upon sixty-two women who regularly listened to *Big Sister* and a "control group" of five who did not. All of the listeners were middle-class housewives, which the authors claim to be the model social position and occupation of the serial audience;[46] the five non-listeners were of a slightly higher socio-economic status.

Personality data were obtained by use of the Thematic Apperception Test, selected portions of which were administered to all subjects. The results led the authors to conclude that certain personality traits, conflicts, value orientations, and behavioral patterns were typical of the sixty-two listeners, but not of the control group. Specifically, the devotees were found to be characterized by "reduced imagination and personal [psychological] resources . . . [and to be given to] impulse suppression." Their outer world was found to be house- and family-centered, monotonous, and personally unrewarding, but they were deeply apprehensive "of the unknown." Their inter-personal relations were found to be "stereotyped" and "strained." They felt that they were engaged in "a struggle for personal control" in which they feared they were not succeeding, and they typically "hope[d] for some externally mediated solution."[47]

Warner and Henry point out that the heroine of *Big Sister* (Ruth) is in many ways like these women, and in other ways embodies what they aspire to be. Ruth is economically completely dependent upon her husband; she has chosen to live a life of moral rectitude and service to her family, and has rejected a career, egocentricity, or any exercise of sexual impulse. Her world is centered in her family and the outer world impinges upon her only as it affects family activities and attitudes. Her problems are more frequent and dramatic than are the listeners', but the listeners see them, the authors believe, as real and possible within the framework of their own lives. Ruth attacks these problems through the exercise of honesty, patience, and moral rectitude—traits on which the listeners themselves customarily rely. Ruth differs from the listeners in that she takes active control of the situation and succeeds in making justice prevail,[48] whereas the listeners typically feel that they are failing to control their family problems.

To determine the functions which *Big Sister* serves for its devotees, Warner and Henry administered what they regarded as a "verbal projective test,"[49] in which the subjects were asked to complete fragmentary episodes involving the serial characters, under the pretense that actual program possibilities were being explored. Devotees supplied conclusions typical of *Big Sister,* while the five non-listeners produced very different and, in the opinion of the researchers, more realistic conclusions.

Warner and Henry believe that the results of these tests indicate "how . . . *Big Sister* . . . functions as a symbol system" and, to some extent, how the women expect such incidents would or should turn out in real life.[50] The present author is inclined to wonder, however, whether the projective potential of the test may not have been strongly compromised by the degree to which the subjects were familiar with the serial itself. A devotee of *Big Sister,* given an incomplete incident that was allegedly being considered for actual use, might very reasonably be expected to hew to the kind of development she knew to be typical of the program. To regard such fealty to the familiar as a projection of the respondent's own values does not seem to the author to be wholly justified.

Warner and Henry, however, attribute considerable validity to the completion test as a true projection of the subject's own values. They feel, on the basis of the test results, that the listeners believe that the problems that beset Ruth might arise in their own lives. They also find in the interview and test responses evidence that the serial performs various positive and supportive functions for the listeners.

(1) It "decreases their feeling of futility" and "increases [their] . . . feeling of importance" by

> dramatizing the significance of the wife's role in basic human affairs, . . . by showing that the family is of the highest importance and that she has control over the vicissitudes of family life.[51]

(2) It increases their "sense of security" in several ways.

(a) It "provides moral beliefs, values, and techniques for solving emotional and interpersonal problems."[52]

(b) It reaffirms "the security of the marriage ties."[53]

(c) It permits the listeners to identify with Ruth and her active control of her family environment, and so to compensate for their own inability to exercise similar control.

(d) It renders the listeners optimistic about their own problems by demonstrating "that those who behave properly and stay away from wrong-doing exercise moral constraint over those who do not," and "that wrong behavior is punished."[54]

(3) It "permits sublimated impulse satisfaction by the listeners, first, unconsciously identifying with the bad woman, and later consciously punishing her through the action of the plot" and identification with Ruth.[55]

The authors therefore conclude that the influence of the program is both individually and socially positive. It helps the individual listeners adjust to the realities of their own lives. In addition, it serves

> . . . to strengthen and stabilize the basic social structure of our society, the family. It so functions by dramatizing family crises and the ideals and values involved, as they are understood and felt, by the women who listen, and by making the good wife (Ruth) the center of action and power.[56]

The two classic studies by Herzog (1944) and Warner and Henry (1948) can now be seen to be not "contradictory," but rather in some ways mutually confirmative, and in other ways extremely unlike. Both are in general agreement as to the function which serials serve for their listeners, but they disagree in respect to the social values in relation to which these functions are judged. Herzog (1944), in effect, criticizes the serials for failing to render their devotees more socially aware and more capable of controlling their environment. Warner and Henry (1948), on the other hand, in effect commend the serials for helping their devotees adjust to the facts of their lives and their *inability* to control the environment. The relative merits of these two points of view involve value questions which cannot be adjudicated by research and which are beyond the scope of this volume.

The two studies differ also in relation to the question of whether serial listeners are characteristically different from non-serial listeners. Herzog (1944) compares the two groups along lines which emphasize the degree to which they respectively engage in various kinds of overt behavior. She finds no meaningful differences and calls for further research emphasizing the psychological characteristics of the two groups. Warner and Henry (1948) pay little attention to overt activity and focus instead on the attitudes, values, and general psychological make-up of the listener group. They propose that the listeners *do* possess characteristic personality traits and a characteristic *Weltanschauung*.

The two studies taken together thus pose but do not definitively answer a crucial question: does escapist material *produce* particular values and patterns of behavior among its devotees, or do its devotees become devotees because of the values and behavioral tendencies they already possess?

Although this question appears susceptible to research, no study known to the author focuses directly upon it. Numerous pertinent data are, however, provided by studies focused on various other problems.

ADDICTION TO ESCAPISM: CAUSE OR EFFECT?

The findings of research subsequent to Herzog (1944) and Warner and Henry (1948) strongly suggest that escapist media material is not the prime mover in creating the values or behavioral tendencies which may be characteristic of its devotees. Virtually all of the data attest relationships between heavy consumption of escapist material and audience characteristics which seem likely to have stemmed from extra-communication sources.

Katz and Lazarsfeld (1955), for example, found that women with high anxiety tendencies exposed themselves more than did other women to "true story" and movie type magazines and to radio serials. Ricutti (1951) found that fifth through eighth grade children who listened particularly often to radio serials or adventure stories scored slightly lower than non-listeners on tests of

happiness, personal social adjustment, imagination, and general
school achievement. Although the direction of causality is not
defined by these data, such personality manifestations would seem
more likely to impel particular communication preferences than
to result from such preferences.

The pattern of young people's group memberships has also
been shown to be related to their communication preferences and
to the use they make of the material. Riley and Riley (1951)
found that children in grades five through seven reacted to fantasy
in different ways, according to whether they were or were not
members of peer groups. Those who were members only of family
groups were significantly more likely to be fond of little animal
comics and typically described the animal hero (e.g., Bugs
Bunny) as "a rascal," as "happy-go-lucky," and, perhaps more
significantly, as one who "gets away with it."[57] The authors
suggest that family demands are probably more frustrating than
peer group demands, and that the family oriented children thus
admire and identify with the hero who evades responsibility. The
older children among those who were not peer group members
were found, as has been previously noted, to employ such characters as the Lone Ranger as fantasy and escape stimulants, while
peer group members found the same content a source of ideas for
group games. Among the older peer group girls, material on dat-
ing and romance was found to be "just liked" by those who were
more popular but to be looked upon *as a source of advice* by the
less popular. In sum, the Rileys found that escapist material is
likely to be more popular among the children who seem likely to
be more frustrated, and is more likely to be used by them as a
mode of escape by identification and as a source of advice.

Perhaps impelled by such indications as these, Maccoby
(1954) attempted to determine whether any direct relationship
existed between the level of frustration and the degree of TV
viewing among young children. Data were obtained through interviews with 379 middle- and lower-class women who were mothers
of kindergarten children. No mention is made in the report of the

type of material viewed, but considering the age of the children it may perhaps be assumed that much of it was escapist. Maccoby herself considers the study pertinent to the functions served for children by TV fantasy programs.

The interviews inquired into the TV habits of the children and into nine areas of parent-child relationships, including the nature of parental reaction to aggression on the part of the child, permissiveness regarding sex behavior, demands for neatness, "affectional relationship," and the like.[58] Each child was rated as to his degree of frustration on each of the nine indices. A strong relationship was found to exist between the degree of frustration and the amount of TV viewing among the middle-class children, but only a suggestion of such a relationship was found among lower-class children. Maccoby attempts to account for these findings in terms of the differential degree of adult TV viewing among the two classes. In middle-class homes, she suggests, children and parents may do many things together, and the frustrated child who turns to TV thus significantly increases his TV viewing. In lower-class homes, however, TV viewing may be so common an occupation for both children and parents that the children's escape via TV is not statistically apparent.

Children who were particularly heavy consumers of mass media products have been a focus of investigation in at least three studies: Wolf and Fiske (1949); Himmelweit, Oppenheim, and Vince (1958); and Bailyn (1959). Although neither of the first two studies attempted to distinguish addicts of escapism from addicts of other media fare, the over-all nature of the media material involved was such that a great proportion of it must undoubtedly have been escapist. In all the studies, furthermore, the addicts were found to *use* the material for escapist purposes.

Wolf and Fiske (1949) studied "the impact of comic book reading on children."[59] They found that 37 per cent of their sample were "fans,"[60] that is, children whose comic book reading differed qualitatively as well as quantitatively from that of moderate readers. The fan was found typically to "prefer comic book reading to all other activities" and to "become . . . so absorbed . . . while reading a comic . . . that the rest of the world is forgotten."[61] Most children were found to progress, at characteristic ages, from "funny animal" comics to "invincible hero" comics (such as *Superman*) and then to "educational comics of the True or Classic type."[62] The fan, however, was found likely to remain at the second, invincible hero stage regardless of age. He does not seek, like other readers, to identify with the invincible hero as "a means of inflating his ego," but rather regards the hero (frequently Superman) as "an omniscient . . . creature, in extreme contrast to . . . himself."[63] The author notes that

> . . . the fan is apparently a child whose peace and security have been in some way so undermined that he needs not merely an invincible hero with which to identify, but rather a god, a being wholly different from men, a creature of unalterable perfection, dedicated to the protection of the otherwise insecure child.[64]

Fans were found in some cases almost literally to worship their comic book god, and, more often, to find thinking about him "a comfort and solace at times of stress."[65] In retelling comic book stories, 85 per cent of the fans changed the story to insure that all details were settled to their satisfaction. Fans were found more commonly among "neurotic" children than among "normal" or "psychotic" children,[66] and were more than three times as common among "children below normal height" as they were among those who were "tall for their age."[67] These data strongly suggest that the "child's problems existed before he became a fan,"[68] rather than that they occurred as a result of comic book reading.

In the course of their multi-faceted study of British children and British television, Himmelweit, Oppenheim, and Vince (1958) focused their sights upon television "addicts," whom they operationally defined as "the one-third of each age group who spent the longest time viewing."[69] They found, to begin with, that less intelligent children were more likely to be addicts. They then sought additional personality characteristics by comparing addicts with occasional viewers individually matched by intelligence, sex, age, and social class. Addicts, more often than occasional viewers, obtained "moderate-to-high" scores,[70] indicative of greater worry, on inventories completed by themselves and by their teachers which concerned "worries," "fears," "feelings of rejection by other children," "general feelings of social insecurity" and "anxiety about growing up."[71] Addicts were also found to visit or entertain friends less often than did occasional viewers, and to "prefer . . . to have things done for them rather than to do them themselves or explore things on their own."[72] Precisely the same differences were observed by these authors in a parallel comparison of heavy vs. occasional cinema goers. Moreover, both cinema and television addicts were found to be heavy radio users and heavy comic book readers. The television "addicts' tastes on the whole differed little from those of occasional viewers," except that more of them preferred "family serials, adventure, and mystery" plays and fewer "preferred comedy and variety."[73] Statements by both the cinema and television addicts, however, suggest that these children tended to use *all* media material to satisfy an apparent "need to withdraw from real situations."[74] The authors feel that their

> . . . findings suggest that these differences were there before television came to the home and explain why the addict views so much more than others of his age, intelligence, and social background. The parallel analysis of cinema addicts showed them to be very similar kinds of children. Television meets a need which the child without television satisfies through the cinema or the radio.[75]

The authors conclude that the media are not the prime movers. "The television addict," they propose, "turns to viewing because of the kind of person he is."[76]

Bailyn (1959) proposes, in the concluding pages of her elaborate study of elementary school children and pictorial mass media, that these media serve an escape function "for some children and not for others."[77] She had earlier reported that "aggressive hero" content,[78] which is both violent and remote from real life, was a favorite of boys (not girls) who were highly exposed to the pictorial media in general *and* who possessed certain psychological characteristics. These characteristics included numerous problems relative to self, family, and peers; a tendency to blame difficulties on others rather than themselves; some evidence of independence, especially from parents; and a desire for adventurous occupations. Bailyn notes that these characteristics suggest an "orientation away from the immediate situation" and "a desire to escape."[79] She considers that the characteristics themselves are not the results of media exposure, but she believes that the reactions of children with such characteristics who are highly exposed to aggressive hero content indicate that they are using the media material as a means of escape. Such children were observed to become so completely involved in reading a comic book of the aggressive hero type that they were unaware of the observer or of external events. They tended, more than other children, to consider that the kind of events depicted do occur in real life. In retelling the story, they tended, unlike other children, to ignore the details unique to the particular comic book and to concentrate instead on those aspects which were typical of the genre, a mode of behavior Bailyn regards as indicative of their having "organized . . . [such] elements of the content . . . into a fairly stable structure"[80] which helps define the world into which they escape. In judging real people, such devotees of aggressive hero content tended to use stereotypes and to employ values characteristic of the media material: they are more likely to believe, for example, that "people are either all good or all bad,"[81] and there are some indications that this tendency is increased by exposure. In addition, such boys, when asked whom they would like to be if they could be changed into someone else, are far more likely than other children to choose Superman or such media types as an FBI agent or a detective. Bailyn accordingly concludes that the media material is not a prime mover toward escapism, but that for *boys* with escapist tendencies it does serve as an avenue of escape and may intensify their escapist orientation. Both the existence of escapist tendencies *and* high exposure are, however, prerequisite for this effect.

Thus, at least seven studies (Katz and Lazarsfeld, 1955; Ricutti, 1951; Riley and Riley, 1951; Maccoby, 1954; Wolf and Fiske, 1949; Himmelweit, Oppenheim, and Vince, 1958, and Bailyn, 1959) attest relationships between heavy use of escapist media material and various socio-economic, socio-structural, and personality characteristics of the audience members. Riley and Riley additionally reveal a relationship between the group orientations of audience members and their reactions to escapist material.

Any discovered correlation can, of course, betoken a cause and effect relationship in one direction or the other. It seems most unlikely, however, that all of these factors are products of the consumption of escapist media material. It would seem far more likely, as both Wolf and Fiske and Himmelweit, Oppenheim, and Vince propose, that such characteristics help determine the selection which people make from the vast supply of media fare and provide channels by which the media may serve to reinforce those people's existing orientations. The weight of the findings, in short, tends to support the view that escapist media material is not so likely to *create* the kind of orientation which its fans seem to possess, as to be *used* by persons who are already so oriented.

To take such a position is, however, in no way to exonerate escapist material from all possible criticism. Though it does not appear to be the cause of the addict's *Weltanschauung*, it does appear to confirm and intensify what *Weltanschauung*. Thus, though Wolf and Fiske (1949) note that comic books cannot be blamed for comic book addiction any more than "morphine itself can be blamed when a person becomes a drug addict," they also note that the drug addict "might have found a better solution for his problems if there were no morphine available."[82] Himmelweit, Oppenheim, and Vince (1958) go somewhat further and speak of

. . . a vicious circle. Emotional insecurity or inadequate facilities at home cause the child to become a heavy viewer. In this way he restricts his outside contacts and so reduces still further his opportunities to mix. With escape through television so readily available, other sources of companionship may demand too much effort and offer too little promise of success.[83]

The point of view expressed by Wolf and Fiske (1949) and by Himmelweit, Oppenheim, and Vince (1958) suggests a line of further inquiry which might be extremely enlightening, although perhaps methodologically difficult to follow. A moment's reflection suggests that heavy use of escapist media material is only one of any number of ways in which people may exercise escapist tendencies. Drinking, unnecessary sleeping, social intercourse of the gossipy sort, walking in the country, or any of countless other activities can be and frequently are pursued as escapes from the realities of daily living. But none of the studies we have cited have made any attempt systematically to investigate the tendencies of their subjects to indulge in such extra-media escapism, nor has anyone, to the author's knowledge, tried to determine whether the accessibility of media channels of escape has reduced the degree to which these alternative channels are used or altered the manner and consequences of their use.

In any case, the evaluation of media effects is not a purpose of this volume, which is essentially a report of research findings. Proposals for remedial action are likewise outside our present scope. It seems clear, however, that attempts to reduce such effects of escapist material as are considered undesirable are not very likely to be fruitful if they are addressed only to reducing the amount of such material available through the mass media. It would appear that social scientists and social critics interested in the problem might more fruitfully address themselves to the study of the emotional needs of persons addicted to escapism.

ESCAPIST COMMUNICATION AS AN INFLUENCE TOWARD SOCIAL APATHY

A considerable number of both disciplined social researchers and lay critics have expressed the belief that the plethora of escapist material in the mass media may tend to promote social apathy.

The argument typically follows one or both of two paths. Some writers propose that escapist material, by providing habitual mode of relief for the tensions of daily living, acts as a safety valve for all social tensions, and thus greatly reduces the likelihood of social criticism. Other writers believe that habitual attention to the world of escapist fare, which, as we have shown,[8] is largely devoid of social problems, renders devotees blind to such social problems as do in fact exist.

An early but typical statement to these effects is provided, for example, by Waples, Berelson, and Bradshaw (1940) in the course of their discussion of the effects of escapist printed matter. They state that

> Psychologically, the effect is distraction from somewhat habitual anxieties. Sociologically, the effect is to reduce the violence of assaults upon the existing social structure by cooling the discontent of underprivileged groups. The reading of anything at all which takes the reader's mind from his troubles has this cooling effect.[85]

Closely similar views have been expressed by various writers including Dollard (1945), and Lazarsfeld and Merton (1948) who proposed that the media might in this way serve a "narcotizing dysfunction."[86] Seldes (1950) also believes that although the radio serial allays its listeners' anxieties, it does so by glorifying

> . . . the weak, the clinging, the submissive; it accepts misery as the natural state of womankind, and by sponging up the fluid, unchanneled emotions of the listeners it renders them passive, perpetuating the very qualities that limit the imagination and stultify the emotional life.[87]

That escapist material actually produces social apathy among persons who were previously not apathetic, or that it tends to increase the number of people who *are* socially apathetic, has not yet been substantiated by any direct evidence, nor could any such evidence be adduced except by the most prolonged and elaborate experimentation.

The whole question is, however, little more than a specific

topical focusing of the larger question discussed immediately above, viz., whether the way of life characteristic of heavy users of escapist material is a product or a cause of their consumption of such material. On the basis of the foregoing discussion and virtually all previous chapters in this volume, it may be said that two highly pertinent points are reasonably well established by the literature. In the first place, mass communication is not so likely to produce great attitude or personality changes as it is to rein- force existing orientations. In the second place, escapist fare does seem to feed and exercise the asocial orientation of persons who are already socially apathetic. Putting the two points together, it would seem logical to suppose that escapist fare is likely to recon- firm the social apathy of the apathetic, but unlikely to quench the fires of the socially active and ardent. The findings of Riley and Riley (1951) to the effect that peer group members and non-peer group members respectively employ fantasy characters for socially useful and asocial purposes demonstrate, within a limited sphere, what the current direction of research would suggest concerning the larger question.

Theoretical Considerations

The findings of research on "the effects" of escapist com- munication seem to the present author to be wholly in accord with the generalizations advanced in the introductory chapter of this volume.

As pointed out above, research in this specific area has from the first proceeded from an orientation, or from an implicit theoretical background, very like that which we have proposed. From the first, investigators have been prone to deny or ignore the possibilities of direct, immediate effects. They have rather directed their sights upon persons who are confirmed users of the media commodity in question and have asked what gratifications the material provides them and what functions it serves.

Such a line of inquiry is in complete accord, although, as we shall show presently, it is not coterminous, with what we have called "the phenomenistic approach." It is characteristic of that approach in that it begins with the already existing phenomenon (i.e., consumption of escapist material), assumes that such consumption is functional for the consumer, and proceeds to explore in detail both the phenomenon and the functions.

The data which have been adduced by this research are in full accord with the set of generalizations advanced in the introductory chapter. Escapist material appears, as proposed in generalization 1, to function not so much as a single necessary and sufficient cause of direct effect, but rather as one among a nexus of other factors, including audience predispositions, selective exposure and selective perception, the socio-economic and socio-structural position of the audience member, his patterns of group membership, and his personality pattern. These very factors, as proposed in generalization 2, seem to mediate the effects of the media, rendering them agents of reinforcement rather than of change. Warner and Henry (1948), for example, found that the personality of ardent serial listeners affected their perception of the material and channelized its effects upon them. Riley and Riley (1951) found that among audience members with different group orientations, the same material was differently perceived and employed. Wolf and Fiske (1949), Himmelweit, Oppenheim, and Vince (1958), and Bailyn (1959) found that children who were heavy media users were inclined to withdraw from facing real problems and used media material as a means of such withdrawal. In all of these cases the media material apparently served to reinforce the existing *Weltanschauung* of its audience.

Although no study documents pertinent cases, it is not hard to imagine, as proposed in generalization 3, that in exceptional circumstances these same mediating factors might help the media to serve as agents of change. A person in severe stress, for example, or in mental breakdown, might precipitately withdraw from insufferable reality, and escapist media offerings might very conceivably help him to do so. If, for example, as Maccoby's (1954) data suggest, the degree of children's TV viewing is related to their level of frustration, one might hypothesize that suddenly increased and maintained frustration might produce increased withdrawal, with appropriately escapist media material providing one avenue of departure.

Quite aside from participating in these complex processes, escapist fare also appears, as proposed in generalization 4, directly to produce certain psycho-physical effects as, for example, to induce a temporary mood of relaxation.

Almost no research in the public domain pertains to generalization 5, as applied specifically to escapist communications. This generalization is advanced largely to acknowledge certain residual phenomena, and proposes, tritely enough, that the effect of a communication is influenced by various aspects of its presentation, its textual organization, the situation in which it is received, and the like. Practically the only published data pertinent to this generalization and to escapist material are the findings of Lazarsfeld and Dinerman (1949) to the effect that some women who seek relaxation from morning radio broadcasts avoid certain programs because they are "noisy." Other data of this sort have doubtless been accumulated by specific program tests conducted by radio, TV, and agency personnel. It is, in any case, obvious that at least some variations in presentation, in content, or in the situation in which the communication is received would influence the over-all effect. Conjecture regarding the differential efficiency of the media in producing a respite effect, and the possible ability of non-escapist material to serve some of the simpler functions served by escapist fare, are suggestive in this connection.

The generalizations themselves, the author submits, have once again proved organizationally and theoretically helpful. They have enabled us to organize findings which were hitherto widely regarded as anomalous, or at least unrelated. They have again attracted attention to the similar function served in the process of effect by such varied factors as predispositions, group membership, and personality, and have thus underscored the notion that these factors belong to a category distinct from the media content or its sources. By throwing these factors and their operation into relief, the generalizations have made conspicuous the fact that *precisely the same factors* serve in similar ways in relation to all areas of communication effect thus far discussed.

The generalizations thus suggest that the process of communication effect is much the same regardless of the area of effect in question. They are additionally theoretically helpful in that they reveal logically relevant avenues for further research. It would be useful and relevant to know, for example, whether the same mediating factors which help escapist material to serve as an agent of reinforcement may, as the generalizations predict, also serve in exceptional circumstances to abet change.

To answer this question, it would first be necessary to identify changes (or changers) and then to trace the process of their development. Such a procedure would indeed be coterminous with the phenomenistic approach. The research to date has not been coterminous with that approach precisely because it has focused exclusively on static conditions; it has been restricted to describing existing phenomena and has not inquired with any vigor into how they came to exist. A more completely phenomenistic approach would start with an existing condition, but would then attempt to trace its genesis and development.

In reference to the effects of escapist material, this is to say that such an approach would, for example, attempt to trace the development of those various audience *Weltanschauungs* which are known to be associated with ardent consumption of escapist communications. Case histories, sociometric techniques, and other devices beyond the confines of traditional communication research would necessarily have to be brought to bear. To trace the development of so basic an orientation is an immense challenge, and the social sciences may well not yet be capable of fully taking up the gauntlet. The author proposes, however, that only when they can, and do, will it become possible precisely to define the role played by any factor, including escapist mass communication, in producing the effects for which such communication is now variously held to be responsible and not responsible, and for which it is variously condemned and praised.

Summary

1. Both lay critics and social researchers have been long concerned with the effects of "escapist" media material upon its audiences. The alleged effects have been variously condemned, condoned, and commended.

2. "Escapist fare," as discussed by such writers, is not primarily defined in terms of its effects, but implicitly defined in terms of its content. The designation is applied to frank fantasy, and to material which presents an unreal picture of life but might be taken as depicting the world as it really is. Typically included in the genre are TV family comedy, much light fiction, daytime serials, and much of what the mass media consider serious drama.

3. Such material has been alleged by social observers to transform its devotees into addicts, to handicap or prevent their maturation, to render them unable to face real life, and to produce social apathy. The same material, on the other hand, has been alleged to provide healthful relaxation, to promote maturity, and to channel off aggressive impulses.

4. Disciplined content analyses reveal that much media material does depict a world unlike the one which exists about us. This "myth world" is chiefly characterized by an over-representation of the wealthy and an under-representation of the lower classes, a lack of social problems,[88] the triumph of rigid middle-class morality, and the prevalence of poetic justice.

5. Disciplined research on the "effects" of such fare has from the first, for reasons unknown, followed a more or less "functional" approach. It has not sought immediate, direct effects, but has rather focused on the nature of the audience for such material and on the functions which the material serves for that audience.

6. These studies have identified a variety of relatively simple functions served by escapist material. Such content has been observed to:

    a. provide mental and thus psychophysical relaxation.
    b. stimulate the imagination.

    c. provide a means of vicarious interaction.

    d. provide a common ground for social intercourse.

In relation to none of these functions have secondary effects been carefully investigated. In relation to some, the escapist nature of the material seems in part an artifact. In relation to most, the needs which the media material satisfies appear to be engendered by sources other than the communication.

    7. "Effect" studies have also revealed that escapist material serves certain highly complex functions. Daytime serials have been observed to:

    a. provide women with emotional release (1) by indicating that the listener is not alone in her woes and by supplying a more comfortable way of perceiving them; (2) by providing the dream of what might have been; and (3) by providing a complex sort of compensation which may involve self-punishment, aggression, or a kind of borrowed prestige.

    b. serve their listeners as a source of advice concerning real-life problems. The lessons allegedly learned often apply to highly unlikely situations, or involve adoptions of ready-made and superficial formulae for behavior. The chief lesson seems to be that if one remains calm and does nothing, everything will somehow come out all right in the end.

    8. The functions cited above have been variously adjudged to be individually and socially supportive and to be individually and socially unwholesome. These differing appraisals seem in part to reflect different social values of the authors, which cannot here be adjudicated. They seem also to be bound up with the question of whether escapist material *produces* certain values and attitudes among its audience members, or whether audience members already possessing such values and attitudes are therefore attracted to escapist material.

    a. One classic study (Herzog, 1944) finds no meaningful differences between serial listeners and non-listeners in regard to a wide range of presumably pertinent overt activities, expressed interests, and overt personality characteristics. The author calls for more psychologically penetrating inquiry.

b. Another major study (Warner and Henry, 1948) finds that the *Weltanschauung* and way of life of serial listeners is remarkably similar to that of the serial heroine in being home-and-family centered, personally insecure, unimaginative, and morally rigid.

c. Various other studies find that ardent users of escapist material differ in personality characteristics from light users or non-users, and that persons of differing personality or socio-structural position use escapist material in characteristically different ways. Heavy use has been associated with anxiety tendencies, social maladjustment, and frustration. Children who are and who are not peer group members have been found, respectively, to use fantasy for socially useful and for asocial purposes.

The weight of available evidence seems to favor the view that escapist fare is not a prime cause of any particular way of life, but that it rather serves the psychological needs and reinforces the ways of life already characteristic of its audience.

9. Escapist communication has been held to produce social apathy. No research evidence directly supports or disproves this claim. Related findings *suggest* that such fare probably does not create apathy among the non-apathetic, but probably reinforces the apathy of the already apathetic.

10. *Theoretical Considerations.* The data adduced in this chapter directly support the first two and the fourth of the five generalizations proposed in the introduction, and suggest that the third and fifth are probably valid as well. The generalizations help to order a considerable body of hitherto unrelated data, and suggest avenues of new and logically relevant research. These avenues involve an approach which is more truly "phenomenistic" than those hitherto followed, in that it would focus on the *genesis* of existing phenomena, rather than on the existing phenomena exclusively. Such an approach would perforce be interdisciplinary.

The Effects of Adult
TV Fare on Child Audiences

Introduction

ONSIDERABLE SPECULATION EXISTS, although in rather limited circles, regarding the effect upon children of prolonged exposure to what is somewhat loosely called "adult TV fare."

Concern over this matter can hardly be said to be socially prevalent, and is rarely expressed either in the popular or semi-popular journals or in the literature of communication research. It appears to be common, however, among child psychiatrists, psychoanalysts, and clinical psychologists, and among other persons who are both psychologically oriented and concerned with the developing attitudes of children. In a study of socially prevalent concerns relative to children and TV performed by the present author in 1953,[1] the topic was spontaneously cited by all of the six psychoanalysts and clinical psychologists among the respondents.

The term "children," as typically used in this context, is not narrowly limited in regard to age, and may be taken to refer somewhat indiscriminately to young people from the age of five or six through to the early teens.

Except for copious documentation of the fact that children do see many adult shows, communications research apparently offers very few studies at all pertinent to the question at hand. The topic seems to the present author, however, to be peculiarly provocative, and the pertinent allegations and conjecture, for all their lack of documentation, seem to merit at least brief discussion.

The Fact of Exposure

That children do see a considerable amount of adult fare is obvious from the discrepancy between the total time the children spend in viewing and the relatively limited time devoted by the networks and local stations to programs designed expressly for children. Bogart (1956) cites fourteen studies which sought to determine the extent of children's TV viewing by direct study of the children themselves rather than by relying upon parental reports. The times cited as averages vary (as does also the nature of the samples) from two to somewhat over three hours per weekday and range as high as ten hours for Saturday and Sunday, with the heaviest viewing being done by children between the ages of eleven and thirteen. The average station, however, devotes no such amount of time to programs designed primarily for children. While some stations do devote as much as two hours per weekday to such programs, others do no programming for children at all, and virtually none devote massive blocks of weekend time to this purpose. Practically all stations which do produce weekday programs for children, furthermore, exhibit them at approximately the same time. A considerable amount of children's viewing must necessarily, therefore, involve exposure to programs which are not designed primarily for a child audience.

This supposition is substantiated by reports and data from various sources. Network personnel interviewed by the present author in 1953, for example, reported that complaints to the effect that particular material was not suitable for children typically referred to shows intended for adults or mixed audiences; many of these programs were telecast as late as 10 P.M. Various studies of children's program preferences confirm what is obvious to casual observation, viz., that children of all ages, and the overwhelming majority of those beyond the ages of seven and eight, regularly see and like a considerable number of adult shows. Thus Witty (1952) found *I Love Lucy* to be the favorite of both elementary school children and their parents. Seagoe (1951) found three adult shows among the ten most regularly seen by Los Angeles children under the age of twelve, and four among the ten they most liked. A random sample of New Haven parents interviewed by Smythe (1955) indicated that "younger children" watched adult fare during 43.7 per cent of their viewing time, and Smythe feels that the parental report is an underestimate. Four studies cited by Bogart (1956) and performed between 1952 and 1954 indicate that Westerns, comedy and variety shows, and situation comedy rank equally with children's programs in the viewing experience and preferences of children by the time they have reached the age of eight, and that such programs reign supreme among those who are ten or older. The situation, incidentally, is apparently not peculiar to the United States. Abrams (1956) found adult fare preferred to children's shows by the large majority of 1,500 British children between the ages of eight and fifteen. Himmelweit, Oppenheim, and Vince (1958), who also studied British children, found that "from the age of 10 onwards, at least half the children watched adult programmes" in the evenings,[2] and that such programs were more often named as favorites by children than were children's programs.[3]

Finally, Friedson (1953) has shown that TV is the mass

medium which children from kindergarten through the sixth grade are most apt to use in a family situation. A rearrangement of his statistics further indicates that more than three-fourths of the TV viewing by kindergarten children and approximately half of the viewing by children from grades two through six is in fact performed in a family situation. Himmelweit, Oppenheim, and Vince (1958) likewise found that for British children "viewing is more of a family activity than listening to the radio or visiting the cinema."[4]

Frequent exposure of children to adult fare is not, of course, wholly peculiar to TV. Findings similar to those we have cited were reported, for example, by Seagoe (1951) and by Hileman (1953) in reference to radio. Churches, social critics, and parents have perennially expressed concern that the material which children encounter at the movies may be morally unfit for their tender years. But the particular concerns with which we are about to deal are expressed, to the author's best knowledge, only in reference to television.

Motives of Exposure

What motives lead children to such extensive viewing of adult TV programs is a question on which relatively few persons have speculated at considerable length. In accord with the theoretical orientation of the present volume, many of the suggested motives derive from extra-communication aspects of the children's environment. TV is seen not as a prime mover, but as a mode of satisfying needs which are otherwise engendered.

Shayon (1951) approaches the question from two paths, conjecturally assigning one set of motives to teen-agers and another set to younger children. Teen-agers, he believes, occupy a minority group status in the American culture. They are no longer accorded the privileged status of childhood and not yet granted recognition as adults. Accordingly, he believes, the frustrated "teen agers seek, in television, to satisfy a hunger for contact with the grown-up world, a desire to know, to learn, the urge to participate, a yearning for status."[5] Younger children, Shayon thinks, also yearn for contact with the adult world; in addition, their need for adventure and excitement is so frustrated by socially imposed restrictions and discipline that there is created in them an

> . . . "excessive" reservoir of aggression. . . . Such a child . . . develops a craving for violence and fantasy which drives him continually to the mass media, particularly TV. There the child finds unlimited fare but no wholesome satisfaction for an abnormal appetite.[6]

Despite the allure which he attributes to violence, Shayon seems to consider that mere contact with the adult world is the chief attraction. He states that television

> . . . is the shortest cut yet devised, the most accessible backdoor to the grown-up world. Television is never too busy to talk to our children. It never shuts them off because it has to prepare dinner. Television plays with them, shares its work with them. Television wants their attention, needs it, goes to any length to get it.[7]

Maccoby (1954) attempted to relate the extent of television viewing among kindergarten children to the degree of frustration they experienced in their relationships with their parents. As noted in Chapter VII, she succeeded in establishing such a relationship in reference to middle-class children, but came to no conclusive findings in reference to lower-class children. Some degree of frustration is of course an inevitable by-product of socialization in this culture, and it may well play a part in motivating children to watch TV. It cannot, of course, be assumed to be the only influence in that direction, nor is it known to be related to children viewing adult programs as distinct from other material.

Other writers, including Seagoe (1951), Smythe (1955), and Klapper (1954) have suggested that the common situation of family viewing is in itself enjoyed by children who may see themselves as thus participating in a grown-up activity. Klapper (1954) has also noted various other possible contributing causes. Most American children over the age of nine, for example, are not usually in bed before eight or nine in the evening in any case, and TV viewing after that hour is often adult sanctioned, not only implicitly by example, but also quite explicitly because it keeps the children "home and out of harm's way." The extent of children's evening viewing may well be additionally related to such other aspects of their social and physical environment as the degree of parental control ordinarily exercised over the child, the socio-economic status of the family, and even the layout of the house.[8]

In addition to such extra-television influences, evening programs themselves typically provide a great deal of material which is attractive to children and young adolescents—e.g., Westerns, comedy hours, and variety shows featuring popular musical numbers performed by the current favorites of adolescent society. A considerable impetus toward evening viewing is thus probably provided by program content itself.

Some of the motives here offered in explanation for children's attendance upon adult TV fare no doubt apply to other media as well. Detailed analysis of the extent to which they do is perhaps not germane to the present task of considering the effects with which TV has been specifically charged. The author suggests, however, that the total influence of the several motives, and in particular the incidence of family attendance, is probably more influential in regard to television than in regard to any other medium.

Allegations of Effect

Psychoanalysts, psychologists, and others who are concerned by the continual exposure of children to adult programs are not fearful that the content is likely to be in any way unseemly. Much of the material, in fact, is intended by the stations to attract audiences of all ages and so conforms to the rather rigid moral requirements of "family programming." The aspect of the content which concerns the psychologically oriented is its simple and wholly natural preoccupation with adults and their problems, real or humorous.

It is perhaps unnecessary to document the rather obvious fact that situation comedy, Westerns, crime drama, serious drama, and even comedy-variety shows are concerned almost exclusively with adults, and that these adults are very often in problem or conflict situations. Documentation does exist, however. Content analysis of all 86 "indigenous" TV dramas telecast by New York City stations during one week in 1953,[9] for example, revealed that 91 per cent of the characters were adults, with the remainder evenly divided between teen-agers and children.[10] Himmelweit, Oppenheim, and Vince (1958) found the phenomenon to be even more marked in England: ". . . only two children below 14 . . . [and only] five young adolescents" appeared in a random selection of 13 plays telecast by the British networks during two consecutive months in 1956.[11] The authors note also that the heroes of adult plays "are generally dissatisfied and unhappy and take life rather hard";[12] that they "are often unable to control their own lives," and are almost never "fully responsible for a satisfactory outcome";[13] and that in general the plays convey "impressions that life is difficult and that adults are unable to deal with it."[14] No content analysis presents similar data about conflicts in American television drama, but it is perhaps beyond the need of demonstration that such dramas typically deal with conflict situations.

The psychologists and psychoanalysts interviewed by the present author in 1953 all agreed that a certain amount of exposure to the adult world as portrayed by television might well have a salutory effect on children. It might serve, they felt, as a window on reality, making the child aware of conditions that do exist and which, in the course of maturation, he must learn to accept. The psychologists and analysts also pointed, however, to several dangers which they considered inherent to the situation.

The sheer quantity of exposure to the adult world of TV, they felt, might unnaturally accelerate the impact of the adult environment upon the child, leading him to a kind of "premature and superficial maturity." A nodding acquaintance with the adult world might be mistaken by the child for real knowledge and might render less urgent his quest for real understanding of people and their problems.[15] A second danger, the psychologists and analysts proposed, lay in the continual exposure of children to portrayal of adults in social and personal conflicts. Such repeated portrayals might contribute to a distorted view of adulthood on the part of the child. Some analysts held that "television could not possibly produce the pathology to begin with,"[16] although it could reinforce existing concepts. Others were inclined to believe that the television experience might serve as a prime mover, creating and building in the child the concept that adults in general are frequently in trouble, frequently deceitful, mean, and, perhaps most important, very unsure of themselves and in fact incompetent to handle many of the situations which descend upon them.

Once obtained, the psychologists pointed out, such a view of adulthood might lead a child into any number of undesirable behavior tendencies. The child might, for example, feel that both inter-personal and intra-personal conflict had been accorded a seal of social acceptance and, in presumed emulation of adults, might court such conflict. On the other hand, the child might become reluctant or afraid to become an adult and thus be beset by an apparently inevitable and endless series of major problems.

Several psychologists and psychoanalysts additionally suggested that television's continual portrayal of adults in trouble, in conflict, in error, and above all in uncertainty, might reduce the period during which children tend to regard adults—particularly their parents—as more or less omniscient.

To these thoughts the author would like to add a personal observation drawn from his 1954 study: The adults in the child's *real* world appear to be fairly frequently found wanting by children who appeal to them in situations created by the accelerated environmental impact which television produces. Such failure on the part of real adults may well affect the child as much or more than do TV portrayals of adult shortcomings.

A notable number of complaints reaching networks and studios, for example, while manifestly dealing with television program content, seem really to be expressions of displaced aggression stemming from the adults' own inability to handle environmental situations which television happened to introduce or bring to a head. One young couple, for example, wrote to a network objecting to a film which dealt with the problem of whether and how adopted children should be told they were adopted. The film apparently brought to a head the well-founded suspicions of the writers' adopted children who had never been told that they were adopted and who now demanded reassurance which their embarrassed and bewildered elders were loath to provide. In another instance, a moppet show which one day undertook to advise children on how to cross streets safely received letters of vehement protest from parents who claimed that children who had never been permitted to cross streets alone now desired to do so and that the safety advice constituted an abrogation of parental authority. Parents and teachers frequently complained, in pre-Sputnik days, that space programs were too imaginative and were "filling the kids' heads with space stuff" and foolish questions;[17] in point of fact, the astronomical data of such programs has typically been reasonably accurate, but the questions asked by the children are—or were—often simply beyond most members of the non-space-educated older generation.

The significant fact about such complaints is, of course, that the situation for which television is taken to task could and probably would have occurred sooner or later in the course of the child's daily life. The fears of the adopted children, for example, could as well have been evoked by chance conversations over-heard in a bus; the desire to cross streets alone could as easily have been stimulated by a playmate newly granted such privileges. Television, in these instances, merely served as the channel of environmental impact, but the parents, precipitated into situations for which they were manifestly unready and which they were perhaps incompetent to handle, vented their aggression on tele-vision as the conspicuous agent. If television actually does ac-celerate the impact of environment upon children, it will natu-rally stimulate questions and appeals to their elders. The inability of real world elders, particularly parents and teachers, to handle such situations may well impress children at least as strongly as do television portrayals of fictional adults in conflict and un-certainty.

The author would also like to suggest a further possibility of trouble in reference to the effect of portrayed value conflicts. More specifically, the contrast between the behavior of known and familiar adults—particularly parents—and the behavior of adults portrayed on television seems particularly likely to bewilder children in reference to questions of socially accepted attitudes and values.

Inconsistencies in the socially accepted value system, par-ticularly the inconsistencies between verbally sanctioned and actively sanctioned values,[18] may, through the agency of tele-vision, be made manifest to children more early and more fre-quently than they would have through routine social intercourse or through the possibly less extensive or more selective routine ex-posure to other media. Thus the child may see a considerable number of adult TV dramas in which the conflict between the two sets of values is portrayed and the verbally sanctioned values emerge celebrated and triumphant; but at the same time the child may observe that the real world adults, including his parents, while professing the verbally sanctioned values, actually live in accordance with quite contradictory values. The father who, like the television hero, celebrates absolute honesty, may also boast of "putting over" business deals the honesty of which is manifestly not absolute; the adult who verbally approves the space officer's statement that a good American judges people on the basis of individual merit rather than ethnic origin may, in the next hour, complain about members of a minority group taking up residence in the neighborhood.

Such value conflicts, let it be re-emphasized, would also be encountered by the child in the non-television home and the pre-television era. But it seems quite possible that the several daily hours of exposure to adult television shows may render the child more early and more keenly aware of the conflict than he would otherwise have been.

To whatever degree, if any, these speculations may be valid, TV is relieved of the role of prime mover in the alleged process of creating distorted images of adulthood in the minds of children. It becomes simply a part of a whole which includes the actual behavior of real adults in the child's primary group. The dynamics of the process would not depend upon television's producing extensive attitude effects itself, which we know to be improbable, but might involve television's serving as a reinforcing agent, which we know to be quite possible.

All of these allegations of effect are, however, purely speculative. We turn now to the findings of empirical research to determine what effects, if any, are known to be produced in children by continual exposure to adult TV programs.

Research Findings

Very little research bears directly on the questions which have been raised above.

A study by Zajonc (1954) which involves reactions to material designed for children rather than for adults is nevertheless pertinent because it deals with the reactions of children to portrayals of adults.

Zajonc (1954) exposed each of two groups of children, numbering thirty-two and forty-five, to one of two taped versions of an alleged radio broadcast in which a space ship successfully weathers a series of crises. In one version, success is due largely to the authoritative, "power-oriented" behavior of co-commander Rocky, beside whom democratic "affiliation-oriented" co-commander Buddy is a sorry failure.[19] In the other version, the relative successfulness of the two commanders is reversed. Asked whether they would prefer to be like Buddy or like Rocky, 100 per cent of those who had viewed Buddy's successes chose Buddy, while 85 per cent of those who had viewed Rocky's successes chose Rocky. The fact that 15 per cent rejected the authoritarian figure despite his successes is notable, but not as remarkable as the reasons advanced for the choice. Of all the reasons that referred to personal attributes, 84 per cent of those bearing on Buddy noted his democratic qualities, and 8 per cent, his exercise of power. Among those bearing on Rocky, only 49 per cent referred to his power orientation, which he had manifested in 98 per cent of the incidents in which he was involved; while 18 per cent cited his affiliative tendencies, which were in fact manifested in only 2 per cent of the incidents in which he was involved. In short, the culturally valued affiliative behavior was consistently valued by the audience far more highly than it was in the story and impressed the child audience out of all proportion to its treatment in the script. The culturally deprecated power-orientation was consistently undervalued. Provocative as these findings may be, it must not of course be forgotten that Rocky was very widely admired, and often specifically for his authoritarian behavior. It is clearly to be regretted that the experimental design did not provide any way of checking on the tenacity or evanescence of the immediate attitude effects produced.

The Zajonc findings suggest that (1) mass communication can have an extensive immediate effect, which may, of course, be evanescent, on the values of young people, but that (2) culturally normative values are already strong in young people and are likely to prove resistant to attack, or even to be reinforced by attack through selective perception. The 15 per cent of the children in one group who rejected Rocky despite his successes, and those who admired him for his nonexistent democratic behavior, presumably had their own strong ideas of what an admirable adult should be like.

These concepts cannot, of course, be regarded as anything more than hypotheses. The Zajonc study has not been replicated and, perhaps more importantly, it deals with reactions to a single communication. Its findings are thus not necessarily indicative of the effects upon children of repeated, long-term exposure to portrayals of adults in conflict situations.

Bailyn (1959), like Zajonc, deals with the effects upon children of media material intended for children but touches to some extent upon children's views of the adult world. She found, it will be recalled,[20] that boys who possessed certain psychological characteristics and were highly exposed to television, movies, and comic books, tended more than less exposed children to believe that the kind of events depicted occurred in the real world. They were also more likely to judge real world adults in stereotyped terms, as, for example, to agree that "people are either all good or all bad" or that "people tell lies . . . because they are naturally dishonest."[21] Such highly exposed boys were no more inclined than other children to give unrealistic answers when asked what they "would . . . most like to be when . . . grown up,"[22] but when asked whom they "would like to be changed into,"[23] they were more likely than less heavy media users to choose media characters such as Superman or media celebrated occupations such as being an FBI agent or a detective. Both this tendency and the tendency to stereotype appear to be increased by further exposure. The highly exposed *boys* were no more likely than other children to consider that they, their country, or the world were endangered by other peoples or forces, despite media emphasis on such concepts, but highly exposed *girls* did see more threat to their country or the world (not to themselves) than did less exposed girls. Bailyn's data do not, of course, indicate whether or not any of these attitudes persist as the children grow older.

In the course of their multi-faceted study of British children and British TV, Himmelweit, Oppenheim, and Vince (1958) sought to determine whether viewing affects children's ideas about various aspects of adult life. More specifically, the authors investigated the effects of television on children's anxieties about growing up; their "ideal of a grown-up";[24] their desires and expectations regarding marriage, jobs, and "get[ting] on in the world";[25] and certain of their concepts relative to social class differences and to foreigners. The findings in each of these areas will first be presented in some detail, after which the findings in all the areas will be summarized.

ONE STUDY—HIMMELWEIT, OPPENHEIM, AND VINCE

As noted in greater detail above, the "main study" pursued by Himmelweit, Oppenheim, and Vince involved the comparison of 1,854 matched viewers and non-viewers ("controls") in four British cities. A supplementary and ingenious before-and-after study, performed in a city where TV was only then being introduced, enabled the authors to identify those differences between the viewers and controls which had been observed in the "main study" but which were apparently induced by factors other than television. None of the differences cited in the discussion which follows were observed in the pre-television situation, and they may therefore be at least tentatively ascribed to the influence of television itself.

Anxieties about growing up.—Himmelweit, Oppenheim, and Vince (1958) cite the hypothesis advanced by Klapper (1954) to the effect that TV's emphasis on adults in conflict might produce in child viewers a peculiarly early awareness of the complexities of life and some degree of anxiety "about their own competence in facing the demands of adult life."[26] The British authors report that among their subjects, TV did seem

> . . . to produce an earlier intellectual awareness of the complexity and essential unfairness of life . . . fewer viewers than controls, for instance, believed the statement to be true that "good people always come out all right in the end."[27]

More detailed data are provided by the children's responses to a series of questions in which they were asked to indicate the degree to which they were worried or frightened, if at all, by "the thought" of certain events associated with growing up.[28] Among the thirteen-to-fourteen-year-olds, more viewers than controls indicated that they were worried by thoughts of leaving school, leaving home, finding a job, and going to work. The differences were much more marked for the girls than for the boys, and the girls were additionally significantly more often worried about marrying than were their controls. No such consistent differences appeared among the ten-to-eleven-year-olds; girl viewers of that age were, however, again significantly more often worried about marriage than were their controls, and boy viewers were slightly more often worried about leaving home. Responses to the fears inventory (as distinct from the worries inventory) followed a generally similar pattern, with one major exception: the thirteen-to-fourteen-year-old girl viewers were again found to be consistently more often frightened than were the controls by thoughts of growing up, *but no consistent differences appeared among the boys.* The authors' explanation that "boys of that age . . . were reluctant to admit to any fears"[29] is in fact irrelevant, since up to 43 per cent of the boys *did* admit to fears in reference to one or more of the topics. As in the case of the worries inventory, no pattern of significant differences was observed between ten-to-eleven-year-old viewers and controls.

The authors draw particular attention to the different picture presented by the two age groups. They consider this to be an illustration of their often repeated point that "there is an *optimal age of responsiveness* for each attitude or topic presented" on TV.[30]

Given material, they propose, is most likely to affect children who are at an age in which they are keenly interested in the matter at hand and who have as yet acquired little pertinent knowledge from other sources. Television is not likely, the authors believe, to affect children who are at an age when they are not concerned about the specific topic.

The social and psychological significance of these findings about anxiety is by no means clear. The authors present no evidence that the anxieties either hinder or assist the actual maturation of the children, nor are any other psychological sequalae of the anxieties from the data reported.

"The child's ideal of a grown-up."[31]—Himmelweit, Oppenheim, and Vince (1958) report briefly on their inquiry into the effect of viewing upon "the child's ideal of a grown-up." They found that

> contrary to expectation, television did not make children more interested in appearance or in fame and glamour. But it did make them (especially the adolescent boys) more interested in the things they would like to own, such as cars and houses, than in the work they would like to do.
>
> Among 13–14 year old boys, 38 per cent of the viewers mentioned material things (as compared with 27 per cent of controls). Only 30 per cent of viewers described the work they would be doing (as against 37 per cent of controls). . . . The longer the access to television, the more pronounced . . . this more materialistic outlook . . . became.[32]

The implications of these data, are, however, no clearer than the implications of the data on increased anxiety. The documented effect is, in fact, rather rare, having apparently occurred only among 11 per cent of the thirteen-to-fourteen-year-old boys (neither the thirteen-to-fourteen—nor the ten-to-eleven-year-old girls are mentioned in this connection). The significance of the few data presented are further obscured by the authors' statement in another context that "viewers were less concerned [than controls] . . . about the material deficiencies of their homes."[33]

Expectations and desires regarding marriage.—Viewers and

controls differed little, when and if they differed at all, in their expectations and desires relative to marriage and marriage partners. The same proportion of the two groups wanted to marry, and the two groups responded similarly when asked whether they agreed or disagreed with the statement, "Once people are married, they are sure to be happy."[34] The groups also agreed on the qualities which make a good spouse, except that the thirteen-to-fourteen-year-old girl viewers (and they alone) mentioned such qualities as kindness and lack of jealousy more often than did their controls, while the controls themselves more often mentioned matters pertaining to the "partnership aspect" of marriage as, for example, that a good husband is "a good provider" and that he "takes his wife out."[35]

Expectations and desires regarding jobs.—Himmelweit, Oppenheim, and Vince (1958) note, on the basis of content analyses, that

> . . . adult television plays highlight the prestige and the way of life that goes with upper-middle-class occupations. In addition, it invests certain occupations with glamour, notably entertainment, detective work, and journalism.[36]

The three authors accordingly attempted to determine

> . . . how far . . . such bias . . . affects the child's knowledge of various types of jobs, and, secondly, how far it affects his expectations and dreams about his own future career.[37]

Viewing was found to have had no effect on children's concepts of what constituted *"a very glamorous job."* Among both viewers and controls, "nearly every child mentioned fashion modeling or some job connected with the world of entertainment." TV did, however, affect viewers' ideas about what jobs were *"very well paid"*. . . . Compared with controls, viewers drew less often on their own local experience . . . and more often mentioned white-collar jobs."[38] More generally, the medium was found to "broaden . . . the child's knowledge of different occupations and to lead . . . him to a more adult [i.e., realistic] awareness of the prestige attaching to them."[39]

Television also affected, in a rather subtle and unexpected fashion, both the "job expectations and job fantasies" of the thirteen-to-fourteen-year-old age group. The children were asked to indicate both *"the job you think you will do when you leave school"* and the *"work . . . you . . . would . . . most of all wish to do . . . supposing you could be anybody, go anywhere, or do anything."*[40] Initial differences, unattributable to TV, in replies to these questions were discovered in the before-and-after study: "future viewers" (i.e., children who were not viewers in the "before" phase but later became viewers) were found to be considerably less ambitious than controls (i.e., those who never became viewers).[41] The "after" tests, together with the results of the "main survey,"[42] indicated that TV had "made the viewers more ambitious in their expected job choice and also in their dreams about jobs."[43] In reference to expected jobs, the

. . . impact of television lay more in subtly raising their level of ambition rather than in directing their job choice into specific occupations. For the job they expect to take up, children draw for ideas on their immediate environment. "Seeing men coming to our house to do the job" or "My brother is in it" were the type of answers given to the question as to how they came to hear about the job.[44]

The increase in ambition induced by television was, however, "not sufficient to offset completely the pre-existing differences between viewers and controls,"[45] nor to eliminate those differences which were apparently due to social class.

In reference to "wish jobs," television "seemed to make viewers more ambitious to take up a profession or executive job rather than manual work," and to choose a wish job "that carried more prestige than their expected job."[46] Both of these effects were more pronounced among viewers with low I.Q.'s, and were more pronounced among girls than among boys.

None of these effects occurred among the ten-to-eleven-year

age group, who were "not yet very interested in the world of work."[47] Their choices of both expected and wish jobs reflected their "socio-economic background and . . . intellectual maturity,"[48] but reflected no influence attributable to television.

These findings, like various others reported by Himmelweit, Oppenheim, and Vince (1958), open wide vistas for speculation, but, by the same token, leave the reader unsure as to the actual significance of the reported effects. The " 'boost' in enterprise" induced by TV might lead viewers to greater striving and to greater achievement and might conceivably increase their rate of upward social mobility.[49] The same boost, however, might also produce widespread frustration and maladjustment. Until more information is available on how viewers *react to their raised levels of aspiration*, the social significance of these findings cannot be meaningfully assessed.

Views on "how to get on in the world."[50]—Viewers and controls observed by Himmelweit, Oppenheim, and Vince (1958) differed in only the most minor ways in their replies to a question as to which of ten items "is the most important . . . in helping a person get on in the world."[51] Among the thirteen-to-fourteen-year-olds, the four most frequent choices in rank order for both viewers and controls were "good character," "hard work," "education," and "brains."[52] Among the ten-to-eleven-year-olds, the same four items, in different order ("education," "brains," "good character," and "hard work"), were also the most frequently chosen by both viewers and controls. These four choices account for 83 to 92 per cent of the votes of the several groups, with the remaining 8 to 17 per cent spread over six other items. Some variations between viewers and controls did occur in relation to the *relative size* of the votes accorded the four most popular items and two of the less popular items. Viewers, for example, chose "good character" less often and chose "brains" more often than did controls, but the differences between the groups were not enough to affect the rank order of the two items. Viewers in the two age groups also selected "not being afraid" more often than did the controls.[53] A sub-group of ten-to-eleven-year-old viewers with I.Q.'s of over 115 valued "education" much less and "hard work" much more than did their matched controls,[54] but this tendency was not marked among other sub-groups, and findings obtained by "five different techniques" showed no differences in what viewers and controls thought about "school, school work, their relationship to their teachers, and the importance of school marks and attendance."[55]

Concepts of "social-class differences" and foreigners.—Himmelweit, Oppenheim, and Vince found that television rendered ten-to-eleven-year-old viewers more aware of dress as a status symbol and influenced their concept of the appearance of homes in social classes *other than their own*. Neither of these differences was found among older children and in neither age group did viewers and controls differ in regard to what activities they thought were characteristic of people in different social classes. In reference to this entire area, then, television exerted only occasional and highly specific influence—only in regard to topics about which the child could not draw on real life experiences.

The three authors also inquired into the effects of television on children's "ideas about foreigners."[56] The children they investigated in this connection had been exposed to "BBC television only, where much thought is given [and specific programs devoted] to the presentation to children of the way of life of other countries."[57] The findings are thus not very pertinent to the present discussion of the effects upon children of *adult fare*, nor are they indicative of the effect of material, such as most American TV drama, which makes no attempt to be deliberately instructive. It is interesting to note, however, that child viewers of BBC were in general influenced toward the "detached, objective attitude" characteristic of BBC's treatment of the topic, and that their images of specific national, religious, and racial groups were influenced by the way such "people had been presented on television."[58] The views thus acquired by BBC child viewers were in the main neutral or complimentary. The provocative question arises, however, as to what effects are produced on children by the possibly less carefully planned treatment of foreigners by other television networks and stations, both in the United States and abroad.[59]

Summary.—In brief and non-exhaustive summary, Himmelweit, Oppenheim, and Vince found that adult television programs apparently induced some anxieties about growing up in thirteen-to-fourteen-year-old children (but not among younger children), and somewhat raised the levels of job aspiration among children of the same age. Viewing apparently had no very important effects on children's desires and expectations about marriage, on their ideas of what characteristics are important in getting on in the world, or on their concepts of social class differences. The authors also report on television's effect or lack of effect in reference to children's ideas on various other highly specific topics.

These findings, as well as the earlier cited findings of Zajonc (1954) and Bailyn (1959), comprise a set of data which are peculiarly discrete. They indicate whether and in what respects television affects children's concepts about various highly specific aspects of adult life, but the further implications of the findings are unclear. No information is as yet available as to how, if at all, these particular concepts are reflected in the broader attitudes and actual behavior of the children or the adults they inevitably become.

Himmelweit, Oppenheim, and Vince (1958) attempt, mostly on the basis of the findings cited above, to present "a general formulation of the *manner* in which television affects children['s]" values and attitudes about adult life.[60] They propose that

> Television exerts an influence only where the views are put over repeatedly, preferably in dramatic form. . . .

Television exerts an influence only where views are not already firmly fixed, or where it gives information not already obtained from other sources. . . .

There is an *optimal age of responsiveness* for each attitude or topic presented.[61]

This formulation seems to the present author to demonstrate both the level of sophistication and the substantive sparseness of our current knowledge regarding the effect of television on children's concepts of adult life. The formulation transcends the typical and rather naïve stage in which the communication is considered to be in and of itself the sole and sufficient cause of extensive attitude effects. The influence of the communication is rather seen to be mediated by various other factors, including the age and maturity of the child and his knowledge about the topic in question. Research thus indicates that there is little basis for the fear that exposure of children to adult TV shows will *in and of itself* produce any widespread pathology of the kind described earlier in this chapter. But the formulation and the specific findings also suggest that, given the right settings of the several mediating variables, television's portrayal of adults can exert a strong influence upon child viewers. To paraphrase Berelson's classic statement about persuasive communication,[62] adult television fare apparently influences *some* children to *some* extent under *some* conditions.

Research along at least three paths seems necessary before more useful conclusions can be safely drawn. In the first place, as we have already suggested, research must not rest content with noting discrete and topically specific effects; it must inquire as well into the duration of such effects and their possible reflection in broad attitudes and in concrete behavior. Secondly, the extra-communication variables which mediate the effects of television, and the results of such mediation, must be more fully identified. Finally, information is needed regarding the relative incidence of such patterns of effects. Only as information accumulates along all these lines will we become able to speak in psychologically and socially meaningful terms of the effect of adult television fare upon child audiences.

Theoretical Considerations

Relatively little is yet known about the effect of adult television shows upon children's concepts of adults and upon the process of their maturation. Such few data as are currently available appear, however, to support the generalizations advanced in the Introduction.

The influence of television appears, for example, to be mediated, as proposed in generalization 1, by extra-communication factors—including, in this case, the ages, interests, and emotional characteristics of the audience members. Children who already possess ideas about a given aspect of adult life are typically found to be uninfluenced in regard to that topic by television. Such lack of influence seems to be related to, but not identical with, the process of reinforcement described in generalization 2; the mediators do not appear, in this instance, to be rendering mass communication an agent of reinforcement, but they do seem to be acting as insulators and to be preventing conversion or other attitude effects. Where such mediators are absent or inoperative—as in the case of children without previous knowledge of the topic at hand—television is found, as proposed in generalization 3, to exert at least a temporary influence. This latter phenomenon may perhaps be regarded as a special case of mass media's creating opinion on new issues. In sum, then, the few available data support generalizations 1 and 3 and suggest the need for slightly emending generalization 2. None of the data bear upon generalizations 4 and 5.

The data are as yet too sparse for the generalizations to serve the kind of organizational function which they served in reference to findings about persuasive communication. It is interesting to note, however, that Himmelweit, Oppenheim, and Vince (1958), in attempting to organize their discrete findings, present a series of statements which are, in the main, specifications of the phenomenon we have described in generalization 1. The general formulation provided by the British authors is devoted in the main to identifying extra-communication factors, such as the age of the children, which mediate the effect of communications. The attempt to generalize has led these authors to a position very like that assumed by the present author as a result of his own attempts to organize a larger body of more or less similarly discrete findings.

The primitive theoretical framework provided by the generalizations is additionally helpful here, as it has been elsewhere, in drawing attention to gaps in our substantive data and in indicating avenues for logically relevant research. If, for example, generalization 1 is valid, and it appears to be, a considerable number of additional mediating factors await identification, and the results of their mediation await description. We may hypothesize that these factors will include the behavior of adults in the child's primary group, the readiness and ability of such adults to communicate their behavioral goals and criteria, and the nature of the child's relations with adults in general. In addition, such old familiar factors as predispositions, group orientation and group norms, and individual personality patterns seem likely to be found operative here as they have been found to be operative elsewhere.

Generalization 3 proposes that the media serve as agents of change when the mediating factors are inoperative *and* on the relatively atypical occasions when they themselves predispose the audience member toward change. The first of these phenomena is manifested by the documented ability of television to influence children's concepts of adulthood in reference to topics in which they are interested *and about which they have practically no other information.* No attention has yet been given to the postulated second type of change, which may, however, be of considerable social importance. We would predict, for example, that when some real life event causes a child to question some of his previous concepts about adults, the potential of television (or other media) for influencing his views would be, for the time being, at least, increased. Should this prove to be true, a knowledge of the dynamics of the process would obviously be extremely useful for social workers, youth leaders, teachers, and others concerned primarily or peripherally with child guidance and therapy.

Considerable additional research is obviously necessary before we can make any broad statements about the effects of adult television shows upon children's concepts of adulthood and upon their behavior as they become adults. The author proposes that what he has called the "phenomenistic approach" may be more likely to provide socially meaningful findings than is the approach which has been followed by the few pertinent studies to date. Such studies have typically begun with the fact of communication stimulus and proceeded to seek its effects; the search has typically involved the comparison of groups who were not known in advance to differ in regard to the areas of possible effect that were being investigated; the studies have thus been largely fishing expeditions, and such effects as have been observed have, as we have noted, been so discrete that they do not contribute greatly to any over-all knowledge of how television affects young viewers' concepts of adult life. A great many such discrete data must be collected and integrated before it becomes possible to see broad relationships and to discern broad attitude effects.

A more phenomenistic approach would bypass much of this search and preclude the appearance of such discrete findings. Such an approach would begin with the effect under investigation, not with the fact of communication stimulus. In its purest state it would seek first to determine what images of adulthood *are* prevalent among young children and would then inquire into how these various images were acquired. A feasible implementation of such a general approach would probably limit investigation, in any one study, to children holding particular pre-selected images of adulthood, and to the interplay of a few variables which might be reasonably presumed, in advance, to be influential in producing the views in question.

No single study nor group of studies of this sort is likely to produce a complete picture of how children come to think what they do of adult life or of how they behave as they approach adulthood. But a series of studies might well provide significant and useful information on the relative roles played by such forces as the behavior of children and adults in the child's primary groups, the values celebrated in formal pedagogy, and various other factors, including the portraits painted by mass communication.

Summary

1. Considerable speculation exists regarding the effect upon childhood of prolonged exposure to adult TV fare. The concern is prevalent among psychologists and teachers but is rarely expressed in either popular literature or in the literature of communications research.

2. A host of studies indicates that children do in fact devote much of their TV viewing to programs designed for adult audiences.

3. The motives for such viewing are matters of speculation rather than findings of objective research. Various writers variously believe that adult TV programs satisfy children's desires to know the adult world; that family viewing is itself regarded by children as a "grown-up" activity; that late evening viewing is adult-sanctioned both implicitly and explicitly; that evening programs are per se attractive to young people; and that various other factors may also play a part.

4. The concern is wholly centered on the fact that adult programs deal almost exclusively with adults, and usually with adults

in conflict situations. Some psychologists and psychiatrists feel that continued exposure to such material might unnaturally accelerate the impact of the adult environment on the child and force him into a kind of premature maturity, marked by bewilderment, distrust of adults, a superficial approach to adult problems, or even unwillingness to become an adult.

5. The present author has made further observations,

a. Real adults in the child's primary group are often found wanting by children who appeal to them in situations which happen to be produced by TV. He suggests that such inability on the part of real adults may impress the child as much or more than does the lack of assurance characteristic of adults portrayed on TV.

b. The contrast between the behavior of real adults—particularly parents—and the behavior of television-portrayed adults may bewilder children and hamper their perception of what attitudes and values are in fact socially accepted and approved.

6. Very little empirical research bears directly upon the questions here raised.

a. One study (Zajonc, 1954) suggests that media portrayals of adults may have extensive immediate effects on the values of young listeners, but that culturally normative values are already strong in young people and resist attack. The study offers no information on the duration of such effects, nor upon the effects of prolonged exposure to media depictions of adults.

b. A study by Bailyn (1959) indicates that boys who are highly exposed to certain types of violent content in pictorial mass media tend to regard the unrealistic content as realistic, to judge real world adults in stereotyped terms, and to exhibit certain other highly specific modes of thought. There is some indication that these tendencies are increased by further exposure.

c. An elaborate inquiry by Himmelweit, Oppenheim, and Vince (1958) reveals that in Britain adult television programs induced some anxieties about growing up in thirteen-to-fourteen-year-old children (but not among younger children), and slightly raised their levels of job aspiration. Viewing apparently had no important effects upon children's desires and expectations about marriage, upon their ideas of what characteristics are important in getting on in the world, or on their concepts of social class differences. The authors propose that television affects children's views of adult life only if such views are "not already firmly fixed" and only if the children are at "an optimal age of responsiveness" in reference to the specific "attitude or topic."[63]

Research cannot provide socially meaningful answers to the questions raised in this chapter until its current findings are supplemented by data on the duration of the observed attitude effects and their reflection (if any) in broader attitudes and concrete behavior; on the identity of extra-communication variables which mediate the effects of mass communication and the nature of such mediation; and, finally, on the relative incidence of such patterns of effects.

7. *Theoretical Considerations.* The data adduced in this chapter appear to support two of the five generalizations proposed in the Introduction, and to suggest minor modification of a third. None of the data bear upon the other two generalizations. The three pertinent generalizations suggest goals and avenues for future research, and indicate the advantages of pursuing a "phenomenistic" approach.

Media Attendance
and Audience Passivity

$\mathcal{T}$HE THREE PREVIOUS CHAPTERS have all been
devoted to the effects of certain specific types of media material,
specifically, depictions of crime and violence; "escapist" material;
and adult TV shows viewed by child audiences.

The present chapter differs somewhat from the previous three
in that it is devoted not to a particular type of media material, but
to a particular type of alleged effect. Specifically, we will be concerned with the allegation that attendance upon mass media, particularly upon television, is a passive occupation, and therefore
likely to produce undesirable effects upon its audiences.

The Nature and Prevalence of the Concern

Concern over this matter has been frequently voiced by social
observers interested in mass communication, by newspaper and

journal critics, by teachers, and by spokesmen of parent teacher associations and similar groups. The topic occurs also, though far more rarely, in the literature of communication research. The feared potential effects are rarely precisely defined but are rather envisaged as generic and socially nihilistic orientations toward the world. The critics typically speak of a possible or even probable widespread atrophy of creative and critical powers, a socially general lethargic compliance, and a predominantly dependent and passive pattern of behavior.

The concern antedates TV and has been at one time or another expressed in reference to virtually every mass medium, with the possible exception of books.[1] In 1948, for example, Siepman asserted that "most radio listening as now practiced is a bad habit, bad because it is a passive, uncritical, vicarious experience."[2] Seldes (1950) took an essentially similar, though more specifically gloomy view, asserting that the offerings of the media

> . . . are mass produced and we receive them in apathy. We are not required to think. We are not required to select. The thing is poured out on us, and the result is that if we let all these instruments of conditioning the mass go on, we are going to create a nation which, I think, will be half a nation of teen-agers, half a nation of robots, because the necessity of thinking becomes progressively less all the time.[3]

Deshaies (1951) *defended* films against similar accusations, asserting that mere watching required active participation, and that films elicited affective reactions, be they aggressive, erotic, or of some other sort. Those who decry the passive nature of viewing, however, would probably reply that it is precisely such "vicarious excitation" or "excitation in passivity" to which they object.

The concern over passivity apparently became much more widespread with the advent and growth of TV. As early as 1950, Levin, after reviewing the plaints of critics in some of the more intellectual journals, found cause to wonder "whether we are going to be able to adjust to our environment and survive as a creative civilization." The new medium, she felt sure, would intensify the kind of passivity "which is one symptom of a society's failure to realize its responsibility as a democracy."[4] Shayon (1951) quotes a New England grade school teacher who found that her charges

> ... have no sense of values, no feeling of wonder, no sustained interest. Their shallowness of thought and feeling is markedly apparent, and they display a lack of cooperation and inability to finish a task. Could this be the result of passively sitting and watching? Or are minds and bodies alike, too tired?[5]

The concern does not seem to have diminished appreciably as TV came of age. In 1955, for example, Demant saw the future of Britain imperiled by the passive nature of TV viewing and described the future in gloomy terms reminiscent of the earlier fears of Levin (1950). Himmelweit, Oppenheim, and Vince (1958) found that 25 per cent of a sample of British school teachers were concerned by the allegedly passive nature of TV viewing and thought it would have harmful effects upon young children.[6] Here in America, as disciplined a social researcher as Bogart asserted (1956) that both radio "listening and [TV] viewing are passive" because they require little effort, and that the effect of this was "reflected in the receptiveness with which the audience takes in the broadcast message."[7] He revived the earlier charge by Cantril and Allport (1935) to the effect that radio audiences cheerfully attend upon a "plethora of platitudes . . . [which] would be unbearable if . . . encountered . . . in print."[8]

Thus, lay critics, social observers, and occasional social scientists have been asserting for over a decade that movie viewing, radio listening, and especially TV viewing are passive occupations which may wither the critical acumen and creative abilities of the audience; but virtually none of these writers has offered any documentation in substantiation of these fears.

Psychologists and Psychoanalysts on Passivity

Psychologists and psychoanalysts interviewed by the present author in 1953 were considerably more explicit about the possible effects upon children of "excitation in passivity" and about the possible dynamics of such effects.[9] They were generally agreed that the results might be harmful, at least in some cases, but were not very likely to be so.

The psychologists and analysts pointed out that television was a source of excitation which provided only vicarious release. This could, they suggested, produce in a child such undesirable effects as a tendency to withdraw from real problems, a lack of self-knowledge, and contentment with superficiality. All such respondents agreed that in times of increased emotional disturbance, children tended to increase their television viewing and that the viewing itself was in such instances accompanied by increased masturbation or masturbation substitutes.[10]

The analysts were generally agreed, however, that seriously undesirable effects would be unlikely to befall a reasonably well adjusted child unless his television viewing were "extremely excessive," the threshold of which would vary from child to child. Within fairly reasonable limits, they agreed, "excitation in passivity" might be healthful, the vicarious experience stimulating the child to imaginative fantasy play in which he took a variety of roles. Such fantasy, according to the analysts, is a normal childhood activity, and could as well (and as innocuously) be stimulated by fairy tales or traditional children's literature as it could by television. Some analysts pointed out that the more imaginative television programs (e.g., space stories) offered the child greater projective potential for such fantasy than did those which hewed more closely to everyday reality. They suggested that such programs might, furthermore, "channelize" and structure the child's fantasy, preventing unhealthy preoccupation with himself, and possibly even effecting some transfer to the child of the psychological security with which the child invested the hero of the story.[11]

These psychologists and psychoanalysts were presumably drawing on their professional experience. But they comprise only a relatively small number of respondents, and their views, however expert, can hardly be said to be impressively documented. It is further to be noted that the interviews dealt exclusively with the effect of TV on children. Effects upon adults were not discussed.

Findings of Empirical Research

Relatively few research studies bear directly or with any depth upon the problem at hand. The paucity of empirical data is hardly surprising, since the methodological requirements of such research involve the challenging tasks of designing indices of passivity and of attempting to determine whether any causal relationship exists between passivity, as so defined, and the habits of respondents vis-à-vis mass media.

A considerable number of studies have compared TV viewers and non-viewers, both young and old, in reference to such activities as use of other media, participation in sports, visiting, pleasure driving, and various other types of behavior.[12] The studies vary widely in focus, in the nature of the sample employed, and in methodological validity. A large proportion do not seriously attempt to answer the major question of whether observed differences are the product of different TV habits, or whether the different TV habits are products of the observed and very possibly pre-existing differences in behavior and general orientation.

Very few of these studies are explicitly concerned with passivity or the lack of it, and the activities on which they focus are too grossly described to permit their being accurately classified as passive or active. The weight of evidence indicates, for example, that TV owners go visiting less and read less than do non-owners, and possibly less than they themselves did before they became TV owners. But such differences or changes cannot validly be regarded as manifesting increased passivity without further information on the specific nature of such people's behavior while visiting, the kind of material they read, and the kind of psychological experiences they undergo while reading it. The finding that TV owners attend spectator sports less than do non-owners can, again, hardly be classified as an indication of increased passivity unless passivity is somehow so defined as to exclude viewing a ball game in a ball park but to include viewing it on TV. Many of the same studies, it must also be noted, reveal no differences between owners and non-owners in various presumably active pursuits, such as pleasure driving and going to parties. In short, these studies can hardly be regarded as providing any valid evidence either to confirm or to deny the allegation that television viewing promotes a generally more passive orientation among its audience.

Two studies, viz., Hamilton and Lawless (1956) and Belson (1957), present findings which the authors regard as evidence that television induces a passive orientation—or at least decreases the active orientation—of adult viewers. The present author considers the interpretation questionable in both instances.

Hamilton and Lawless (1956) compared the daily activities of 73 television-owning families, randomly selected as representative in Wichita, Kansas, with 75 non-television-owning families residing in the same blocks. The "study was conducted after television broadcasting had been in the community approximately six months" and the "median age of the television sets was six months."[13] The authors report, among other findings, that members of TV families engaged less in creative hobbies involving manipulating the environment than did members of non-TV families, although more members of the TV group engaged in non-creative hobbies. No differences could be discovered between the two groups in regard to participation in games, picnics, or pleasure driving. There were indications that children in television homes performed more household chores than did children in non-television homes, but the difference was not statistically significant. Television owners were found to prefer programs which "easily enabled identification" (e.g., drama, comedy, and movies, as compared with audience participation and sports shows); whereas non-owners preferred "aesthetic" and "educational" programs.[14] Hamilton and Lawless suggest that this difference in program preference "may be interpreted to mean a lessening of cognitive-conquest of the world on the part of television families."[15] The present author questions this interpretation on two grounds. In the first place, there is no indication that Hamilton and Lawless made any attempt to determine whether the differences between television and non-television families antedated the purchase of the television sets. In the second place, the difference in program tastes may be variously interpreted. It may, for example, reflect the experienced viewers' knowledge that presumably "aesthetic" and "educational" offerings are frequently disappointing. To regard such differences in program preference as indicating "a lessening of cognitive-conquest of the world" seems to the present author a conjecture which goes considerably beyond the data. Such conjecturing is, of course, not only permissible, but also desirable, but it remains only conjecture.

An extremely elaborate study performed in England by Belson (1957) inquired into the effects of television upon the interests, activities, and initiative of adult viewers over a five-year period. Usable data were obtained from 440 television viewers and 342 non-viewers randomly selected within Greater London. Ingenious and complex procedures were employed to note differences in the degree and range of interests and activities among non-viewers and among viewers of one, two, three, four, and five years of viewing experience. Additional complex procedures were employed to distinguish those observed differences between the various groups which might have been pre-existing, or which might have been due to extraneous forces, from those differences which might more confidently be regarded as the results of television viewing over periods of time ranging from one to five years.[16]

Belson finds that there are marked reductions in the over-all range and intensity of viewers' interests and in the degree of their initiative activities by the end of the second year of TV ownership, but that a recovery then sets in which leaves only trivial and statistically insignificant differences visible at the end of the fifth year. This general pattern, however, does not necessarily apply to specific individual interests or activities, whose several fates are almost infinitely variable. Thus, while reading, theatre going, and "strolling" suffer at least initial and in some cases lasting declines, a wide range of activities including "attendance at clubs or associations or institutes," "going to see horse racing or horse jumping," and "gardening,"[17] either suffer no significant final loss or are increased.

Belson's general conclusions are to the effect that TV does reduce interests, activities, and initiative among its audiences. The present author agrees that some effects of this sort do seem to occur temporarily, but he points out that significant differences are not lasting. He also fails to see why the activities which are reduced, such as theatre going or "strolling," are any more active or "initiative" than those which are not reduced or which are increased, such as going to horse races or gardening.

In short, neither the findings of Hamilton and Lawless (1956) nor those of Belson (1957) seem to the present author to indicate that TV viewing induces a passive orientation among its adult audiences.

Prior to 1958, no study known to the author had reported findings which bore directly upon the question of whether TV viewing influenced *children* toward passivity. A few earlier studies did occasionally provide some data which might be regarded as relevant to the question, but such data were typically isolated, in some instances crude, and subject to various interpretations. Stewart (1952), for example, reported that 90 per cent of the parents in a sample of Atlanta TV households recalled that their children had imitated someone or something (e.g., puppets) which they had seen on TV, but substantially fewer parents recalled their children imitating anything they had encountered on the radio, in comic books, or in real life. Battin (1951), in an unpublished study cited by Bogart (1956), reported that approximately one-third of a group of children interviewed in Ann Arbor claimed that TV had stimulated new hobbies and others claimed to have learned about such active pursuits as "making things" and cooking; a few children, however, claimed that TV had reduced their pursuits of hobbies.[18] Various librarians have reported that television stimulated children to increased reading in astronomy, handicrafts, and other fields with which media programs had specifically dealt.

These discrete data and subjective reports do of course suggest that television viewing may stimulate some children to some specific active pursuits. The data can hardly be regarded, however, as indicative of any broad effect, nor can they be said to refute the allegation that viewing may, on the whole, influence children toward passivity.

In the course of her study of pictorial mass media and American elementary school children, Bailyn (1959) sought to determine whether heavy users of such material were more passively oriented than were light users. She found no meaningful difference between the groups in relation to preferred activities or in relation to whether they preferred the active or passive role in various social situations. (Boys who were heavy users of pictorial media did tend more than others to prefer using those media to reading books or playing indoor games, but Bailyn acutely observes that this finding is tautological since the group in question includes only heavy media users.) Bailyn also found that heavy users—particularly boys with many problems—were less apt than light users to aspire to an occupation of higher social status than that pursued by their fathers. She regards such an attitude as an index of passivity. It must be noted, however, that the index relates to a very highly specialized and rather unusual concept of passivity, and that, furthermore, the attitude in question appears to be a correlate rather than an effect of high exposure.

Himmelweit, Oppenheim, and Vince (1958) attacked the passivity question directly, explicitly, and elaborately, in the course of their extensive research on British children and British television. As has been previously noted, their observations were based upon a sample of 1,854 viewers and matched controls, supplemented by two other matched groups, totaling 370 children, who were observed both before and after the introduction of television into the area in which they lived.

The three British authors analyzed teachers' statements to the effect that television rendered children passive and found that five different, if related, types of behavior were involved in the expressed fears. Following the reporting technique of the three authors, we shall here cite the five alleged effects and briefly summarize the findings as to whether or not each of the effects actually occurs.

(1) *"Viewing itself is a passive mental activity—the child . . . absorbs the content of television like a sponge."*[19] The authors feel that "this assertion can be readily dismissed in the light of our findings about the effects of television on values and outlook."[20] As we have noted in the preceding chapter, such effects were found to be extremely limited and did not involve unquestioned acceptance of the values celebrated on television. The British authors further contend that

> There is no evidence whatever that viewing is of necessity a mentally passive affair. It is no more passive than watching a play in the theatre; it may be no more passive than reading a light book.[21]

(2) *"Viewing may lead the child to prefer an edited version of life to life itself . . . he acquires a taste for seeing things second-hand rather than making the effort to see (or do) the real thing for himself."*[22] Viewers (not controls) were given a list of twenty-seven events, places, and personalities and asked to indicate, for each of the twenty-seven, whether they would prefer to see it (or

them) "in real life, or on TV."[23] The items were grouped into six topical classes.[24] In reference to five out of the six classes "some 80 per cent chose to see . . . more than half the items" in the class "for themselves," rather than on TV. "Only for plays, ballet, and concerts did the figures drop to 60 per cent."[25] These findings are the more noteworthy considering the fact that in reference to all twenty-seven items TV offered certain definite advantages, such as a close-up view of events which could ordinarily not be seen at such close range. The authors feel that this "evidence . . . suggests that fears on this score are unnecessary."[26]

(3) *"Viewing leads to 'spectatorism' and loss of initiative . . . when television is not available, the child will turn to other forms of spectator entertainment—the radio or the cinema—rather than engage in active play."*[27] Viewers did not differ significantly from controls in their responses to a series of questions on what they would like to do in free time and whether they would prefer to participate in certain activities or assume a spectator role. In all sub-groups of children, furthermore, and in reference to all activities but one,[28] the majority chose active participation, and in no sub-group was use of the media preferred to outdoor play. Viewer and control groups were rated similarly by teachers on a scale of initiative. The authors additionally note that

> where time has to be found for viewing, it is the other mass media, especially radio and the cinema, which suffer, and not playing with friends or taking part in some sport. Club attendance was hardly affected—with the possible exception of the cinema club [where children see movies].[29]

The authors suggest that the loss of viewers' interest in cinema clubs may indicate that children's "thirst for spectator entertainment is not insatiable."[30]

(4) *"Television leads to a jaded palate. The child is being bombarded by a great diversity of stimuli; one or the other may interest him, but he will not translate it into action because im-*

mediately afterwards something else is offered which diverts his attention."[31] Himmelweit, Oppenheim, and Vince (1958) sought information on this topic in the responses of the children to three questionnaires: the "preference for television versus real life" device described in relation to "spectatorism";[32] a series of questions about the kinds of books and films the children preferred; and "an inventory listing eighty different types of interests,"[33] which seems to be nowhere further described. On the basis of these data, the three authors conclude that television does *not* "lead . . . to a jaded palate," and that

> . . . if anything, the reverse is true: viewers were more curious, more ready to interest themselves in a wide diversity of things—a difference which did not exist between future viewers and controls in Norwich [i.e., in the 'before' phase of the supplementary before-and-after study]. The livelier interest of viewers was shown in their responses to [all] three different questionnaires.[34]

The researchers found no evidence, however, that television very often *inspired* children actively to pursue new interests, other than reading in the suggested areas. A few children were said by their parents to have been led to new hobbies by television, but the effect on the group as a whole was minimal. A series of specific inquiries revealed that viewers, as compared with controls, did not "go in more for hobbies, making things, entering for competitions, or visiting interesting places."[35] In brief, television appeared neither to decrease or increase the likelihood that children would take up new pursuits.

(5) *"Viewing dulls the imagination. It provides the child with ready-made fantasy material so that he makes less use of his creative imaginative abilities."*[36] The authors had the children rated by their teachers as "unusually imaginative, moderately imaginative, or unimaginative. . . . Once again no differences were found between viewers and controls."[37]

In sum, Himmelweit, Oppenheim, and Vince found "no evidence that viewing makes children passive"[38] in any of the five senses of the word suggested by teachers' statements about passivity. They found some evidence that viewing actually increased the diversity of children's interests, but no evidence that it stimulated them to engage in a greater range of hobbies or active pursuits than did non-viewers.

The findings of the three British authors cannot, of course, be casually generalized to American children. Replication of the research is obviously desirable. Pending its accomplishment, however, the findings of the British study strongly *suggest* that Americans are unduly fearful of television influencing children toward passivity.

Theoretical Considerations

If the generalizations proposed in the introductory chapter are at all valid, and if findings regarding the role of mass communication in other areas are at all generalizable, then it might be hypothesized that TV viewing would neither create passivity among those hitherto active nor stimulate great activity among those hitherto essentially passive. The limited amount of empirical research which bears upon this problem tends to support this hypothesis.

The generalizations also suggest the hypothesis that viewers make their selections from TV's vast offerings and react to these selections in ways which help them to exercise their personal and otherwise-engendered passive or active orientations. Riley and Riley (1951) have shown that the same media material is used by socially oriented children as a source of ideas for group games, and by more isolated children as a stimulant to eerie and individualistic fantasy.[39] The present author suggests that television probably serves, in a similar manner, to stimulate the creative hobbyist and to supply the passive consumer. But these are suggestions which empirical research has as yet neither confirmed nor denied. The few studies reported to date all in one way or another compare groups of viewers and groups of non-viewers; none attempt to distinguish between viewers who are essentially passively oriented and those who are more actively oriented.

The most fruitful line for further inquiry into this matter may well lie through psychoanalytic and case history techniques, rather than through controlled experiments or surveys. Such an approach would be "phenomenistic," and would obviate the necessity of attempting to define "passivity" in terms sufficiently precise to permit the construction of indices and the classification or scaling, according to such indices, of vast ranges of human behavior.

Summary

1. Lay critics, social observers, and occasional social scientists have been asserting for over a decade that movie viewing, radio listening, and especially TV viewing are passive occupations which may wither the critical acumen and creative abilities of the audience. The more alarmistic have foreseen a populace reduced to lethargic acquiescence and a nation in which active democracy has atrophied. Virtually none of these writers has offered any documentation in substantiation of these fears.

2. A number of psychologists and psychoanalysts, interviewed in regard to this topic, agreed that "excitation in passivity" *could* be harmful to children, but is unlikely to be so. They felt that the viewing situation was more likely to afford children healthful opportunity for vicarious role-playing. These experts offered no documentation for their beliefs, and did not offer opinions regarding the effect of viewing on adults' orientations.

3. Relatively little empirical research bears directly on the question at hand.

   a. Numerous studies have compared the behavior of TV viewers and non-viewers, or have compared the behavior of viewers with their own behavior before they became viewers. These studies vary widely in methodological validity, and the behavior with which they deal is too grossly described (e.g., "visiting") for observed differences to be validly regarded as manifesting increased or decreased passivity.

b. Two studies (Hamilton and Lawless, 1958, and Belson, 1957) respectively propose that television viewers experience a "lessening of cognitive conquest of the world"[40] and that television reduces viewers' interests, activities, and initiative. The present author considers that neither of these conclusions is justified by the data which the authors report.

Bailyn (1959) found that children who were highly exposed to pictorial mass media were less likely than light users to aspire to an occupational status higher than that of their fathers. She regards such an attitude as an index of passivity. Bailyn found no meaningful differences between the two groups in relation to preferred activities.

c. An elaborate study of British children and British television (Himmelweit, Oppenheim, and Vince, 1958) indicates that viewing does not produce any of five types of effects which British teachers regard as kinds of passivity.

The present author considers that empirical research to date indicates that television viewing does not induce passivity. Implicit in this view, however, is the present author's rejection of the conclusions of Hamilton and Lawless and of Belson, as noted in paragraph 3b above. If the conclusions of these authors are taken at face value, empirical research to date must be regarded as having provided contradictory answers to the question at hand.

4. *Theoretical Considerations.* The generalizations advanced in the introductory chapter of this book are supported by the weight of existing data, as those data are interpreted by the present author. The generalizations also suggest that further research might fruitfully take a phenomenistic and psychoanalytic approach, and that such an approach would find that all media, including television, are selectively utilized by passive and active persons to reinforce and exercise their existing and otherwise-engendered orientations.

Concluding Note

$\mathcal{I}$T WOULD SEEM DESIRABLE to conclude this volume with an evaluative note on the five generalizations which were proposed in the introduction. What follows is, like the various notes on the subject sprinkled throughout the text, a purely subjective and personal offering. As in all previous such contexts, the author here submits rather than asserts.

On the positive side, the generalizations appear to have served three major functions.

First, as the various notes on "theoretical considerations" have been at some pains to demonstrate, the generalizations have permitted us in some measure to organize, or to "account for," a considerable number of communications research findings which have previously seemed discrete and anomalous. The author submits, tentatively, that the set of generalizations has in fact made possible organization of several different orders:

It has enabled us to relate the *processes* of effect and the *directions* of effect. Put another way, it has provided us with a concept of the process of effect in which both reinforcement and change are seen as related and understandable outcomes of the same general dynamics. This concept enabled us to account for the relative incidence of reinforcement and change in reference to attitudes on specific issues, and provided an orientation which was found to be applicable in one or another degree to reinforcement and change in regard to a wide variety of audience orientations.

It has enabled us to view such diverse phenomena as audience predispositions, group membership and group norms, opinion leadership, personality patterns, and the nature of the media in this society, as serving similar functions in the process of effect—as being, so to speak, all of a certain order, and distinct from such other factors as the characteristics of media content.

It has enabled us to view other seemingly unrelated phenomena, such as the efficacy of the media in creating opinions on new issues and the effect of role-playing, as manifestations of the same general process—as specific combinations of known variables, the outcomes of which were predictable.

So much for the organizational capabilities of the generalizatons. But note that this organization of existing data, even within so sketchy a framework as these generalizations provide, permitted us to see gaps—to discover, for example, that certain presumed outcomes have to date been neither documented nor shown not to occur. This points to a second contribution: the generalizations seem capable of indicating avenues of needed research which are logically related to existing knowledge. But virtually *any* set of generalizations, or any theoretical framework, will point to gaps and needed research. The fact that these generalizations do so thus in no way gainsays the fact that future thought and research must inevitably change the generalizations themselves. As presently formulated, they constitute only a single tentative step forward, and it may reasonably be hoped that their refinement or emendation would enlarge rather than reduce the area of their applicability.

Finally, it is in the extent of the applicability of the generalizations, coupled with their present primitive nature, that the author finds particular basis for hope. Sketchy and imperfect as they are, these propositions regarding the process and direction of effect seem applicable to the effects of persuasive communications and to the effects of various kinds of non-persuasive media content upon a wide range of audience orientations and behavior patterns. Furthermore, the mediating variables to which the generalizations point—variables such as predispositions, group membership, personality patterns, and the like—seem to play essentially similar roles in all these various kinds of effects. Even if the generalizations turn out to be wholly in error, they seem nevertheless sufficiently useful and sufficiently applicable to justify the faith that *some* generalizations can in due time be made. And the author has indicated, from the outset, that he is "less concerned with insuring the viability of these generalizations than he is with indicating that the time for generalization is at hand."

For certainly these particular generalizations do not usher in the millennium. They are imperfect and underdeveloped, they are inadequate in scope, and in some senses they are dangerous.

They do not, for example, cover the residuum of direct effects, such as the creation of moods, except to note that such effects exist. They recognize, but in no way illuminate, the dynamism of the variety of effects stemming from such contextual and presentational variables as order, timing, camera angles, and the like. They are less easy to apply, and are conceivably inapplicable, to certain other broad areas of effect, such as the effect of the media upon each other, upon patterns of daily life, and upon cultural values as a whole. To be sure, we have spoken of cultural values as a mediating factor which in part determines media content, but certainly some sort of circular relationship must exist, and media content must in turn affect cultural values.

Such concepts suggest what is perhaps the greatest danger inherent both in these generalizations and in the approach to communications research from which they derive. And that danger, which has been mentioned in the Introduction but is well worth repeating, is the tendency to go overboard in blindly minimizing the effects and potentialities of mass communications. In reaping the fruits of the discovery that mass media function amid a nexus of other influences, we must not forget that the influences nevertheless differ. Mass media of communication possess various characteristics and capabilities distinct from those of peer groups or opinion leaders. They are, after all, media of *mass* communication, which daily address tremendous cross-sections of the population with a single voice. It is neither sociologically unimportant nor insignificant that the media have rendered it possible, as Wiebe (1952) has put it, for Americans from all social strata to laugh at the same joke, nor is it insignificant that total strangers, upon first meeting, may share valid social expectations that small talk about Lucy and Desi, or about Betty Furness, will be mutually comprehensible. We must not lose sight of the peculiar characteristics of the media nor of the likelihood that of this peculiar character there may be engendered peculiar effects.

We must remember also that under conditions and in situations other than those described in this volume, the media of mass communication may well have effects which are quite different and possibly more dramatic or extensive than those which have here been documented.

For example, the research here cited which bears upon mass communication as an instrument of persuasion has typically dealt with non-crucial issues and has been pursued either in laboratories or in naturalistic situations within a relatively stable society. Little attention has here been given to the potentialities of persuasive mass communication at times of massive political upheaval or in situations of actual or imminent social unrest. Given the rumblings of serious social malcontent—or, in terms of our current orientation, given individuals with predispositions toward change, unstructured as the envisaged change may be—mass communication would appear to be capable of molding or "canalizing" the predispositions into specific channels and so producing an active revolutionary movement. Some such process, in miniature, appears to have occurred in the previously cited cases of Nazi and North Korean soldiers who, upon the dissolution of their primary groups, became susceptible to Allied propaganda. A similar process of greater social width may well have occurred in under-developed countries in which the Communist party has recently become a major political force. Mass communication in such areas has of course been deliberately and carefully abetted by personal influence and by the formation and manipulation of reinforcing primary and secondary groups. Although it cannot therefore be said to have been a sufficient cause of the observed social changes, it may well have been an extremely important or even a crucial cause. Its effects may have been largely restricted to the activation and focusing of amorphous unrest, but these effects appear to have had consequences far beyond those normally associated with the reinforcement of pre-existing and specific attitudes. The fear that a similar activation process may occur, or that the media might actually create new attitudes, presumably lies behind the totalitarian practice of denying media access to voices of the political opposition.[1]

Even within a relatively stable social situation, the media of mass communication may well exercise extensive social effects upon the masses by the indirect road of affecting the elite. Particular vehicles of mass communication (e.g., *The New York Times*) and other vehicles directed toward a more specialized audience (e.g., *The Wall Street Journal* or *U.S. News and World Report*) may reasonably be supposed to affect the decisions and behavior of policy-making elites. Individual business and political leaders may or may not be "opinion leaders" in the sense in which the term is used in communications research—i.e., they may or may not critically influence a handful of their peers. But their decisions and their consequent behavior in themselves affect society at large, and the mere fact of their taking a particular stand frequently serves to make that stand and the issue to which it pertains a topic of media reporting and debate, and a topic in regard to which personal influence, in the more restricted sense of the term, is exercised. The media may, in short, stimulate the elite to actions which affect the masses and which incidentally restimulate and so affect both the media and channels of inter-personal influence.

It has also been suggested that the classic studies of how voters make up their minds—e.g., Lazarsfeld, Berelson, and Gaudet (1948) and Berelson, Lazarsfeld, and McPhee (1954)—provide an incomplete picture of the total effects of mass communication because they concentrate only on effects which occur *during* the campaign itself. Lang and Lang (1959), for example, point out that although most of the voters observed in such studies apparently kept to a decision made before the campaign began, shifts in voting behavior sufficient to produce changes of administration do occur. They suggest that such changes take place slowly *between* the campaigns, as new issues arise and as the images of the parties change or fail to change. Mass communication, they propose, makes these issues salient and builds the party images, and may thus exercise a much more extensive effect than is revealed in the classic voting studies. The Langs call for research designed to investigate the possibility of such effects and of various other types of effect which they believe mass communication may exercise upon political opinion.

Some elections, furthermore, may be more "critical" than others. Key (1955), for example, notes that there is "a category of elections," including those of 1896 and 1928, in which

. . . voters are, at least from impressionistic evidence, unusually deeply concerned, in which the extent of electoral involvement is rel-atively quite high, and in which the decisive results of the voting reveal a sharp alteration of the pre-existing cleavage within the electorate. Moreover, and perhaps this is the truly differentiating characteristic of this sort of election, the realignment made manifest in the voting in such elections seems to persist for several succeeding elections.[2]

The elections on which the classic voting studies focus are not "critical" by these criteria, but are rather occasions on which previously manifested alignments held more or less stable. What role mass communication may play in determining voter's decisions before a "critical" election is not yet known.

Mass media may also have extensive but as yet undocumented effects of various non-political sorts. We have already alluded, for example, to the probable but unmapped interplay between the mass media and cultural values. To look more closely into one aspect of this matter, one might postulate that the media play a particularly important role in the socialization and acculturation of children. Such studies of children as are cited in this volume have dealt with children aged five and older, and have focused on highly specific attitudes or patterns of behavior. But to what degree do the media structure, even for younger children, the society and the culture which they are entering? The influence of the media in these respects is no doubt modified by the influence of the family, of the school, and of peer groups; but the question of ultimate media effect is complicated, perhaps beyond the possibility of simplification, by the fact that the persons comprising these very sources of extra-media influence are themselves exposed to and affected by the media. The role and the effects of the media in the socialization of the child can perhaps no longer be accurately assessed, but some concept of its possible scope may be obtained by performing the mental experiment of imagining the process of socialization occurring in a society in which mass media did not exist. Our knowledge of primitive cultures and of pre-media years suggests that the present social system and the present culture are at least in part a product of the existence of mass communication, and may be dependent upon such communication for their continued existence.

One may also speculate on the possibility that some of the

functions served by mass communication may, perhaps indirectly and perhaps only after a long period, have certain effects both upon the audience as individuals and upon integral elements of the social structure. We have noted, for example, that certain light media material, such as comic strips, serves certain audience members by providing a common ground for social discourse. It is interesting to speculate on what alternative systems of serving the same function may be thereby replaced, may be reduced in importance, or may simply fail to develop for lack of being needed. If no comic strips or other mass media material existed to serve the conversational needs of the adult males observed by Bogart (1955), might they and others like them perhaps be more actively interested in each other's real life goals and problems? Do mass media, by providing an easily available and common ground for chit-chat, perhaps reduce or retard the development of interest in one's fellow men? And to what degree, if any, has the serving of such functions by mass media affected the functions previously served by such institutions as the neighborhood bar and barber shop?

Other situations and conditions which are not covered in this volume in which mass communication may have extensive effects may be readily imagined. For many of these situations and conditions, the primitive theoretical framework we have sketched may prove to be an inadequate model. It is to be hoped that its shortcomings may serve to stimulate the development of other models, at once refined and more widely applicable.[3]

The phenomenistic approach, which our generalizations suggest, also has its dangers and limitations. As we have noted, the identification of conditions under which mass communication has different effects is only a step in the direction of answering the basic questions about the incidence of such effects. If the influence of mass communication is to be described in socially meaningful terms, research must also inquire into the relative prevalence of the conditions under which the several effects occur.

The need of recognizing such limitations and of taking precautions against such dangers does not seem to the author, however, to compromise the usefulness of either the generalizations or the phenomenistic approach. The most fruitful path for communications research appears to him to be neither the path of abstract theorizing nor the path, which so many researchers have deserted, of seeking simple and direct effects of which mass communication is the sole and sufficient cause. The author sees far greater hope in the new approach which begins with the existing phenomenon—an observed change of opinion, for example—and which attempts to assess the roles of the several influences which produced it. He sees similar hope in the pursuit of logically related controlled experiments in which the multifarious extra-media factors being investigated are built into the research design. These are the paths which seem to him to have brought us to the point of tentative generalization and which seem likely to lead further toward the still distant goal of empirically-documented theory.

Bibliography

NOTE: Items are listed alphabetically by author. Series of works by the same author(s) *are listed chronologically by publication dates, not alphabetically by title.* Agencies are treated as authors in cases where they are so treated on the title pages of the documents cited. For articles contained in books, the publication date of the article pertains to the book as well, unless a second date is cited.

Abrams, Mark (1956). "Child Audiences for TV in Great Britain," *Journalism Quarterly*, XXXIII, 35–41.

Albert, R. S. (1957). "The Role of Mass Media and the Effect of Aggressive Film Content upon Children's Aggressive Responses and Identification Choices," *Genetic Psychology Monographs*, LV, 221–85.

Albig, William (1939). *Public Opinion.* New York: McGraw-Hill Book Company.

Allport, Gordon and Postman, Leo J. (1945). "The Basic Psychology of Rumor," *Transactions of the New York Academy of Sciences*, VIII, Series II, 61–81.

Annis, A. D. and Meier, N. C. (1934). "The Induction of Opinion through Suggestions by Means of Planted Content," *Journal of Social Psychology*, V, 65–81.

Arnheim, Rudolf (1944). "The World of the Daytime Serial," in Lazarsfeld, Paul F. and Stanton, Frank N., eds., *Radio Research, 1942–1943*. New York: Duell, Sloan and Pearce.

Asch, S. E. (1952). *Social Psychology*. New York: Prentice-Hall, Inc.

Asheim, Lester (1951). "Report on the Conference on Reading Development," *Public Opinion Quarterly*, XV, 305–21.

—— (1952). "From Book to Film: Mass Appeal," *Quarterly of Film, Radio and Television*, VI, 258–73.

Asher, R. and Sargent, S. S. (1941). "Shifts in Attitude Caused by Cartoon Caricatures," *Journal of General Psychology*, XXIV, 451–55.

Bailyn, Lotte (1959). "Mass Media and Children: A Study of Exposure Habits and Cognitive Effects," *Psychological Monographs*, LXXI, 1–48.

Bartlett, F. C. (1940). *Political Propaganda*. Cambridge: Cambridge University Press.

Bateman, Richard M. and Remmers, H. H. (1941). "A Study of the Shifting Attitude of High School Students When Subjected to Favorable and Unfavorable Propaganda," *Journal of Social Psychology*, XIII, 395–406.

Battin, T. C. (1951). *The Use of the Diary Method Involving the Questionnaire-Interview Technique to Determine the Impact of Television on School Children in Regard to Viewing Habits and Formal and Informal Education*. Unpublished Ph.D. dissertation, University of Michigan.

Bauer, Raymond A. (1958). "The Communicator and the Audience," *Journal of Conflict Resolution*, II, 67–77.

Belson, William Albert (1956). "A Technique for Studying the Effects of a Television Broadcast," *Journal of Applied Statistics*, V, 195–202.

—— (1957). *A Study of the Effects of Television upon the Interests and the Initiative of Adult Viewers in Greater London*. Unpublished Ph.D. dissertation, Birkbeck College, University of London.

—— (1958). "Measuring the Effects of Television: A Description of Method," *Public Opinion Quarterly*, XXII, 11–18.

Berelson, Bernard (1941). *Content, Emphasis, Recognition, and Agreement: An Analysis of the Role of Communication in Determining Public Opinion*. Unpublished Ph.D. dissertation, University of Chicago.

—— (1942). "The Effects of Print upon Public Opinion," in Waples, Douglas, ed., *Print, Radio, and Film in a Democracy*. Chicago: University of Chicago Press.

—— (1948). "Communications and Public Opinion," in Schramm,

Wilbur, *Communications in Modern Society*. Urbana, Ill.: University of Illinois Press.

———, Paul F. Lazarsfeld and McPhee, William N. (1954). *Voting: A Study of Opinion Formation in a Presidential Campaign*. Chicago: University of Chicago Press.

——— and Salter, Patricia J. (1947). "Majority and Minority Americans: An Analysis of Magazine Fiction," *Public Opinion Quarterly*, X, 168–90.

Berlo, David K. and Kumata, Hideya (1956). "The Investigator: The Impact of a Satirical Radio Drama," *Journalism Quarterly*, XXXIII, 287–98.

Bettelheim, Bruno and Janowitz, Morris (1950). "Reactions to Fascist Propaganda: A Pilot Study," *Public Opinion Quarterly*, XIV, 53–60.

Bloch, Herbert A. and Flynn, Frank T. (1956). *Delinquency: The Juvenile Offender in America Today*. New York: Random House.

Blumer, Herbert (1933). *Movies and Conduct*. New York: The Macmillan Company.

——— and Hauser, Philip (1933). *Movies, Delinquency, and Crime*. New York: The Macmillan Company.

Bogardus, Emory S. (1952). "Television and the Political Conventions," *Sociology and Social Research*, XXXVII, 115–21.

Bogart, Leo (1955). "Adult Talk about Newspaper Comics," *American Journal of Sociology*, LXI, 26–30.

——— (1956): *The Age of Television*. New York: Frederick Ungar Publishing Company.

Brombaugh, Florence N. (1950). "Books and TV," *Publisher's Weekly*, CLVII, 2638–44.

Bruel, Oluf (1953). "Psychic Trauma through the Cinema," *International Journal of Sexology*, VII, 61–63.

Bruner, Jerome S. and Goodman, Cecile C. (1947). "Value and Need as Organizing Factors in Perception," *Journal of Abnormal and Social Psychology*, XLII, 33–44.

Bryson, Lyman, ed. (1948). *The Communication of Ideas*. New York: Harper and Brothers.

Bureau of Applied Social Research (1944). *Naples Is A Battlefield*. New York: Bureau of Applied Social Research, Columbia University.

——— (1953). *A Controlled Study of the Impact of Anti-Discrimination Car Cards*. New York: Bureau of Applied Social Research, Columbia University, and Department of Research and Evaluation, Anti-Defamation League of B'nai B'rith.

——— (1954). *The Effects of Oil Progress Week, 1952: A Summary of a Supplemental Report*. New York: Bureau of Applied Social Research, Columbia University.

Cannell, Charles F. and MacDonald, James C. (1956). "The Impact of

Health News on Attitudes and Behavior," *Journalism Quarterly*, XXXIII, 315–23.

Cantril, Hadley and Allport, Gordon W. (1935). *The Psychology of Radio.* New York: Harper and Brothers.

Carpenter, C. Ray and Greenhill, Lester P. (1955). *An Investigation of Closed Circuit Television for Teaching University Courses.* Instructional Television Research Project No. One. University Park, Pennsylvania: Pennsylvania State University.

Cartwright, Dorwin (1949). "Some Principles of Mass Persuasion: Selected Findings of Research on the Sale of United States War Bonds," *Human Relations*, II, 253–67.

Charters, W. W. (1933). *Motion Pictures and Youth.* New York: The Macmillan Company.

Chen, W. K. (1933). "Influence of Oral Propaganda Material on Student Attitudes," *Archives of Psychology*, No. 150.

Clinard, Marshal B. (1949). "Secondary Community Influence and Juvenile Delinquency," *Annals of the American Academy of Political and Social Science*, CCLXI, 42–54.

Coffin, Thomas E. (1948). "Television's Effects on Leisure Time Activities," *Journal of Applied Psychology*, XXXII, 550–58.

Coleman, A. Lee and Marsh, C. Paul (1954). "Practice Adoption Rates of Farmers and Leaders in a Kentucky Rural Community," *Rural Sociology*, XIX, 180–81.

Coleman, James; Katz, Elihu; and Menzel, Herbert (forthcoming). *Doctors and New Drugs.* Glencoe: The Free Press.

Cooper, Eunice and Dinerman, Helen (1951). "Analysis of the Film 'Don't Be A Sucker': A Study in Communication," *Public Opinion Quarterly*, XV, 243–64.

————— and Jahoda, Marie (1947). "The Evasion of Propaganda," *Journal of Psychology*, XXIII, 15–25.

Cousins, Norman (1949). "The Time Trap," *Saturday Review of Literature*, XXXII, December 24, 1949, p. 20, as excerpted in Marx, Herbert L., Jr. (ed.) (1953), *Television and Radio in American Life.* New York: H. W. Wilson Company.

Demant, V. A. (1955). "The Unintentional Influences of TV," *Cross-Currents*, V, 220–25.

Deshaies, Gabriel (1951). "Les Fonctions Psychologiques du Cinema," *Annales Medico-Psychologiques*, I, 553–73.

Dollard, John (1945). "The Acquisition of New Social Habits," in Linton, Ralph, *The Science of Man in the World Crisis.* New York: Columbia University Press.

Doob, Leonard W. (1935). *Propaganda: Its Psychology and Technique.* New York: Henry Holt and Company.

————— (1948). *Public Opinion and Propaganda.* New York: Henry Holt and Company.

―――― (1950). "Goebbels' Principles of Propaganda," *Public Opinion Quarterly*, XIV, 419–42.

―――― (1953). "Information Services in Central Africa," *Public Opinion Quarterly*, XVII, 7–19.

Dysinger, W. S. and Ruckmick, Christian A. (1933). *The Emotional Responses of Children to the Motion Picture Situation*. New York: The Macmillan Company.

Eisenstadt, S. N. (1955). "Communications Systems and Social Structure: An Exploratory Comparative Study," *Public Opinion Quarterly*, XIX, 152–67.

Elkin, Frederick (1950). "The Psychological Appeal of the Hollywood Western," *Journal of Educational Sociology*, XXIV, 72–86.

―――― (1954). "The Value Implications of Popular Films," *Sociology and Social Research*, XXXVIII, 320–22.

Fearing, Franklin (1947). "Influences of the Movies on Attitudes and Behavior," *Annals of American Academy of Political and Social Science*, CCLIV, 70–79.

―――― (1954). "Social Impact of the Mass Media of Communication," *Fifty-Third Yearbook, Part II, Mass Media and Education*. Chicago: National Society for the Study of Education, pp. 165–91.

Festinger, Leon; Schachter, Stanley; and Back, Kurt (1950). *Social Pressures in Informal Groups*. New York: Harper and Brothers.

Flowerman, Samuel H. (1949). "The Use of Propaganda to Reduce Prejudice: A Refutation," *International Journal of Opinion and Attitude Research*, III, 99–108.

Ford, Joseph B. (1953). "Is There Mass Communication?" *Sociology and Social Research*, XXXVII, 4.

―――― (1954). "The Primary Group in Mass Communication," *Sociology and Social Research*, XXXVIII, 3.

Forer, Raymond (1955). "The Impact of a Radio Program on Adolescents," *Public Opinion Quarterly*, XIX, 184–94.

Freeman, Howard E.; Weeks, H. Ashley; and Wertheimer, Walter I. (1955). "News Commentator Effect: A Study in Knowledge and Opinion Change," *Public Opinion Quarterly*, XIX, 209–15.

Freidson, Eliot (1953). "The Relation of the Social Situation of Contact to the Media of Mass Communication," *Public Opinion Quarterly*, XVII, 230–38.

Gesselman, Daisy B. (1951). "Television and Reading," *Elementary English*, XXVIII, 385–91.

Glock, Charles Y. (1953). "The Comparative Study of Communication and Opinion Formation," *Public Opinion Quarterly*, XV, 512–23.

Goldberg, H. D. (1950). "Liking and Retention of a Simulcast," *Public Opinion Quarterly*, XIV, 141–42.

Goldensen, Robert M. (1954). "Television and Our Children—The Experts Speak Up," *Parents Magazine*, XXIX, 12.

Goldstein, Harry (1940). *Reading and Listening Comprehension at Various Controlled Rates.* New York: Teachers College, Columbia University, Bureau of Publications.

Gould, Jack (1951). "What TV Is Doing to Us," *New York Times,* June 24 and 30, 1951.

Graalfs, Marilyn (1954). *A Survey of Comic Books in the State of Washington.* Seattle: Department of Sociology, University of Washington.

Graham, Saxon (1954). "Cultural Compatability in the Adoption of Television," *Social Forces,* XXXIII, 166–70.

Hamilton, Robert V. and Lawless, Richard H. (1956). "Television Within the Social Matrix," *Public Opinion Quarterly,* XX, 393–403.

Handel, Leo (1950). *Hollywood Looks at Its Audience.* Urbana: University of Illinois Press.

Haugh, Oscar M. (1952). "The Relative Effectiveness of Reading and Listening to Radio Drama as Ways of Imparting Information and Shifting Attitudes," *Journal of Educational Research,* XLV, 489–98.

Head, Sidney W. (1954). "Content Analysis of Television Drama Programs," *Quarterly of Film, Radio and Television,* IX, 175–94.

Herz, Martin F. (1949). "Some Psychological Lessons from Leaflet Propaganda in World War II," *Public Opinion Quarterly,* XIII, 471–86.

Herzog, Herta (1944). "What Do We Really Know about Daytime Serial Listeners," in Lazarsfeld, Paul F. and Stanton, Frank N., eds., *Radio Research, 1942–1943,* New York: Duell, Sloan and Pearce.

Hileman, Donald G. (1953). "The Young Radio Audience: A Study of Listening Habits," *Journalism Quarterly,* XXX, 37–43.

Himmelweit, Hilde T.; Oppenheim, A. N.; and Vince, Pamela (1958). *Television and the Child.* London and New York: Oxford University Press.

Hoban, C. F. and Van Ormer, E. B. (1951). *Instructional Film Research (Rapid Mass Learning) 1918–1950.* (Technical Report No. SDC 269-7-19). Washington, D.C.: Department of Commerce, Office of Technical Services.

Holaday, Perry W. and Stoddard, George D. (1933). *Getting Ideas From the Movies.* New York: The Macmillan Company.

Hoult, T. F. (1949). "Comic Books and Juvenile Delinquency," *Sociology and Social Research,* XXXIII, 279–84.

Hovland, Carl I. (1954). "Effects of the Mass Media of Communication," in Lindzey, Gardner ed., *Handbook of Social Psychology.* Cambridge, Mass.: Addison-Wesley Publishing Company, Inc., II, 1062–103.

————; Janis, Irving L., and Kelley, Harold H. (1953). *Communication and Persuasion.* New Haven: Yale University Press.

————; Lumsdaine, Arthur A.; and Sheffield, Fred D. (1949). *Experiments on Mass Communication*, "Studies in Social Psychology in World War II." Vol. III. Princeton: Princeton University Press.

———— and Weiss, W. (1951). "The Influence of Source Credibility on Communication Effectiveness," *Public Opinion Quarterly*, XV, 635–50.

———— *et al* (1957). *The Order of Presentation in Persuasion.* New Haven: Yale University Press.

Hudson, Robert B. and Wiebe, Gerhart D. (1948). "A Case for Listener Participation," *Public Opinion Quarterly*, XIII, 201–8.

Hyman, Herbert H. and Sheatsley, Paul B. (1947). "Some Reasons Why Information Campaigns Fail," *Public Opinion Quarterly*, XI, 412–23.

International Research Associates, Inc. (1953). *Media of Communication and the Free World as Seen by Czechoslovak, Hungarian and Polish Refugees: A Report prepared for the Division of Radio Program Evaluation of the Department of State.* New York: International Research Associates, Inc.

Janis, Irving L. (1954). "Personality Correlates of Susceptibility to Persuasion," *Journal of Personality*, XXII, 504–18.

———— and Feshbach, S. (1953). "Effects of Fear-Arousing Communications," *Journal of Abnormal and Social Psychology*, XLVIII, 78–92.

———— (1954). "Personality Differences Associated with Responsiveness to Fear-Arousing Communications," *Journal of Personality*, XXIII, 154–66.

———— and Herz, M. (1953). "The Influence of Preparatory Communications on Subsequent Reactions to Failure." Summarized in Hovland, Carl I.; Janis, Irving L., and Kelley, Harold H. *Communication and Persuasion.* New Haven: Yale University Press.

———— and King, B. T. (1954). "The Influencing of Role-Playing on Opinion Change," *Journal of Abnormal and Social Psychology*, XLIX, 211–18.

———— and Milholland, H. C. (1954). "The Influence of Threat Appeals on Selective Learning of the Content of a Persuasive Appeal," *Journal of Psychology*, XXXVII, 75–80.

———— *et al* (1959). *Personality and Persuasibility.* New Haven: Yale University Press.

Johnstone, John and Katz, Elihu (1957). "Youth and Popular Music," *American Journal of Sociology*, LXII, 563–68.

Jones, H. E. (1934). "The Influence of Motion Pictures upon the Social Attitudes of Children," *Journal of the American Association of University Women*, XXVII, 221–26.

Jorden, William J. (1956). "Moscow's Jet Set Rides High," *New York Times Magazine*, November 4, 1956, p. 14.

Kaiser, Walter H. (1951). "Television and Reading," *Library Journal*, LXXVI, 348–50.

Katz, Elihu (1957). "The Two-Step Flow of Communication: An Up-to-Date Report on an Hypothesis," *Public Opinion Quarterly*, XXI, 61–78.

——— and Lazarsfeld, Paul F. (1955). *Personal Influence: The Part Played by People in the Flow of Mass Communications*. Glencoe, Ill.: The Free Press.

Kaufmann, Helen J. (1952). "Implications of Domestic Research for International Communications Research," *Public Opinion Quarterly*, XV, 553–60.

Kecskmeti, Paul (1950). "Totalitarian Communications as a Means of Control: A Note on the Sociology of Propaganda," *Public Opinion Quarterly*, XIV, 224–34.

Kelley, Harold H. (1950). "Communication in Experimentally Created Hierarchies," in Festinger, Leon *et al*, *Theory and Experiment in Social Communication*. Ann Arbor: Research Center for Group Dynamics, University of Michigan.

——— (1958). "Salience of Membership and Resistance to Change of Group Anchored Attitudes," *Human Relations*, VIII, 275–89.

——— and Volkart, Edmund H. (1952). "The Resistance to Change of Group Anchored Attitudes," *American Sociological Review*, XVII, 453–65.

Kelman, Herbert C. (1953). "Attitude Change as a Function of Response Restriction," *Human Relations*, VI, 185–214.

——— and Hovland, Carl I. (1953). "Reinstatement of the Communicator in Delayed Measurement of Opinion Change," *Journal of Abnormal and Social Psychology*, XLVIII, 327–35.

Kendall, Patricia L. and Wolf, Katherine M. (1946). *The Personification of Prejudice as a Device in Educational Propaganda*. New York: Bureau of Applied Social Research, Columbia University.

——— (1949). "The Analysis of Deviant Cases in Communications Research," in Lazarsfeld, Paul F. and Stanton, Frank N., eds., *Communications Research, 1948–1949*. NewYork: Harper and Brothers.

Key, V. O. (1955). "A Theory of Critical Elections," *Journal of Politics*, XVII, 3–18.

King, B. T. and Janis, Irving L. (1953). "Comparison of the Effectiveness of Improvised Versus Non-Improvised Role-Playing in Producing Opinion Changes." Paper presented before the Eastern Psychological Association.

Kishler, John (1950). "Prediction of Differential Learning from a Motion Picture by Means of Indices of Identification Potentials Derived from Attitudes toward the Main Character," *American Psychologist*, V, 298–99.

Klapper, Joseph T. (1948). "Mass Media and the Engineering of Consent," *American Scholar*, XVII, 419–29.

—— (1949). *The Effects of Mass Media*. New York: Bureau of Applied Social Research, Columbia University.

—— (1954). *Children and Television: A Review of Socially Prevalent Concerns*. New York: Bureau of Applied Social Research, Columbia University.

—— (1957–58). "What We Know About the Effects of Mass Communication: The Brink of Hope," *Public Opinion Quarterly*, XXI, 4.

Knower, Franklin R. (1935). "Experimental Studies of Changes in Attitudes—I: A Study of the Effect of Oral Argument on Changes of Attitude," *Journal of Social Psychology*, VI, 315–47.

—— (1936). "Experimental Studies of Changes in Attitudes—II: A Study of the Effect of Printed Argument on Changes in Attitude," *Journal of Abnormal and Social Psychology*, XXX, 522–32.

Kracauer, Siegfried and Berkman, Paul L. (1956). *Satellite Mentality*. New York: Frederick A. Praeger, Inc.

Kriesberg, Martin (1949). "Cross-Pressures and Attitudes: A Study of the Influence of Conflicting Propaganda on Opinions Regarding American-Soviet Relations," *Public Opinion Quarterly*, XIII, 5–16.

Kumata, Hideya (1956). *An Inventory of Instructional Television Research*. Ann Arbor: Educational Television and Radio Center.

Lang, Gladys Engel and Lang, Kurt, (1955). "The Influential Structure of Political Communications: A Study in Unwitting Bias," *Public Opinion Quarterly*, XIX, 168–84.

Lang, Kurt and Lang, Gladys Engel (1953). "The Unique Perspective of Television and Its Effect: A Pilot Study," *American Sociological Review*, XVII, 3–12.

—— (1959). "The Mass Media and Voting," in Burdick, Eugene and Brodbeck, Arthur J., eds., *American Voting Behavior*. Glencoe, Ill.: The Free Press.

Larson, Otto N. and Hill, Richard (1954). "Mass Media and Interpersonal Communication in the Diffusion of a News Event," *American Sociological Review*, XIX, 426–33.

Lazarsfeld, Paul F. (1940). *Radio and the Printed Page*. New York: Duell, Sloan and Pearce.

—— (1942). "The Effects of Radio on Public Opinion," in Waples, Douglas, ed., *Print, Radio, and Film in a Democracy*, Chicago: University of Chicago Press.

—— (1947). "Audience Research in the Movie Field," *Annals of the American Academy of Political and Social Science*, CCLIV, 160–68.

—— (1947). "Some Remarks on the Role of the Mass Media in So-called Tolerance Propaganda," *Journal of Social Issues*. III, 17–25.

——— (1948). "Communication Research and the Social Psychologist," in Dennis, Wayne, ed., *Current Trends in Social Psychology*. Pittsburgh: University of Pittsburgh Press.

———; Berelson, Bernard; and Gaudet, Hazel (1948). *The People's Choice*. New York: Columbia University Press.

——— and Merton, Robert K. (1948). "Mass Communication, Popular Taste and Organized Social Action," in Bryson, Lyman, ed., *The Communication of Ideas*, New York: Harper and Brothers.

——— and Schneider, Helen Dinerman (1949). "Resarch for Action," in Lazarsfeld, Paul F. and Stanton, Frank N., eds., *Communications Research, 1948–1949*. New York: Harper and Brothers.

——— and Stanton, Frank N., eds. (1941). *Radio Research, 1941*, New York: Duell, Sloan and Pearce.

———, eds. (1944). *Radio Research, 1942–1943*. New York: Duell, Sloan and Pearce.

——— eds. (1949). *Communications Research, 1948–1949*. New York: Harper and Brothers.

Lerner, Daniel (1953). "A Scale Pattern of Opinion Correlates: Communication Networks, Media Exposure and Concomitant Responses," *Sociometry*, XVI, 266–71.

Levin, Betty (1950). "Television and the Schools," *Harvard Educational Review*, XX, 255–70.

Levine, Jerome M. and Murphy, Gardner (1943). "The Learning and Forgetting of Controversial Material," *Journal of Abnormal and Social Psychology*, XXXVIII, 507–17.

Lewin, Herbert S. (1953). "Facts and Fears about the Comics," *Nation's Schools*, LII, 46–48.

Likert, Rensis (1954). "A Neglected Factor in Communications," *Audio-Visual Communication Review*, II, 163–77.

Lionberger, Herbert F. (1952). "The Diffusion of Farm and Home Information as an Area of Sociological Research," *Rural Sociology*, XVII, 132–40.

Lipset, S. M. (1953). "Opinion Formation in a Crisis," *Public Opinion Quarterly*, XVII, 20–46.

Logan, Clara S. (1950). "What Our Children See," in Olsen, O. Joe, ed., *Education on the Air: Twentieth Yearbook of the Institute for Education by Radio and Television*. Columbus: Ohio State University Press.

Lorge, Irving (1936). "Prestige, Suggestion, Attitudes," *Journal of Social Psychology*, VII, 386–402.

Lowell, A. L., (1939), in Albig, William, *Public Opinion*. New York: McGraw-Hill Book Company.

Lowenthal, Leo (1942–43). "Biographies in Popular Magazines," in Lazarsfeld, Paul F. and Stanton, Frank N., eds., *Radio Research, 1942–1943*. New York: Duell, Sloan and Pearce.

Luchins, Abraham S. (1957). "Primacy-Recency in Impression Formation," in Hovland, Carl I. *et al, The Order of Presentation in Persuasion*. New Haven: Yale University Press.

Lumsdaine, Arthur A. and Janis, Irving L. (1953). "Resistance to 'Counter Propaganda' Produced by One-Sided and Two-Sided 'Propaganda' Presentations," *Public Opinion Quarterly*, XVII, 311–18.

Lund, F. H. (1925). "The Psychology of Belief: IV. The Law of Primacy in Persuasion," *Journal of Abnormal and Social Psychology*, XX, 183–91.

Lundberg, George A. (1926). "The Newspaper and Public Opinion," *Social Forces*, IV, 709–15.

Lyness, Paul I. (1952). "The Place of the Mass Media in the Lives of Boys and Girls," *Journalism Quarterly*, XXIX, 43–54.

Maccoby, Eleanor E. (1951). "Television: Its Impact on School Children," *Public Opinion Quarterly*, XV, 421–44.

——— (1954). "Why Do Children Watch TV?" *Public Opinion Quarterly*, XVIII, 239–44.

McKeachie, Wilbert J. (1954). "Individual Conformity to Attitudes of Classroom Groups," *Journal of Abnormal and Social Psychology*, XLIX, 282–89.

McKellar, Peter and Harris, Ralph (1952). "Radio Preferences of Adolescents and Children," *British Journal of Educational Psychology*, XXII, 101–13.

McPhee, William N. (1953). *New Strategies for Research in the Mass Media*. New York: Bureau of Applied Social Research, Columbia University.

——— and Meyersohn, Rolf (1955). *Futures for Radio*. New York: Bureau of Applied Social Research, Columbia University.

Mandell, Wallace and Hovland, Carl I. (1952). "Is There a Law of Primacy in Persuasion?" *American Psychologist*, VII, 538.

Marx, Herbert L., Jr., ed. (1953). *Television and Radio in American Life*. New York: H. W. Wilson Company.

Menzel, Herbert and Katz, Elihu (1955). "Social Relations and Innovations in the Medical Profession: The Epidemiology of a New Drug," *Public Opinion Quarterly*, XIX, 337–52.

Merton, Robert K. (1946). *Mass Persuasion*. New York: Harper and Brothers.

——— (1949). *Social Theory and Social Structure.* Glencoe, Ill.: The Free Press.

Meyersohn, Rolf B. (1956). "Social Research in Television," in Rosenberg, Bernard and White, David Manning, eds., *Mass Culture: The Popular Arts in America.* Glencoe, Ill.: The Free Press.

Michael, Donald N. and Maccoby, Nathan (1953). "Factors Influencing Verbal Learning from Films under Varying Conditions of Audience Participation," *Journal of Experimental Psychology*, XLVI, 411–18.

Mirams, Gordon (1951). "Drop That Gun," *Quarterly of Film, Radio and Television*, VI, 1–19.

Mott, Frank Luther (1944). "Newspapers in Presidential Campaigns," *Public Opinion Quarterly*, VIII, 348–67.

—— (1947). *Golden Multitudes.* New York: The Macmillan Company.

Muhlen, Norbert (1949). "Comic Books and Other Horrors: Prep School for Totalitarian Society?" *Commentary*, VI, 80–87.

Newcomb, Theodore M. (1943). *Personality and Social Change.* New York: Dryden Press.

New York State Joint Legislative Committee (1955). *Report of the New York State Joint Legislative Committee to Study the Publication of Comics* (Legislative Document No. 37 of 1955). Albany: Williams Press, Inc.

North Central Rural Sociology Sub-Committee for the Study of Diffusion of Farm Practices (1960). *The Adopters of New Practices: Characteristics and Communications Behavior.* Columbia, Mo.: Missouri Extension Service.

Palter, Ruth (1948). "Radio's Attraction for Housewives," *Hollywood Quarterly*, III, 248–57.

"Parents, Children, and Television: The First Television Generation," (1954) *Information Service* (Bulletin of the Central Department of Research and Survey, National Council of Churches of Christ in the United States of America), XXXIII, 7.

Parker, Edward C.; Barry, David W.; and Smythe, Dallas W. (1955). *The Television-Radio Audience and Religion.* New York: Harper and Brothers.

Parrish, Jack A. and Campbell, Donald T. (1953). "Measuring Propaganda Effects with Direct and Indirect Attitude Tests," *Journal of Abnormal and Social Psychology*, XLVIII, 3–9.

Perentesis, John L. (1949). "Effectiveness of a Motion Picture Trailer as Election Propaganda," *Public Opinion Quarterly*, XII, 465–69.

Peterson, Ruth C. and Thurstone, L. L. (1933). *Motion Pictures and the Social Attitudes of Children.* New York: The Macmillan Company.

Pittman, David J. (1958). "Mass Media and Juvenile Delinquency," in Roucek, Joseph C., ed., *Juvenile Delinquency.* New York: Philosophical Library, Inc.

Purdue Opinion Panel (1954). *Four Years of New York Television.* Urbana: National Association of Educational Broadcasters.

Raths, Louis E. and Trager, Frank N. (1948). "Public Opinion and Crossfire," *Journal of Educational Sociology*, XXI, 345–68.

Renshaw, Samuel; Miller, Vernon L.; and Marquis, Dorothy (1933). *Children's Sleep*. New York: The Macmillan Company.

Ricutti, Edward A. (1951). "Children and Radio: A Study of Listeners and Non-Listeners to Various Types of Radio Programs in Terms of Selected Ability, Attitudes, and Behavior Measures," *Genetic Psychology Monographs*, XLIV, 69–143.

Riley, John W., Jr.; Cantrell, Frank V.; and Reittiger, Katherine F. (1949). "Some Observations on the Social Effects of Television," *Public Opinion Quarterly*, XII, 233–34.

——— and Riley, Mathilda White (1959). "Mass Communication and the Social System," in Merton, Robert K.; Broom, Leonard; and Cottrell, Leonard S., Jr., eds., *Sociology Today: Problems and Prospects*. New York: Basic Books.

Riley, Mathilda White and Riley, John W., Jr. (1951). "A Sociological Approach to Communication Research," *Public Opinion Quarterly*, XV, 444–60.

Robinson, Karl F. (1941). "An Experimental Study of the Effects of Group Discussion upon the Social Attitudes of College Students," *Speech Monographs*, VIII, 34–57.

Roody, S. I. (1952). "The Effect of Radio, Television, and Motion Pictures on the Development of Maturity," *English Journal*, XLI, 245–50.

Rose, Arnold M. (1948). "The Use of Propaganda to Reduce Prejudice," *International Journal of Opinion and Attitude Research*, II, 220–29.

Rosen, Irwin C. (1948). "The Effect of the Motion Picture *Gentlemen's Agreement* on Attitudes toward Jews," *Journal of Psychology*, XXVI, 525–26.

Rosenthal, S. P. (1934). "Changes in Socio-Economic Attitudes under Radical Motion Picture Propaganda," *Archives of Psychology*, No. 166.

Saenger, Gerhart (1955). "Male and Female Relations in the American Comic Strip," *Public Opinion Quarterly*, XIX, 194–205.

——— (1955). "The Effect on Intergroup Attitudes of the UNESCO Pamphlets on Race," *Social Problems*, III, 21–27.

Schank, R. L. and Goodman, Charles (1939). "Reactions to Propaganda on Both Sides of a Controversial Issue," *Public Opinion Quarterly*, III, 107–12.

Schramm, Wilbur (1948). *Communications in Modern Society*. Urbana: University of Illinois Press.

——— (1954). *The Process and Effects of Mass Communication*. Urbana: University of Illinois Press.

——— (1958). Unpublished and untitled study described to author in a personal communication.

——— and Carter, Richard F. (1959). "Effectiveness of a Political Telethon," *Public Opinion Quarterly*, XXIII, 121–26.

——— and Merritt, Ludwig (1951). "The Weekly Newspaper and Its Readers," *Journalism Quarterly*, XXVIII, 301–14.

——— and Riley, John W., Jr. (1951). "Communication in the Sovietized State as Demonstrated in Korea," *American Sociological Review*, XVI, 757–66.

Seagoe, May V. (1951). "Children's Television Habits and Preferences," *Quarterly of Film, Radio and Television*, VI, 143–53.

Seeleman, Virginia (1941). "The Influence of Attitude upon the Remembering of Pictorial Material," *Archives of Psychology*, No. 258.

Seibert, Joseph (undated). *The Influence of Television on the Election of 1952*. Oxford, Ohio: Miami University.

Seldes, Gilbert (1950). *The Great Audience*. New York: Viking Press.

Shayon, Robert Lewis (1950). "The Pied Piper of Video," *Saturday Review of Literature*, XXXIII, November 25, 1950, 9–11 and continued.

——— (1951). *Television and Our Children*. New York: Longmans, Green and Company.

Sherif, Muzafer (1936). *The Psychology of Social Norms*. New York: Harper and Brothers.

Shils, Edward A. and Janowitz, Morris: (1948). "Cohesion and Disintegration in the Wehrmacht in World War II," *Public Opinion Quarterly*, XII, 280–315.

Shuttleworth, Frank N. and May, Mark A. (1933). *The Social Conduct and Attitudes of Movie Fans*. New York: The Macmillan Company.

Siepmann, Charles S. (1948). "Radio," in Byrson. Lyman., ed., *The Communication of Ideas*. New York: Harper and Brothers.

——— (1948). *The Radio Listener's Bill of Rights: Democracy, Radio, and You*. New York: Anti-Defamation League of B'nai B'rith.

Silvey, Robert (1951). "The Intelligibility of Broadcast Talks," *Public Opinion Quarterly*, XV, 299–304.

Sims, Verner Martin (1938). "Factors Influencing Attitudes Toward the TVA," *Journal of Abnormal and Social Psychology*, XXXIII, 34–56.

Smith, Bruce L.; Lasswell, Harold D.; and Casey, Ralph D. (1946). *Propaganda, Communication and Public Opinion*. Princeton: Princeton University Press.

Smythe, Dallas W. (1951). "Analysis of Television," *Scientific American*, CLXXXIV, June, 15–17.

—— (1952). "What Television Programming Is Like," *Quarterly of Film, Radio and Television*, VII, 25–31.

—— (1953). *Three Years of New York Television*. Urbana, Ill.: National Association of Educational Broadcasters.

—— (1954). "Some Observations on Communications Theory," *Audio-Visual Communications Review*, II, 23–37.

—— (1955). "Dimensions of Violence," *Audio-Visual Communications Review*, III, 58–63.

Sorokin, Pitirim and Baldyreff, J. W. (1932). "An Experimental Study of the Influence of Suggestion on the Discrimination and the Valuation of People," *American Journal of Sociology*, XXXVII, 720–37.

Spiegelman, Marvin; Terwilliger, Carl; and Fearing, Franklin (1952). "The Content of Comic Strips: A Study of a Mass Medium of Communication," *Journal of Social Psychology*, XXXV, 37–57.

Star, Shirley A. and Hughes, Helen McGill (1950). "Report of an Educational Campaign: The Cincinnati Plan for the United Nations," *American Journal of Sociology*, LV, 389–400.

Staudohar, Frank T. and Smith, Robert G., Jr. (1956). "The Contribution of Lecture Supplements to the Effectiveness of an Attitudinal Film," *Journal of Applied Psychology*, XL, 109–11.

Stewart, Raymond F. (1952). *The Social Impact of Television on Households*. Emory, Ga.: Emory University, Division of Journalism.

Stouffer, Samuel (1940). Untitled report on radio and newspapers as news sources, summarized in Lazarsfeld, Paul F., *Radio and the Printed Page*. New York: Duell, Sloan and Pearce.

Stycos, J. Mayone (1952). "Patterns of Communication in a Rural Greek Village," *Public Opinion Quarterly*, XVI, 59–70.

Swanson, Charles E.; Jenkins, James; and Jones, Robert L. (1950). "President Truman Speaks: A Study of Ideas vs. Media," *Journalism Quarterly*, XXVII, 251–62.

—— and Jones, Robert L. (1951). "Television Owning and Its Correlates," *Journal of Applied Psychology*, XXXV, 352–57.

Tannenbaum, Percy H. (1953). "The Effect of Headlines on the Interpretation of News Stories," *Journalism Quarterly*, XXX, 189–97.

—— (1956). "Initial Attitude Towards Source and Concept as Factors in Attitude Change through Communication," *Public Opinion Quarterly*, XX, 413–25.

—— and Kerwick, Jean (1954). "Effects of Newscasts' Item Leads upon Listener Interpretation," *Journalism Quarterly*, XXXI, 33–37.

Thistlewaite, Donald L.; deHaan, Henry; and Kamenetzky, Joseph (1955). "The Effects of 'Directive' and 'Non-Directive' Communication Procedures on Attitudes," *Journal of Abnormal and Social Psychology*, LI, 107–13.

—— and Kamenetzky, Joseph (1955). "Attitude Change Through Refutation and Elaboration of Audience Counterarguments," *Journal of Abnormal and Social Psychology*, LI, 3–12.

Thrasher, Frederick M. (1949). "The Comics and Delinquency: Cause or Scapegoat," *Journal of Educational Sociology*, XXIII, 195–205.

"TV Lifts Students' Grades in Texas But Lowers Them in New Jersey" (1950). *Advertising Age*, March 20, 1950, p. 48.

UNESCO (1953). "Three Experiments in the Spreading of Knowledge about the Universal Declaration of Human Rights," *International Social Science Bulletin*, V, 583–602.

U.S. Congress Senate Committee on the Judiciary (1955). *Comic Books and Juvenile Delinquency. A Part of the Investigation of Juvenile Delinquency in the United States*. 84th Congress, First Session. Washington, D.C.: Government Printing Office.

—— (1955). *Television and Juvenile Delinquency. Interim Report of the Subcommittee to Investigate Juvenile Delinquency*, 84th Congress, First Session. Washington, D.C.: Government Printing Office.

Waples, Douglas, ed. (1942). *Print, Radio, and Film in a Democracy*. Chicago: University of Chicago Press.

——; Berelson, Bernard; and Bradshaw, Franklyn R. (1940). *What Reading Does to People*. Chicago: University of Chicago Press.

Warner, W. Lloyd and Henry, William E. (1948). "The Radio Day Time Serial: A Symbolic Analysis," *Genetic Psychology Monographs*, XXXVII, 3–71.

Wertham, Frederick C. (1954). *Seduction of the Innocent*. New York: Rinehart & Company, Inc.

Westley, Bruce H. and Barrow, Lionel C., Jr. (1959). *Exploring the News: A Comparative Study of the Teaching Effectiveness of Radio and Television* (Research Bulletin No. 12). Madison: University of Wisconsin Television Laboratory.

Wheeler, D. and Jordan, H. (1929). "Changes of Individual Opinion to Accord with Group Opinion," *Journal of Abnormal and Social Psychology*, XXIV, 203–15.

Wiebe, Gerhart D. (1951). "Merchandising Commodities and Citizenship on Television," *Public Opinion Quarterly*, XV, 679–91.

—— (1952). "Mass Communications," in Hartley, Eugene L. and Hartley, Ruth E., *Fundamentals of Social Psychology*. New York: Alfred A. Knopf, Inc.

—— (1952). "Responses to the Televised Kefauver Hearings," *Public Opinion Quarterly*, XVI, 179–200.

Wiese, Mildred J. and Cole, Stewart G. (1946). "The Study of Children's Attitudes and the Influence of a Commercial Motion Picture," *Journal of Psychology*, XXI, 151–71.

Wilke, W. H. (1934). "An Experimental Comparison of the Speech, the

Radio, and the Printed Page, as Propaganda Devices," *Archives of Psychology*, No. 169.

Williamson, A. C. and Remmers, H. H. (1940). "Persistence of Attitudes Concerning Conservation Issues," *Journal of Experimental Education, VIII*, 354–56.

Wilner, Daniel M. (1951). *Attitude as a Determinant of Perception in the Mass Media of Communication: Reactions to the Motion Picture, "Home of the Brave."* Unpublished Ph.D. dissertation, University of California, Los Angeles Library.

Wilson, Elmo C. (1948). "The Effectiveness of Documentary Broadcasts," *Public Opinion Quarterly*, XII, 19–29.

Winick, Charles (1959). *Taste and the Censor in Television*. New York: Fund for the Republic.

Witty, Paul A. (1951). "Television and the High School Student," *Education*, LXXII, 242–51.

—— (1952). "Children's Interest in Comics, Radio, Motion Pictures, and TV," *Educational Administration and Supervision*, XXXVIII, 138–47.

—— (1952). "Children's Reactions to TV: A Third Report," *Elementary English, XXIX*, 469–73.

—— (1954). "Comparative Studies of Interest in TV," *Educational Administration and Supervision*, XL, 321–35.

Wolf, Katherine and Fiske, Marjorie (1949). "The Children Talk about Comics," in Lazarsfeld, Paul F. and Stanton, Frank N., eds., *Communications Research, 1948–1949*. New York: Harper and Brothers.

Zajonc, Robert B. (1954). *Cognitive Structure and Cognitive Tuning*. Unpublished Ph.D. dissertation, University of Michigan.

—— (1954). "Some Effects of Space Serials," *Public Opinion Quarterly*, XVIII, 367–74.

Zimmerman, Claire and Bauer, Raymond A. (1956). "The Effect of an Audience upon What Is Remembered," *Public Opinion Quarterly*, XX, 238–48.

Notes

Preface

Note: All works referred to in the Notes are given in full in the Bibliography.

1. The earlier work consisted of four discrete memoranda, each of which presented data relevant to a specific question (in one case two questions) posed by the Director of the Public Library Inquiry of the Social Science Research Council. No attempt was made to relate the four memoranda, except to note that certain phenomena relevant to one area of effect applied to other areas as well.

The persuasive effects of mass communication, treated in one memorandum in the 1949 work, is here the topic of all four chapters of Part One.

The functions and effects of escapist media material are also treated here at considerably greater length than they were in the 1949 monograph.

Three topics unmentioned or barely mentioned in the 1949 work are here accorded a chapter each. These are: (1) the effects of media depictions of crime and violence; (2) the effects of adult TV fare upon child audiences; and (3) the media as influences toward audience "passivity."

One of the memoranda in the 1949 volume discussed the "comparative effects" of the various media, books, and face-to-face discourse "as instruments of informal pedagogy . . . and persuasion." Data on the relative persuasive efficacy of the media appear here in Chapter V. The relative efficacy of the media in "informal pedagogy," however, is not discussed. The author is not certain that valid distinctions can be made between formal, quasi-formal, and informal pedagogy by mass media. The findings of the vast research on formal pedagogy by mass media cannot, in any case, be assumed to be irrelevant to the use of the media in "informal pedagogy." But, as pointed out below (pp. 122–23), the collation and summarizing of such research appeared to be a task clearly beyond the possibilities of the present study. The interested reader is, however, directed to certain pertinent bibliographies and partial collations (see note 21 to Chapter V).

One memorandum in the 1949 volume dealt with the effect of mass media content on the level of public taste. The author has since become convinced that meaningful treatment of that topic can be achieved only in connection with an analysis of the functions and effects of popular culture. The research which would be involved is again clearly beyond the scope of the present study, and the topic is accordingly not treated in this volume.

2. Two elaborate studies of the effects of British television on British audiences are, however, discussed at some length. Both focus upon questions which are of current concern in the United States, but upon which American research has very little to offer. The two studies are Belson (1957) and Himmelweit, Oppenheim, and Vince (1958).

CHAPTER I

Introduction

NOTE: *All studies cited in the notes to this chapter are discussed at greater length at various other points in this volume, and many are discussed in several different contexts. The page locations of such discussions may be easily gleaned from the Index.*

1. Most of this chapter has been previously published in almost identical form in *Public Opinion Quarterly*, XXI (Winter, 1957–58). The material there served as the beginning of a paper entitled "What We Know About the Effects of Mass Communication: The Brink of Hope," which was first delivered as an address at the National Education Association's Centennial Seminar on Communications, at Dedham, Mass., May 21–23, 1957. Permission to republish has been graciously granted by *Public Opinion Quarterly*.

2. e.g., Arnheim (1944) and Herzog (1944).

3. e.g., Warner and Henry (1948).

4. This is a typical conclusion of surveys of pertinent literature and comment, e.g., Bogart (1956), pp. 258–74.

5. e.g., Lazarsfeld and Merton (1948); Klapper (1948).

6. Klapper (1949), pp. II–25, IV–52.

7. Merton (1946).

8. The efficacy as well as the limitations of media in this regard are perhaps most exhaustively documented in the various unclassified evaluation reports of the United States Information Agency.

9. Kelley and Volkart (1952).

10. Lasswell proposed in 1946 (Smith, Lasswell, and Casey, p. 121) that communications research might be described as an inquiry into *"Who says what, through what channels* (media) of communication, *to whom,* [with] what . . . results."* This now classic formulation was widely adopted as an organizational framework for courses and books of readings in communications research and greatly influenced research orientations as well.

11. e.g., Hovland (1954); Hovland *et al* (1957).

12. e.g., Merton (1946), p. 61 ff.; Freeman, Weeks, and Wertheimer (1955); Hovland, Janis, and Kelley (1953), chap. ii, which summarizes a series of studies by Hovland, Weiss, and Kelman.

13. Hovland, Lumsdaine, and Sheffield (1949) *in re* "sleeper effects" and "temporal effects."

14. e.g., Kelley and Volkart (1952); Riley and Riley (1951); Ford (1954); Katz and Lazarsfeld (1955) review a vast literature on the subject (pp. 15–133).

15. Katz (1957) provides an exhaustive review of the topic.

16. e.g., Friedson (1953). For an early insight, see Cooper and Jahoda (1947).

17. Janis and King (1954), King and Janis (1953), and Kelman (1953), all of which are summarized and evaluated in Hovland, Janis, and Kelley (1953); also Michael and Maccoby (1953).

18. e.g., Janis (1954); Hovland, Janis, and Kelley (1953), chap. vi; Janis *et al* (1959).

19. e.g., Maccoby (1954).

20. e.g., Klapper (1948); Klapper (1949), pp. IV–20–27; Wiebe (1952–B).

21. Wiebe (1951).

22. Berelson (1948), p. 172.

23. See Berelson, Lazarsfeld, and McPhee (1954), p. 234, for "hypodermic effect."

24. Klapper (1957–58).

25. Berelson, Lazarsfeld, and McPhee (1954), p. 234.

26. Katz and Lazarsfeld (1955).

27. Riley and Riley (1951), and Maccoby (1954).

28. e.g., the experimental programs described in Hovland, Janis, and Kelley (1953), Hovland *et al* (1957), and Janis *et al* (1959).

29. Occasions on which it does so serve are noted in generalizations 3, 4, and 5.

PART ONE

Introductory Note

1. Any attempt to present a digest of such vast material involves extensive organizational problems. The question arises, for example, as to whether the basic organizational scheme should reflect *types of effects* or the *causes* which create them. It has seemed to the author that this volume would be most use-

ful if it were organized according to types of effects, with the major identified causes noted as well.

But the organizational problems peculiar to Part One are not so much solved by this decision as simply postponed a step. We are brought face to face with the task of formulating some kind of *typology of attitude effects.* A list of topical categories is obviously unfeasible, since it would necessarily involve all topics of human thought. A distinction in terms of immediate effects, short range effects, and long range effects involves difficult and perhaps arbitrary classifications, and would suffer, at least at present, from the virtual lack of objective studies of anything that might properly be called long term effect. Various other possibilities present similarly complex classification problems, all of which are intensified by the fact that the pertinent studies were never planned to fit into any such overall structure. Mass communications research has, in fact, been notoriously devoid of any organizing theoretical framework. But the data themselves do suggest an organizational scheme. If the findings are viewed in reference to what might be called the *directions of effect,* marked consistencies are discernible; cross topical findings can be brought into some sort of order; and many of the identified causative factors can be treated in relation to the directional typology. Such an organizational scheme, in short, appears to offer wide possibilities of integration with few organizational trappings.

Logic and common sense indicate that the possible "directions of effect" are limited. In reference to any given topic, a persuasive communication may:

a. create opinions or attitudes among persons who previously had none on the topic in question; *or*

b. reinforce (i.e., intensify or buttress) attitudes which already exist; *or*

c. diminish the intensity of existing attitudes without actually accomplishing conversion; *or*

d. Convert persons to a point of view opposite to the one they held; *or*

e. (at least theoretically) have no effect at all.

The data of Part One are organized and the chapters titled in accord with this simple typology.

2. Katz and Lazarsfeld (1955), p. 17.

CHAPTER II

Reinforcement, Minor Change, and Related Phenomena

1. The efficacy of mass comunication in *creating* opinions among persons possessing none on the topic in question is discussed in Chapter III. We are here concerned exclusively with the influence of mass communication upon existing opinions.

2. Lazarsfeld, Berelson, and Gaudet (1948), p. 102. The percentages cited in the present volume are drawn from Table V, p. 102 and refer to stated vote intentions only. Lazarsfeld, Berelson, and Gaudet deal also with the relation-

ship of vote intentions to "predispositions." Their use of the terms "reinforcement" and "conversion" and the percentages they cite are accordingly not precisely identical with the usages and percentages here. The dominance of reinforcement and the rarity of conversion is, however, equally apparent in either context.

3. Berelson, Lazarsfeld, and McPhee (1954), p. 23. Persons who remained neutral are not here regarded as reinforced, nor are ex-neutrals counted as convertees.

4. *Ibid.*, p. 252.   5. *Ibid.*, p. 248.

6. See p. 254 below.

7. Bureau of Applied Social Research (1954).

8. The effect of role-playing upon the effectiveness of persuasive communication is discussed below, pp. 80–84.

9. In so summarizing the findings of the research, we are virtually repeating the first two of the five generalizations proposed in the introductory chapter of this book.

10. "Selective exposure" seems to the author a somewhat more realistic term than the classic "self-selection." It is, in a sense, true that a given media product "selects its audience before it affects it" (Lazarsfeld, 1940, p. 134), i.e., that it acts like a sieve in screening its particular audience from among the vast potential audience of all media offerings. But the sieve works, after all, only because the people, rather than the program, are, consciously or unconsciously, selective.

11. Lazarsfeld, Berelson, and Gaudet (1948), pp. 89 ff.

12. Lazarsfeld (1942), p. 69.

13. The studies of Sherif (1936) and of Bruner and Goodman (1947) are classic. The latter cites some twenty other earlier and pertinent investigations. Many of the earlier findings have been refined and extended by Asch (1952).

14. Allport and Postman (1945), p. 81.

15. See, for example, Kriesberg (1949), who reports on the failure of certain persons under cross-pressures to perceive that the cross-pressures existed. More recently Luchins (1957) found that of 70 subjects exposed to a communication including incompatible bits of information, 23 professed unawareness of the incompatible elements, and 17 others reported that they were able to reconcile the conflict. Zajonc (1954) reports a curious instance of selective perception in the interest of cultural values, rather than in reference to controversial topics. His study is summarized in another context on pp. 216 f., below.

16. Levine and Murphy (1943), p. 510.

17. The increase in differences between the groups is not as regular for the anti-Communist material as it is for the pro-Communist material, but both initial and final differences are larger. Other differences between the findings in reference to the two passages are discussed by Levine and Murphy but are not germane to the point here under discussion. The authors consider that some of those differences, including the more marked reactions to the anti-communist material, are probably related to the fact that the two selections are not in themselves comparable, differing not only in point of view but also in intensity of attitude and in textual difficulty.

18. Lazarsfeld, Berelson, and Gaudet (1948), p. 89.

19. See pp. 7 f.

20. Katz and Lazarsfeld (1955), p. 33.

21. *Ibid.*, p. 63.

22. Conditions under which groups may help communications to produce opinion changes are discussed on pp. 65–68 below.

23. Lazarsfeld, Berelson, and Gaudet (1948), p. 142.

24. *Ibid.*, p. 141.   25. r = —.71.

26. Johnstone and Katz (1957).

27. Inter-personal dissemination of the contents of communications is itself likely to abet reinforcement and is discussed separately immediately below.

28. See pp. 30–38 and pp. 68–72.

29. pp. 7 f.

30. See, for example, Festinger, Schachter, and Back (1950). For a review of that study and other pertinent studies in small group research, see Katz and Lazarsfeld (1955), pp. 94 f. The cited findings suggest that primary groups may provide an ideal arena for inter-personal dissemination of the content of communications.

31. Berelson, Lazarsfeld, and McPhee (1954), pp. 246–48. Quotations are from p. 248.

32. *Ibid.*, p. 106.

33. Schramm and Carter (1959) did find that Republican viewers of a Republican sponsored telecast were more apt to have talked about the program than were Democrats. They propose that "since a . . . larger percentage of the Republicans [who saw the program] heard of the program from a friend, we can assume that Republicans told Republicans about it" (p. 124). The Schramm and Carter study, however, involved only 65 viewers and the evidence is inferential rather than direct. The present author believes that partisan audiences of partisan communications probably do tend to discuss the communications with persons of similar views, but the Schramm and Carter study can hardly be considered a conclusive demonstration.

34. See pp. 32–38.   35. See pp. 7 f.

36. Lazarsfeld, Berelson, and Gaudet (1948), p. 151.

37. Katz (1957), p. 63.   38. *Ibid.*, p. 63 f.

39. Lazarsfeld, Berelson, and Gaudet (1948), p. 151.

40. Personal influence with respect to public issues, marketing, fashion, and movie attendance is exhaustively treated in Katz and Lazarsfeld (1955), Part II. The role of personal influence in physicians' adoption of new drugs is detailed in Coleman, Katz, and Menzel (1960). The role of personal influence in agricultural innovation is the subject of considerable literature, much of which is summarized in North Central Rural Sociology Sub-Committee for the Study of Diffusion of Farm Practices (1960); see Bibliography for detailed listing.

41. Katz (1957), p. 77. Some deviation from this tendency is noted by Katz and Lazarsfeld (1955) in regard to those women in their sample who had been influenced to change their minds on a public opinion issue. The authors found "that the real locus of public affairs influence for our female respondents is within the household unit" and "the proportion of influencing that goes on outside the family is minimal" (pp. 227 f). However, of 37 cases of extra-family influence in which the relative social status of influential and influencee could be checked, 54 per cent involved a flow of influence from persons of higher social status to persons of lower social status. It must be remembered,

however, that the major arena of public affairs influence was found to be within the immediate family and that the number of cases of extra-family influence which could be analyzed was extremely small.

Katz and Lazarsfeld also investigated the status of self-designated women public affairs opinion leaders, and of "general influentials"—i.e., those who were named as being good sources of advice on public affairs, rather than as having exerted influence in reference to a specific issue. The self-designated opinion leaders were found to be proportionately three times as common among high status as low status women, but no data are available on whom they influenced. In reference to general influence, the authors conclude that they "can . . . describe the flow . . . as follows. People are most likely to choose their experts from within their own social group. But as we move up the ladder of prestige to each succeeding expert group, we find a tendency toward vertical influence—an increasing probability that persons from higher strata will be designated as general influentials" (p. 286).

A finding common to two other studies is also pertinent here. Lazarsfeld, Berelson, and Gaudet (1948) and Berelson, Lazarsfeld, and McPhee (1954) both found that opinion leaders in reference to election issues tended to belong to the same socio-economic class as their followers, although they more typically came from the higher levels of that class; blue collar workers, for example, tended to follow opinion leaders who were on the upper levels of the blue collar range.

42. Television was not a major medium of mass communication in Decatur when the field work was pursued.

43. Opinion leaders interviewed by Lazarsfeld, Berelson, and Gaudet (1948) claimed to have been more influenced in their own decisions by mass communication than they were by other people. Later and more refined studies have typically found, however, that though opinion leaders are more *exposed* to mass communication than are their followers, they are more *influenced* by other opinion leaders than they are by mass communication. These findings have suggested that the term "two-step flow of influence" should probably be expanded. Katz and Lazarsfeld (1955) found that fashion leaders alone, among the several types they studied, were more influenced by mass media than by other influentials.

44. The nature of opinion leaders and the extent of their influence vary markedly from one socio-cultural situation to another. Stycos (1952) reports that in rural Greece, for example, the opinion leaders are liable to be the few people who have intellectual and physical access to the news. In the village of Kalos, a teacher and a priest are opinion leaders by virtue of being the only literate residents. They are required by the villagers to transmit and evaluate news and are regarded with "respect and near awe" (Stycos, 1952, p. 60). Various other studies of opinion leadership in other cultures are cited in Katz (1957).

45. Lazarsfeld, Berelson, and Gaudet (1948), pp. 150 f.
46. Katz (1957), p. 71 f.   47. *Ibid.*
48. Berelson, Lazarsfeld, and McPhee (1954), p. 113.
49. *Ibid.*
50. Katz (1957), p. 73.   51. *Ibid.*, n.
52. Berelson, Lazarsfeld, and McPhee (1954), p. 117. The authors also note (pp. 116 f) the relative frequency of deviations, e.g., that where discussion is

not among people of like age, "young people look more to older people than the opposite." They make similar observations in reference to occupational status and political majority and minority groups, but find that "most political discussion goes on among people of like characteristics."

53. *Ibid.*, p. 106.

54. Katz (1957), pp. 71 f. Homogeneity may also occur and persist in support of change. Coleman, Katz, and Menzel (1960), for example, found that "doctors who were sociometrically connected tended to adopt . . . a new drug at virtually the same time" (Katz, 1957, p. 72).

55. Wiebe (1952-B) reaches a roughly similar point by way of a somewhat different path. He is concerned with the socio-cultural rather than the economic character of the media and proposes that "they provide . . . an enormous fund of shared vicarious experiences" (p. 166). He points out that should they transcend the limits of such quasi-universal experience, their appeal would be restricted to a smaller and more specialized audience, and they would thus cease to be media of *mass* communication.

56. For example, in relation to daytime serials, Arnheim (1944); in relation to popular magazine fiction, Berelson and Salter (1947); in relation to TV drama, Smythe (1953) and Head (1954). Smythe, incidentally, found that American women were *underrepresented* in TV dramas and were presented as in some ways less admirable than the foreign ladies.

57. Asheim (1952).   58. Klapper (1949), p. IV–26.

59. See the discussion of Warner and Henry (1948) in Chapter VI below. Herzog (1944), which is discussed in the same chapter, does not explicitly ascribe a causal influence to the serials themselves.

60. Smythe (1953) provides data on such questions as the ethnic distribution of characters and the values and ideals celebrated in television programs available in New York City in January, 1953. Head (1954) deals with TV dramas presented in 1952. The present author has encountered no equally or more recent systematic analyses of the content of any American media. A pertinent but non-quantitive report by Winick (1959) is mentioned immediately below.

61. Winick (1959), p. 32.

62. *Ibid.*, p. 33. The "study" here mentioned is not further identified, but appears to be Winick (1959) itself.

63. Such a reaction to panel programs was in fact postulated by Hudson and Wiebe as early as 1948.

64. And following Wiebe's path (see note 55 above), their socio-cultural character.

65. The data summarized in this paragraph are set forth in greater detail and the cited studies identified on pp. 16–18.

66. See pp. 84–90.

67. The findings of the study are more fully cited on pp. 29 f.

68. See pp. 77–80 below.

69. John Crosby, as quoted without further identification of source in Bogart (1956), p. 215.

70. Pertinent studies discussed elsewhere in this volume include Cooper and Jahoda (1947), and Kendall and Wolf (1946 and 1949, pp. 23 f.); also Raths and Trager (1948, p. 41). See also Seeleman (1941), Flowerman (1949), and Bureau of Applied Social Research (1953).

71. Tannenbaum (1956), p. 425.
72. As reported, for example, in the studies cited in note 70 above.

CHAPTER III

The Creation of Opinion on New Issues

1. Doob (1950), p. 435.
2. The literature on what has come to be known as the "order of presentation in persuasion" (Hovland et al, 1957) deals in the main with the relative effectiveness of different orders of pro and con arguments about issues in regard to which the audience is already likely to have some sorts of ideas. The topic is discussed in Chapter V. We are here concerned, however, with the efficacy of mass communication in creating attitudes about new issues.
3. Hovland cites Lundberg (1926) and Mott (1944) both of whom empirically document such a lack of relationship.
4. As reported, for example, by Sims (1938), Bateman and Remmers (1941), and various others.
5. As detailed in Lazarsfeld, Berelson, and Gaudet (1948), passim.
6. Berelson, Lazarsfeld, and McPhee (1954), p. 23 (derived from Table 3).
7. Berelson (1948), p. 176.
8. Both of these studies are primarily concerned with other matters. They are discussed in Chapter V, p. 101, and pp. 117–18.
9. See pp. 90–91.
10. Lang and Lang (1955), p. 181.
11. *Ibid.*, p. 169.
12. The findings of Lang and Lang (1955) are in some sense reminiscent of the findings of Lang and Lang (1953). In this early study, the investigators compared telecasts of a visit by General MacArthur to Chicago and what actually took place in the city. They found that the TV depiction was not in accord with reality and presumably created an erroneous impression in the minds of viewers. The study, though fascinating, is not too pertinent here, however. The events depicted related to an issue which was in no sense new, but rather already emotionally laden for many people. In addition, the findings bear almost exclusively on the difference between the TV depiction and reality, rather than on audience reaction to the telecasts or on audience attitudes toward the underlying issue.
13. See pp. 114–16.
14. The study by Himmelweit, Oppenheim, and Vince (1958) is discussed in considerable detail at several points in Part II of this book. See the Index for a complete listing of such discussions.
15. Himmelweit, Oppenheim, and Vince (1958), pp. 240–43.
16. See pp. 84–90.
17. See, however, footnote 21, Chapter V, which cites bibliographies and partial collations of that literature.

18. See p. xvi above.   19. See pp. 252 f., below.

20. Quoted from p. 8 above, with punctuation slightly modified and numerals added.

CHAPTER IV

Conversion

1. Lazarsfeld, Berelson, and Gaudet (1948), p. 102. See note 2 to Chapter II, regarding slight dissimilarities in meanings of terms as used by these investigators and by the present author.

2. Berelson, Lazarsfeld, and McPhee (1954), p. 23 (derived from Table 3).

3. Bureau of Applied Social Research (1944).

4. Katz and Lazarsfeld (1955), p. 142. The study is discussed at length on pp. 69–70 below.

5. The present author has deliberately refrained from citing specific examples of such reporting. The measures used are often adequate to the stated purposes of the studies, though not as useful as they might be to us.

6. The terms "net change" and "net effect" are also used by some writers to indicate the proportion of potential converts who were in fact converted. Thus, if 10 of 50 persons changed their views, the "net effect" is said by such writers to be .20. This device facilitates comparisons of the effectiveness of several communications, but, like other types of net change measures, obscures whatever degree of change may have been balanced by boomerang effect.

7. Bureau of Applied Social Research (1954).

8. Seibert (undated) as summarized by Bogart (1956), p. 226.

9. See, for example, conjectural rationales offered in connection with the effect of cross-pressures (pp. 79 f., below) and of role-playing (pp. 83 f., below), and in connection with the communication of facts without consonant opinion change (pp. 88–90 below).

10. See, for example, the discussions which follow immediately below of opinion leadership, personal influence, and personality, in processes of conversion.

11. The concept of "dysfunction" is formulated and discussed by Merton (1949). Readers unfamiliar with the concept may consider the word to mean something on the general order of "destructively malfunctional." Merton's concept, however, does not lend itself to brief summary.

12. International Research Associates, Inc. (1953).

13. Katz and Lazarsfeld (1955), p. 67.

14. See pp. 29 f., above.

15. Katz and Lazarsfeld (1955), p. 142.

16. *Ibid.*, Part II, chap. v.

17. Lazarsfeld, Berelson, and Gaudet (1948), chap. xvi.

18. Coleman, Katz, and Menzel (1960).

19. These experiments are briefly discussed on p. 106.

20. For a summary of the pertinent parts of Katz' summary, see p. 32 f., above.

21. This point is discussed at greater length in reference to reinforcement on pp. 33–37 above.

22. See, for example, Katz and Lazarsfeld (1955), Part I, chap. vii, and Stycos (1952).

23. Some attempt has been made deliberately to use previously identified opinion leaders in securing acceptance of improved farming practices. The as yet sparse data suggest that as soon as the leader's followers realize that the leader is being so manipulated, they cease to follow him. See Coleman and Marsh (1954).

24. Janis *et al* (1959), p. 1.

25. Hovland, Janis, and Kelley (1953), p. 175.

26. *Ibid.*, pp. 174–214, 277.   27. *Ibid.*, p. 185.

28. *Ibid.*   29. *Ibid.*, pp. 185 f.

30. Janis *et al* (1959), p. 244.   31. *Ibid.*, p. 237.

32. i.e., Janis and Field (chap. iii), Janis and Rife, Linton and Graham, and Lesser and Abelson.

33. Lazarsfeld, Berelson, and Gaudet (1948), p. 70.

34. Janis *et al* (1959), p. 233.

35. *Ibid.*, p. 234. The studies are Janis (1954), Janis (1955), and Janis and Field (in *ibid.*, chap. iii).

36. *Ibid.*, p. 232. The studies, all reported only in *ibid.*, are Janis and Field (chap. iii), Janis and Rife, Linton and Graham, and King.

37. These studies, reported only in *ibid.*, are Janis and Field (chap. iii) and King.

38. Abelson and Lesser, reported exclusively in *ibid.*

39. *Ibid.* (1959), p. 238. These particular findings are summarized pp. 238–40. 238–40.

40. *Ibid.*, p. 237.

41. The studies, reported only in *ibid.*, are Janis and Field (chap. iii) and Janis and Rife.

42. Linton and Graham, reported only in *ibid.* Quote is from p. 235.

43. *Ibid.*, p. 248.

44. Lazarsfeld, Berelson, and Gaudet (1948), p. 68 (derived from Chart 24).

45. Herz (1949), p. 471.

46. The point is documented in various unclassified reports prepared by or for the U.S. Information Agency and is suggested in Kracauer and Berkman (1956).

47. Lazarsfeld, Berelson, and Gaudet (1948), p. 62.

48. See note 15 to Chapter II.

49. Janis and King (1954), as reported in Hovland, Janis, and Kelley (1953), p. 278.

50. King and Janis (1953), as reported in Hovland, Janis, and Kelley (1953), p. 279.

51. Kelman (1953), as reported in Hovland, Janis, and Kelley (1953), p. 279.

52. Hovland, Janis, and Kelley (1953), p. 278.

53. *Ibid.*, pp. 228–37 and 278–80.

54. Cooper and Dinerman (1951), p. 255.

55. *Ibid.*   56. *Ibid.*
57. *Ibid.*, p. 263.   58. *Ibid.*
59. Hovland, Lumsdaine, and Sheffield (1949), pp. 33–37.
60. *Ibid.*, p. 42.   61. *Ibid.*, p. 64.
62. *Ibid.*, p. 65.
63. Cooper and Dinerman (1951), p. 263.
64. See pp. 126 f.
65. Hovland, Lumsdaine, and Sheffield (1949), p. 71.
66. Such a study would compare the degree to which the facts (*not the conclusions*) were accepted by persons exposed to a communication which drew explicit conclusions to which those persons were opposed, and the degree to which the same facts were accepted by persons of similar attitude exposed to a similar communication without explicit conclusions.
67. A. L. Lowell, as quoted with no further identification of source in Albig (1939), p. 217.
68. Waples, Berelson, and Bradshaw (1940, p. 119 and p. 78.
69. Lazarsfeld, Berelson, and Gaudet (1948), p. 98.
70. Waples, Berelson, and Bradshaw (1940), p. 121.
71. As previously stated on p. 48.
72. As stated above, p. 49.
73. Janis *et al* (1959), p. 1.
74. Hovland, Janis, and Kelley (1953), p. 175.

CHAPTER V

Contributory Aspects of the Communication
and the Communication Situation

1. Research in this tradition was, however, being pursued over twenty years ago. Lorge (1936), for example, found that people interpreted the same statements differently when they were ascribed to such different sources as Abraham Lincoln and then current labor leaders.
2. Hovland and Weiss (1951), p. 648.
3. Hovland, Janis, and Kelley (1953), p. 35.
4. Merton (1946), p. 3.   5. *Ibid.*, p. 150.
6. Lazarsfeld, Berelson, and Gaudet (1948), p. 136.
7. Coleman, Katz, and Menzel (1960).
8. Lazarsfeld and Merton (1948), pp. 101–2.
9. Waples, Berelson, and Bradshaw (1940), p. 119.
10. Merton (1946), p. 84.
11. Studies comparing only the degree of retention elicited by the several media are not here included as they are not clearly relevant to persuasion. Goldstein (1940) reviews much of the literature on the topic.
12. Various such studies have, of course, been pursued in reference to the capabilities of the two media in advertising consumer goods. As explained in

the Preface to this volume, the findings of advertising studies are not ordinarily generalizable to the purveying of ideas and no attempt is made to cover that vast literature, published and unpublished, in this volume.

13. Katz and Lazarsfeld (1955), p. 142.

14. See Schramm and Riley (1951) for a description of how the system was instituted in North Korea.

15. Cf. Lazarsfeld and Merton (1948), quoted on p. 121.

16. A series of such experiments are summarized in Goldstein (1940).

17. These points of view are expressed with varying degrees of conviction and emphasis by numerous writers, including, among others, Lazarsfeld (1940), Doob (1935 and 1948), and Berelson (1942).

18. Typical expressions of these several points of view will be found in Lazarsfeld (1940); Stouffer (1940); Lazarsfeld, Berelson, and Gaudet (1948); McPhee (1953); Bogart (1956); and various other writers.

19. See, among the older works, Blumer (1933), Holaday and Stoddard (1933), Charters (1933), and Doob (1935). Related points of view have been more recently expressed by Goldberg (1950), and Bogart (1956). The vast literature on instructional films bears occasionally on the degree of retention elicited by the medium and certain other points here touched upon. A veritable host of such studies, performed between 1918 and 1950, are individually summarized in Hoban and Van Ormer (1951). Experiments in educational television have produced an equally massive and occasionally relevant literature. A vast number of such studies are individually summarized in Carpenter and Greenhill (1955), Kumata (1956), and Westley and Barrow (1959).

As explained in some detail in the Preface to this volume, no attempt has here been made to survey the literature on formal pedagogical use of mass media. The findings of such studies are only rarely generalizable to communications with persuasive rather than instructional goals.

20. Such "unique advantages" of face-to-face contact are spelled out in detail in Lazarsfeld, Berelson, and Gaudet (1948), chap. xvi. The relative persuasive power of personal influence as compared with other media has recently been the subject of a considerable literature which is cited at length at other places in this volume, including pp. 32–38 and pp. 68–72.

21. See, for example, Hoban and Van Ormer (1951) in regard to films. and the works cited in footnote 19 above in regard to television.

22. Hovland, Lumsdaine, and Sheffield (1949), p. 225.

23. Waples, Berelson, and Bradshaw (1940), p. 109. It is to be emphasized that these experiments compare the effect of two types of propaganda which actually favor the same point of view, differing only in the degree to which opposing arguments are recognized. Actually opposing propagandas tend to nullify each other's effects. Schank and Goodman (1939), for example, found that persons exposed to propaganda on both sides of an issue underwent no significant attitude changes. Surveys of election campaigns—e.g., Lazarsfeld, Berelson, and Gaudet (1948), and Berelson, Lazarsfeld, and McPhee (1954)— typically reveal that opposing political propagandas have very little effect upon the proportionate distribution of partisan vote intentions.

24. As used in this chapter, "net change" expresses the percentage of the group which changed in the direction intended by the communication, minus the percentage which changed in the opposite direction.

25. Hovland *et al* (1957), pp. 23–32.

26. Hovland, Janis, and Kelley (1953), p. 110.
27. Cartwright (1949), p. 264.
28. Katz and Lazarsfeld (1955), p. 214.
29. This rather odd term was apparently coined by Hovland, Janis, and Kelley (1953, p. 56, and *passim*) and has become standard terminology for content which attempts to persuade by frightening the listener.
30. Hovland, Janis, and Kelley (1953), p. 271.
31. The Cannell and MacDonald (1956) findings are cited in greater detail on pp. 21, 23. Some of the relatively recent studies in the effect of different degrees of threat are perhaps an outgrowth and refinement of the much earlier investigations of "rational" vs. "emotional" appeals. Literature on that topic blossomed during the mid-1930's and is reviewed by Hovland (1954). He points out that the findings were inconsistent and suggests the need for more theoretically refined and more carefully controlled research.
32. Bureau of Applied Social Research (1954).
33. As stated in a manuscript allegedly dictated by him (Doob, 1950).
34. Barlett (1940), p. 69.   35. Merton (1946), p. 36.
36. Cartwright (1949), p. 262.   37. *Ibid.*, p. 261.
38. Doob (1950), p. 419.
39. Lazarsfeld and Merton (1948), p. 114.
40. *Ibid.*, pp. 114–15.
41. Wiebe (1951) is, however, less concerned with this distinction than with the relative availability of "action outlets" for the two types of persuasion.
42. Merton (1946), p. 119.   43. *Ibid.*, p. 55.
44. e.g., Herz (1949) and various others.
45. See, for example, the reviews of the literature in Hovland (1954) and Hovland *et al* (1957).
46. e.g., Hudson and Wiebe (1948); Hovland, Lumsdaine, and Sheffield (1949); Parrish and Campbell (1953); and various others.
47. e.g., Thistlewaite, deHaan, and Kaminetzky (1955), and various others.
48. A great number of such studies are cited in periodical summary reports of the program. See, for example, the summaries cited in note 21, above.
49. As reported in Hovland *et al* (1957).
50. Hovland *et al* (1957), p. 154–55.
51. Lazarsfeld, Berelson, and Gaudet (1948), p. 108.
52. Hovland, Janis, and Kelley (1953), p. 298.
53. Wiebe (1951), p. 679.

PART TWO

CHAPTER VI

The Effects of Crime and Violence in the Media

1. Bogart (1956), p. 258.   2. Klapper (1954), p. 22.
3. i.e., popular weeklies and monthlies, Sunday supplements, and the more popular magazines on child raising, family life, and the like.

4. e.g., Logan (1950).

5. Four reports were published bearing on television content in 1951, 1952, 1953, and 1954. Violence was tallied in the last three of these and is most elaborately discussed in the last two, viz., Smythe (1953) and Purdue Opinion Panel (1954).

6. Purdue Opinion Panel (1954), p. 38.

7. *Ibid.*, p. 40.

8. Himmelweit, Oppenheim, and Vince (1958), p. 176.

9. For bibliographical listing and details, see "New York State Joint Legislative Committee (1955)."

10. U.S. Congress Senate Committee on the Judiciary, *Comic Books and Juvenile Delinquency*, (1955), p. 7. Examples of "pathologically weird" material will be found on pp. 8–10 of the same document.

11. Purdue Opinion Panel (1954), p. 37.

12. *Ibid.*

13. Cf. Smythe (1953), p. 61; and Purdue Opinion Panel (1954), p. 41.

14. Himmelweit, Oppenheim, and Vince (1958), whose findings on this point are discussed in detail below.

15. Purdue Opinion Panel (1954), p. 39.

16. Bogart (1956), p. 269.   17. Logan (1950), p. 173.

18. Cousins (1949), as quoted in Marx (1953), p. 69.

19. New York State Joint Legislative Committee (1955), p. 29.

20. *Ibid.*, p. 31.

21. *Code of the Comic Magazine Association of America*, as reproduced in New York State Joint Legislative Committee (1955), p. 172.

22. Blumer and Hauser (1933), p. 198.

23. Such testimony will be found, for example, at various points in U.S. Congress Senate Committee on the Judiciary, *Television and Juvenile Delinquency* (1955). A number of such statements from that document are more conveniently available in Bogart (1956), chap. xii.

24. Mirams (1951), pp. 12–13.   25. See note 23, above.

26. e.g., Dysinger and Ruckmick (1933), and Renshaw, Miller, and Marquis (1933).

27. Himmelweit, Oppenheim, and Vince (1958), title page.

28. *Ibid.*, p. 5.   29. *Ibid.*, pp. 4–5.

30. *Ibid.*, pp. 8–9.   31. *Ibid.*, p. 206.

32. *Ibid.*, p. 200.   33. *Ibid.*, p. 210.

34. *Ibid.*, p. 191.   35. *Ibid.*, p. 210.

36. *Ibid.*, p. 194.   37. *Ibid.*, p. 196.

38. *Ibid.*, pp. 194–95.

39. *Ibid.*, p. 196. These findings are confirmed and in fact extended by Albert (1957), who administered projective tests to young boys before and after exposure to a conventional Western film. His "subjects . . . show[ed] a decrease in their aggression" (p. 279). The change was not statistically significant, however.

40. Himmelweit, Oppenheim, and Vince (1958), p. 204.

41. *Ibid.*, pp. 461–62.   42. *Ibid.*, p. 203.

43. *Ibid.*, p. 461.   44. *Ibid.*, p. 204.

45. *Ibid.*   46. *Ibid.*, p. 203.

47. i.e., the studies cited in note 26 of this chapter.

48. e.g., Bruel (1953), who describes the role allegedly played in the development of a young girl's neurosis by the picture *The Hunchback of Notre Dame*.

49. Bogart, for example, tells a delightful story of his own daughter being terrified at the age of two-and-a-half "by an illustration in a delightful little nursery story (with the usual advisory board of educators and child psychologists) . . . [of] a bed which flew through the air like a magic carpet. The picture of the two children, with their dog and toy animals merrily sailing through the clouds on this bed produced only terror in my daughter's heart. She required assurance for several evenings that her bed would not fly away" (Bogart, 1956, p. 273).

50. Himmelweit, Oppenheim, and Vince (1958), p. 193.

51. *Ibid.*, p. 210.   52. *Ibid.*, p. 201.

53. Thrasher (1949), p. 199.

54. Himmelweit, Oppenheim, and Vince (1958), p. 215.

55. Bailyn (1959), title page.

56. *Ibid.*, pp. 9, 13. Italics added.

57. *Ibid.*, pp. 5, 14.   58. *Ibid.*, p. 3.

59. Bailyn (1959), p. 37.

60. This particular study by Maccoby has not been published, but is described in Bogart (1956). Another study by Maccoby (1954) explored the relationship between children's level of frustration and their degree of television viewing. The findings do not bear upon violent content per se, and the study is accordingly discussed elsewhere, viz, p. 191–92.

61. Maccoby, as summarized by Bogart (1956), p. 272.

62. Riley and Riley (1951), p. 451.

63. Himmelweit, Oppenheim, and Vince (1958), p. 150.

64. *Ibid.*, p. 215.

65. See pp. 194–96, below.

66. See pp. 194–96, below.

67. Bailyn (1959), p. 37.

68. See note 25, above, for printed sources of such testimony. Explicit mention must be made of Dr. Frederick Wertham, who is probably the world's most voluble castigator of media-depicted violence, and in particular of comic books. Wertham claims to have diagnosed or treated numerous delinquent children in whose downfall comic books were the chief impetus. He does not seem to consider that emotional disturbance or abnormal aggressive tendencies are necessary prerequisites to comic book influence but rather seems to believe, as the title of his best known work asserts, that such fare in and of itself achieves "seduction of the innocent" (Wertham, 1954). Wertham is not generally regarded, however, as having substantiated his very extreme views. Thrasher (1949), for example, is typical of the critics in pointing out that Wertham provides no description of his samples of comic books or of human cases, apparently deals only with a small and highly deviant minority of both, provides no description of his case study techniques, uses no control groups, and, in short, provides no acceptable scientific evidence for his ascription of comic book influence.

69. See Goldenson (1954), Bloch and Flynn (1956), Pittman (1958), and, to some extent, Klapper (1954).

CHAPTER VII

The Effects of Escapist Media Material

1. Charles Earle Funk, ed., *New Practical Standard Dictionary of the English Language* (New York & London: Funk & Wagnall's Co., 1946), p. 451.
2. Mott (1947), p. 262.   3. Siepmann (1948), p. 196.
4. Seldes (1950), p. 76.   5. *Ibid.*, p. 251.
6. Arnheim (1944), p. 41.   7. Saenger (1955), p. 198.
8. Smythe (1955), p. 61.   9. Herzog (1944), pp. 3 f.
10. Waples, Berelson, and Bradshaw (1940), p. 123.
11. Asheim (1951), p. 318.
12. The McPhee and Meyersohn (1955) study is a particularly fine example of the functional approach. Not only is the entire investigation devoted to determining the functions which radio serves, but the fare is itself described in functional rather than purely contextual categories. The authors divide radio's offerings into three broad categories: music, which provides a background mood for entertainment; most "talk," which provides occasions of vicarious interaction and which is here further discussed below, and material such as news and weather reports, which provides specific information.
13. Asheim (1951), p. 309.   14. Bogart (1956), p. 34.
15. Katz and Lazarsfeld (1955), p. 378.
16. A very similar sort of function has, in fact, been ascribed to the weekly newspapers. Their contents, which are locally oriented but hardly escapist, are believed by Schramm and Merritt (1951), to "knit . . . together . . . readers with the little understandings which are the essence of both communication and community." Siepmann (1948) has also suggested that by creating a well-informed public, the media could restore the feeling of belonging which has been progressively lost as society has grown in size and complexity.
17. Bogart (1955) proposes that any popular fiction might serve the same function. He notes that Georg Simmel long ago observed that jokes served in this way.
18. Herzog (1944), p. 3.   19. *Ibid.*, p. 24.
20. *Ibid.*, p. 28.   21. *Ibid.*, pp. 24–25.
22. *Ibid.*, p. 24.   23. *Ibid.*
24. Albig (1939), p. 384.
25. Waples, Berelson, and Bradshaw (1940), p. 72.
26. Herzog (1944), p. 25.   27. *Ibid.*, p. 30.
28. Quoted in *ibid.*, p. 27. Herzog questions the benefit of this woman's "learning" that "husbands do not really understand what a wife goes through." It is to be observed, however, that the woman herself has allegedly learned to be more tolerant and less ego-centered.
29. Quoted in *ibid.*, p. 27.   30. Quoted in *ibid.*, pp. 27–28.
31. Quoted in *ibid.*, p. 27.   32. Quoted in *ibid.*, p. 28.
33. Quoted in *ibid.*   34. Quoted in *ibid.*, p. 31.
35. Quoted in *ibid.*, p. 30.   36. *Ibid.*, p. 29.
37. *Ibid.*, p. 31.   38. *Ibid.*, p. 4.
39. *Ibid.*, pp. 5–6.   40. *Ibid.*, p. 17.

41. *Ibid.*   42. *Ibid.*, p. 8.
43. *Ibid.*, p. 15.   44. *Ibid.*, p. 18.
45. This claim is based on the belief that the social class composition of the serial audience is essentially similar to that of the population as a whole.
46. Bailyn (1959) notes that child devotees of violent content in the pictorial media tend more than light users to believe that the improbable events depicted actually do occur in life. They tend also to judge real people in stereotyped terms reminiscent of media depictions of heroes and villains. Bailyn's findings relative to whether addiction to such material creates escapist tendencies are discussed below.
47. Warner and Henry (1948), pp. 50–51.
48. Ruth appears to attack problems somewhat more actively than the typical serial heroine described by Arnheim (1944).
49. Warner and Henry (1948), p. 11.
50. *Ibid.*, p. 18.   51. *Ibid.*, p. 63.
52. *Ibid.*   53. *Ibid.*
54. *Ibid.*   55. *Ibid.*
56. *Ibid.*, p. 64.   57. Riley and Riley (1951), p. 451.
58. Maccoby (1954), p. 242.   59. Wolf and Fiske (1949), p. 3.
60. *Ibid.*, p. 22.   61. *Ibid.*, p. 23.
62. *Ibid.*, pp. 5, 26.   63. *Ibid.*, p. 27.
64. *Ibid.*   65. *Ibid.*, p. 29.
66. *Ibid.*, p. 28.   67. *Ibid.*, p. 35.
68. Himmelweit, Oppenheim, and Vince (1958), p. 385.
69. *Ibid.*, p. 389.   70. *Ibid.*
71. *Ibid.*, p. 390.   72. *Ibid.*, p. 391.
73. *Ibid.*, p. 390.   74. *Ibid.*, p. 395.
75. *Ibid.*   76. Bailyn (1959), p. 33.
77. *Ibid.*, p. 13.   78. *Ibid.*, p. 34.
79. *Ibid.*, p. 35.   80. *Ibid.*, p. 44.
81. Wolf and Fiske (1949), p. 35.
82. Himmelweit, Oppenheim, and Vince (1958), p. 394.
83. See pp. 169–71.
84. Waples, Berelson, and Bradshaw (1940), p. 123.
85. Lazarsfeld and Merton (1948), p. 105. On the concept of "dysfunction," see also note 13, chap. iv of the present book.
86. Seldes (1950), p. 245.
87. "Myth world" is from Seldes (1950), p. 76.

CHAPTER VIII

The Effects of Adult TV Fare on Child Audiences

1. Klapper (1954), for which field work was performed in 1953.
2. Himmelweit, Oppenheim, and Vince (1958), p. 13.
3. *Ibid.*, p. 125.   4. *Ibid.*, p. 377.

5. Shayon (1951), pp. 26–27.

6. *Ibid.*, p. 35.   7. *Ibid.*, p. 37.

8. Small or crowded living quarters, for example, may offer a child no escape from the soundtrack of television so long as the set is in use. Under such circumstances children may often watch because it is virtually impossible for them to do anything else.

9. The term "indigenous" refers to dramas produced especially for TV, as opposed to being adopted from some other medium. Smythe (1953), p. 77.

10. *Ibid.*, p. 80.

11. Himmelweit, Oppenheim, and Vince (1958), p. 225.

12. *Ibid.*, p. 223.   13. *Ibid.*, p. 225.

14. *Ibid.*, p. 227.

15. This concept is essentially similar to the "narcotizing dysfunction" concept propounded by Lazarsfeld and Merton (1948) in relation to adult radio listeners. See index.

16. Klapper (1954), p. 34.   17. *Ibid.*, p. 41.

18. *Ibid.*, p. 31, and Klapper (1949), pp. IV–60 ff. The distinction is between values which people profess but do not live by (i.e., values which they only verbally sanction), and those by which they actually guide their behavior (i.e., which they actively sanction).

19. Zajonc (1954), p. 369.

20. See pp. 194–96.   21. Bailyn (1959), pp. 44 f.

22. *Ibid.*, p. 40.   23. *Ibid.*, p. 43.

24. Himmelweit, Oppenheim, and Vince (1958), p. 248.

25. *Ibid.*, p. 243.

26. Himmelweit, Oppenheim, and Vince (1958), p. 249.

27. *Ibid.*   28. *Ibid.*, p. 250.

29. *Ibid.*, p. 250 n.   30. *Ibid.*, p. 260.

31. *Ibid.*, p. 248.   32. *Ibid.*

33. *Ibid.*, p. 250.   34. *Ibid.*, p. 247. Italics deleted.

35. *Ibid.*   36. *Ibid.*, p. 233.

37. *Ibid.*   38. *Ibid.*

39. *Ibid.*, p. 258.   40. *Ibid.*, p. 234.

41. *Ibid.*, p. 235.   42. *Ibid.*, p. 5. Italics deleted.

43. *Ibid.*, p. 235.   44. *Ibid.*, p. 236.

45. *Ibid.*   46. *Ibid.*, p. 237.

47. *Ibid.*, p. 239.   48. *Ibid.*

49. *Ibid.*, p. 236.   50. *Ibid.*, p. 243.

51. *Ibid.*, p. 244. Italics deleted.   52. *Ibid.*, p. 468.

53. *Ibid.*   54. *Ibid.*

55. *Ibid.*, p. 246.   56. *Ibid.*, p. 253.

57. *Ibid.*, p. 256.   58. *Ibid.*, p. 255.

59. The treatment of foreigners and minority groups by American media, and the effects of such content upon audience attitudes, are discussed at several points in this volume, including especially pp. 39–42. For a complete listing, see Index entries under *Minority groups* and *foreigners.*

60. Himmelweit, Oppenheim, and Vince (1958), p. 260. Italics added.

61. *Ibid.*   62. See p. 5.

63. Himmelweit, Oppenheim, and Vince (1958), p. 260. Italics deleted.

CHAPTER IX

Media Attendance and Audience Passivity

1. Even comic books, which are more typically feared as stimulants to violent behavior, have been looked upon askance by those fearful of passivity. Muhlen (1949) concludes, after reviewing earlier studies, that some children identify with the hero's protégé, rather than with the hero himself, and that this may betoken and stimulate a passive orientation and a dependence on omnipotence figures. Muhlen considers such a *Weltanschauung* more suited to a totalitarian state than to a democracy. He does not explicitly charge comic books with *creating* such an orientation, although his article is entitled "Comic Books and Other Horrors: Prep School for Totalitarian Society?"

2. Siepmann (1948), p. 47.

3. Seldes, in a speech quoted by Brombaugh (1950), p. 2644.

4. Levin (1950), p. 250.   5. Shayon (1951), p. 20.

6. Himmelweit, Oppenheim, and Vince (1958), p. 352.

7. Bogart (1956), p. 34.   8. *Ibid.*

9. Klapper (1954), for which interviewing was done in 1953.

10. Maccoby (1954) has empirically demonstrated a relationship between TV viewing and frustration among middle-class children, but failed, possibly because of spurious factors, to demonstrate such a relationship among lower-class children. Her study is described at some length above (see Index).

11. It may be noted that this specific effect conjectured by psychologists and psychoanalysts is diametrically opposite to the effect conjectured by Muhlen (1949), and outlined in note 1, above. Available conjectures, it would seem, are nothing if not varied.

12. An exhaustive array of such studies are cited and summarized in Bogart (1956) and are there classified in reference to specific activities, such as reading, attendance at spectator sports, etc.

13. Hamilton and Lawless (1956), p. 394.

14. *Ibid.*, pp. 402 f.   15. *Ibid.*, p. 403.

16. The description of Belson's involved methodology covers over 100 pages in Belson (1957) and is virtually insusceptible of brief summary. A shorter description of the technique will be found in Belson (1956), and a rather general statement of the procedure occurs in Belson (1958), from which the following paragraphs are quoted:

[The technique] begins with a straight comparison of the test scores of viewers and non-viewers, and then partials out as much as possible that portion of the difference in test score which is attributable not to TV, but to the viewers and non-viewers *being different to start with.*

This correction of the non-viewers score is achieved through a refinement of the matching technique—though it differs from ordinary matching in two important ways: *first*, the matching criteria are selected empirically and *second*, there is no discarding of unmatched subjects. Instead, the test score of the non-viewer group is adjusted through a regression equation, or through simple weighting, to give an estimate of what it would have been had the two groups (viewers and non-viewers) been the same in respect to the chosen criteria. A comparison of this adjusted test score with the test score of the viewer group then provides a direct estimate of television's real effect.

The empirical selection of the matching criteria of course requires the inclusion in the questionnaire of a large number of proposed matching criteria (perhaps up to a hundred) with subsequent analysis to select that composite of them most predictive of test score. It is essential that the predictors not be open to influence by television. (p. 14).

17. Changes here cited refer to active pursuit of the listed interests, which is not always related to degree of expressed interest. Quotes are from Belson (1957), pp. 177 and 182 f.

18. Bogart (1956), pp. 255 f.

19. Himmelweit, Oppenheim, and Vince (1958), p. 352. Italics added.

20. *Ibid.*, p. 353.   21. *Ibid.*

22. *Ibid.* Italics added.   23. *Ibid.*, p. 354. Italics deleted.

24. Specifically, "ceremonial events," "sports events," "plays and entertainment," "famous personalities," "exhibitions and art galleries," and "special places of work." (*Ibid.*, p. 355).

25. Non-viewers were not questioned, presumably because they had no basis for making a choice.

26. *Ibid.*, pp. 353 f.

27. *Ibid.*, p. 353. Italics added for benefit of format.

28. "Learning to play a musical instrument (rather than 'listening to music')." *Ibid.*, p. 356.

29. *Ibid.*   30. *Ibid.*, p. 349.

31. *Ibid.*, p. 353. Italics added.   32. *Ibid.*, p. 357.

33. *Ibid.*   34. *Ibid.*

35. *Ibid.*, p. 361.   36. *Ibid.*, p. 353. Italics added.

37. *Ibid.*, p. 358. Punctuation modified.

38. *Ibid.*, p. 361.

39. The Riley and Riley (1951) study is discussed at some length on pp. 154–56.

40. Hamilton and Lawless (1956), p. 403.

CHAPTER X

Concluding Note

Approximately three pages of this chapter have been previously published in almost identical form in *Public Opinion Quarterly*, XXI (Winter, 1957–58), 4. They occurred within an article entitled "What We Know about the Effects of Mass Communication: The Brink of Hope," which was first delivered as an address at the National Education Association's Centennial Seminar on Communications, at Dedham, Mass., May 21–23, 1957. Permission to republish has been graciously granted by *Public Opinion Quarterly*.

1. Monopoly propaganda, as practiced by totalitarian governments, and a kind of unwitting monopoly propaganda practiced in democracies in favor of

certain cultural values, are believed by some authors to be in themselves very effective persuasive procedures. See, for example, Lazarsfeld (1942), Lazarsfeld and Merton (1948), and Klapper (1948) and (1949, IV–20–27). In general, these writers suggest that the monopoly propaganda continually reinforces the attitudes it espouses, while simultaneously handicapping the birth and preventing the spread of opposing views. The argument is logically appealing and has been advanced as a conjectural explanation of various attitude and opinion phenomena, but it has been neither substantiated nor refuted by empirical research.

2. Key (1955), p. 4.

3. A particularly provocative and already well developed model for the study of mass communication as a process occurring within a social system has been recently provided by Riley and Riley (1959).

Index